Unstoppable

Proven Leadership Strategies to Scale Your Business and Leave a Lasting Impact.

Ben Botes

Unstoppable Growth: How Top Leaders Achieve Lasting Impact and Scale Beyond Limits

Copyright © 2024 by Ben Botes.

All rights reserved.

No part of this book may be reproduced, stored in a retrieval system, or transmitted in any form or by any means, electronic, mechanical, photocopying, recording, or otherwise, without the prior written permission of the publisher, except for brief quotations in reviews or articles.

ISBN: 978-1-0683103-0-0

Published by Impact Thinking Press

Printed and distributed by IngramSpark

Disclaimer:

This book is intended to provide general information and inspiration. The author and publisher are not responsible for any actions taken based on the information in this book.

Printed in the United Kingdom.

Dedication

To my children,

May you lead with impact wherever you go, find your voice in the world, and always stay true to your purpose. This book is a testament to what's possible when we grow with intention, resilience, and heart—qualities I see in each of you every day.

Table of Contents

Foreword: A Guide for Leaders Who Dare to Grow 2

   Why This Book Matters Now 3

   What You'll Discover 3

   An Invitation 4

Introduction: A New Paradigm for Transformative Leadership 6

   The Leadership Crossroads: Challenges of Scaling in a Complex World. 7

   Why This Book Matters: Grounded in Evidence, Built for Action 11

Chapter 1: Setting the Stage for Unstoppable Growth 15

   The Challenges of Leadership Today 17

   Defining Unstoppable Growth 19

   Why Traditional Growth Models Fall Short 21

   The Power of Purpose: Insights from Research 22

   Framework for Cultivating Adaptability: The PIVOT Model 26

   Maintaining Focus in the Growth Journey 28

Chapter 2: The Growth Mindset: From Survival to Scaling 31

   Understanding the Survival Mentality 33

   Defining the Growth Mindset 35

   Transforming Challenges into Catalysts for Development 37

   Reflective Pause 38

   Cultivating the Growth Mindset Within Teams 39

   The Power of Culture: Pixar's Commitment to Creativity and Growth ... 39

   The Role of Resilience in Scaling 40

   Case Study: Netflix—Reinventing Resilience in the Face of Disruption .. 40

   A Cautionary Tale: Blockbuster's Collapse 41

   Building Resilience Within Teams and Systems 41

Embracing the Unknown *43*

The Pioneer's Path: A Narrative of Bold Exploration *44*

The Growth Mindset in Uncertainty *45*

Framework: The Expansion Cycle *47*

Reflective Questions for Leaders *48*

Chapter 3: Rediscovering Core Purpose for Lasting Impact 50

The Erosion of Purpose During Growth *51*

The Dynamic Nature of Purpose *53*

Aligning Purpose with Action *55*

The Business Case for Purpose *58*

Leading with Purpose During Uncertainty *61*

Case Reflection: Grameen Bank – Scaling Purpose-Driven Impact through Microcredit *63*

The Expansion Cycle Applied to Purpose *66*

An Invitation to Reflect *70*

Chapter 4: Building Scalable Systems and Processes for Seamless Expansion 72

The Case for Scalable Systems *75*

Turning Complexity into Clarity *78*

Turning Chaos into Seamless Expansion *82*

Expert Spotlight: Indra Nooyi – Scaling with Vision and Purpose *85*

Leadership Perspectives: The Fork in the Road *88*

Reflection for Leaders *90*

Beyond the Traditional Blueprint *90*

Building the Foundation for Enduring Growth *94*

Reflect and Refocus: Designing Systems That Reflect Your Vision *96*

Chapter 5: Leadership in Turbulent Times: Thriving Through Change .. 99

The Leadership Imperative in Times of Change 100

Tools for Leading Through Turbulence 104

Real-World Applications: Thriving Through Turbulence 108

Jacinda Ardern – Leading with Empathy and Clarity in Turbulent Times 112

The Two Roads of Leadership in Turbulence 115

Beyond the Familiar Approaches 117

Thriving Through the Storm 121

Leading Through the Waters of Change 123

Chapter 6: Effective Communication in a Noisy World 126

The Science of Communication in a Noisy World 128

Frameworks in Action: Navigating the Noise 131

From Framework to Action 135

Expert Spotlight: Satya Nadella – Redefining Communication to Transform Culture 140

Leadership Perspective: The Fork in the Road – Two Paths of Communication 143

Reflective Questions for Leaders 145

Expanding Possibilities: New Frontiers in Communication 146

Illuminating the Path Forward 150

Finding Your Voice 152

Chapter 7: The Power of Multidisciplinary Teams 155

Research-Based Insights: The Science Behind Multidisciplinary Success 157

Real-World Applications: Collaboration in Action 163

Expert Spotlight: Reed Hastings – Reinventing Collaboration for Global Impact 166

The Multidisciplinary Dilemma 169

New Horizons for Multidisciplinary Teams 172

Conducting the Symphony of Collaboration 176

Chapter 8: The Inner Game of Leadership 178
Exploring Inner Challenges: Facing the Shadows of Leadership 180
The Impact of Self-Awareness, Emotional Intelligence, and Resilience in Leadership 184
Frameworks for Inner Mastery: Strengthening Leadership from Within . 187
The Power of Inner Mastery 192
Inner Growth in Action 192
Navigating the Dilemma of Short-Term Wins vs. Long-Term Growth 195
Expanding Possibilities: Broadening the Path to Inner Growth 198
Mindfulness Practices: Cultivating Presence in Chaos 200
Strengthening Your Inner Game 203

Chapter 9: Health as a Foundation for Resilient Leadership 205
Building Resilience Through BALANCE 210
Health as Leadership's Invisible Power 215
Innovating Health for Leadership Resilience 218
Health as Leadership's Bedrock 221
Reflect and Refocus: Building Your Leadership Resilience Through Health 222

Chapter 10: Empowering People for Unstoppable Performance 224
The Power of Empowerment 226
The TRUST Approach 229
Leaders Who Embody Empowerment 233
Alternative Strategies for Empowering Teams 236

Chapter 11: Cultivating a Culture of Innovation and Impact 242
The Cultural Foundations of Innovation and Impact 244
Leaders Who Embody Innovation and Impact 251
The Power of Inclusion 257

Shaping a Culture of Innovation and Impact.. 260

Chapter 12: Strategic Funding for Unstoppable Growth 263

The Pillars of Strategic Funding... 265

Frameworks for Funding Success: The GROWTH Model...................... 268

Funding as a Catalyst for Transformative Growth................................... 272

Reflections on Funding for Growth.. 274

The Dilemma of Growth vs. Sustainability 275

Exploring Alternative Funding Strategies... 278

Funding as a Strategic Lever for Growth 281

Chapter 13: Financial Planning and Intelligent Resource Allocation 284

The Strategic Role of Financial Planning... 286

The ALIGN Approach 289

Intelligent Financial Leadership in Action... 292

Chapter 14: Building Strong Partnerships with Investors and Stakeholders 304

The Foundations of Strong Partnerships 306

TRUST in Action.. 308

The Art of Building Transformative Partnerships..................................... 311

Balancing Investor Expectations and Organizational Values................. 314

Reimagining Partnerships for a Dynamic Future..................................... 316

Strengthening the Ties That Drive Growth 319

Chapter 15: Sustaining Growth Momentum in Changing Markets..... 322

Key Factors for Sustaining Growth in Changing Markets....................... 324

Using The ADAPT Approach 326

Sustaining Growth in Changing Markets.. 329

Balancing Agility with Strategic Focus 331

Exploring Alternative Strategies for Sustained Momentum 333

Sustaining Momentum in Changing Markets..336

Chapter 16: Beyond Growth: Evolving Leadership for Lasting Success 339

The Role of Leadership in Shaping Legacy...341

Using The LEGACY Framework..343

People Building Legacies That Last..347

Broadening the Path to Legacy 353

The Leadership Legacy: Creating Impact That Endures........................356

Conclusion: Your Roadmap to Lasting Impact and Unstoppable Growth 359

Opening Reflection: Revisiting the Journey...359

The Core Principles for Unstoppable Growth...360

Vision for the Future: A Call to Continuous Evolution..............................362

Invitation to Engage and Additional Resources 362

Final Words: Leaving a Legacy of Impact and Inspiration.....................363

Bibliography..365

Appendix: Tools, Exercises, and Additional Resources for Unstoppable Growth 376

Glossary...379

About the Author..385

"True growth is not about what you gain, but what you build—within yourself, your team, and the world you touch. Leadership is the art of expanding possibility, not just profits."

Foreword

A Guide for Leaders Who Dare to Grow

"Growth is never by mere chance; it is the result of forces working together."
—James Cash Penney

Growth. It's a word that evokes both excitement and apprehension, especially for those leading businesses through the ever-changing landscape of scale-ups. As someone who has worked with countless leaders navigating the complexities of growth, I've seen how success demands more than ambition or strategy—it requires adaptability, resilience, and above all, purpose.

This book, is not just another guide to business scaling. It's a roadmap for leaders who understand that the challenges of scale aren't simply operational—they're personal, cultural, and deeply human. It speaks to those at the helm of scale-ups, startups, and even established organizations looking to reignite their growth potential. In today's volatile and unpredictable world, where markets evolve faster than ever and competition is fierce, this book is an essential guide for navigating the journey ahead.

Why This Book Matters Now

We live in an era of unparalleled complexity. Technology accelerates change, globalization shifts markets, and consumer expectations continue to rise. For leaders of growing organizations, these changes present opportunities—but only if they are met with clarity and courage.

Unstoppable Growth recognizes that scaling a business is about more than chasing revenue or increasing headcount. It's about building something meaningful and sustainable. This book invites you to consider growth not as a straight line but as an evolving process—a series of decisions, reflections, and transformations that require you to lead with purpose and adaptability.

Through its pages, you'll find insights that bridge the worlds of leadership, innovation, and strategy. You'll learn how to balance the demands of growth with the core purpose that drives your organization. You'll also explore the personal transformations required of leaders to navigate change and inspire those around them.

This is a book that doesn't just tell you what to do; it shows you how others—real leaders facing real challenges—have done it.

What You'll Discover

What makes Unstoppable Growth truly stand out is its blend of practical frameworks, thought-provoking insights, and human-centred storytelling. You'll follow the journeys of Laila, a founder of a sustainable packaging enterprise in Kenya, and Chris, a health tech entrepreneur from the UK. These fictional yet deeply relatable characters bring the book's concepts to life, offering perspectives that transcend industries and geographies.

Each chapter is packed with actionable strategies and reflective exercises designed to help you:

- Align your purpose with actionable goals.
- Build systems and processes that scale without losing your entrepreneurial spirit.
- Foster resilience and adaptability in the face of market changes.
- Empower your team to thrive and innovate.
- Balance the demands of growth with the values that define you.

And perhaps most importantly, this book challenges you to think beyond growth itself. What kind of leader do you want to become? What kind of legacy do you want to leave?

This is not a book that promises shortcuts or guarantees. Instead, it offers something far more valuable: a framework for thoughtful leadership and purposeful growth. It's a book you'll return to as your challenges evolve and your vision expands.

An Invitation

If you're holding this book, chances are you're ready to embrace the next stage of your journey. Whether you're leading a fast-growing startup, a scale-up grappling with complexity, or an established business seeking reinvention, Unstoppable Growth will meet you where you are and challenge you to grow in new ways.

This is a book for leaders who dare to think bigger—not just about their businesses but about themselves, their people, and their impact. I encourage you to dive in with an open mind, ready to engage, reflect, and take action. Growth isn't just something that happens to your business; it's something that happens to you.

Let this book be your guide.

Ben Botes

Introduction

A New Paradigm for Transformative Leadership

Imagine standing at the edge of a vast, uncharted forest. You're armed with a compass and a rough map, yet the terrain ahead is unfamiliar—marked with opportunities to discover but also challenges that demand resilience and adaptability. The path behind you, the one you've already walked, represents survival: the hard-fought battles of establishing something meaningful, enduring setbacks, and learning through trial and error. But now, you're ready for something more—something transformative. Ahead lies the possibility of growth, not just in size but in depth, impact, and purpose.

Leadership in today's world is a lot like navigating that forest. The ground beneath us constantly shifts—markets evolve, industries disrupt, and the very definition of success transforms. Leaders of scale-ups and growth-focused organizations often find themselves at this crossroads, where the skills and strategies that once brought success now feel inadequate for the journey ahead. It's not just about getting bigger or faster; it's about redefining how to lead, inspire, and create lasting change.

Yet, many leaders approach this moment armed with the same old tools: quick fixes, short-term strategies, or frameworks built for stability, not scale. They rush forward, trying to replicate success while losing sight of the bigger picture. Like explorers who ignore the compass in favor of shortcuts, they risk getting lost in the dense foliage of growth's complexities.

But what if we reframed the journey entirely? What if growth wasn't about conquering the forest but about cultivating it? Leaders who thrive in this new paradigm understand that growth isn't a linear race; it's an ecosystem. It requires nurturing, adaptability, and the humility to embrace uncertainty. Scaling a business isn't just about clearing a path—it's about creating systems, building trust, and planting seeds for a future that thrives long after you've walked away.

Here's the question: What kind of leader will you be as you navigate this forest? Will you rush through, chasing the next milestone, or will you cultivate something lasting and transformative?

This book is your compass—a guide to help you reimagine leadership not as a destination but as a dynamic process. Through stories, frameworks, and actionable insights, we'll explore what it means to lead with purpose, resilience, and vision in a world that demands nothing less. Let's step into the forest together.

The Leadership Crossroads: Challenges of Scaling in a Complex World

The modern world has never been more connected—or more complicated. Leaders of scale-ups and growth-focused businesses stand at the intersection of unprecedented opportunity and overwhelming complexity. The promise of scaling is enticing:

expanding impact, reaching new markets, and building something enduring. Yet, the road to growth is fraught with challenges that test even the most seasoned leaders.

Market volatility looms large, reshaping industries overnight. One moment, demand surges; the next, supply chains fracture under pressure. Technology, once a clear advantage, is now a double-edged sword—offering incredible potential for efficiency and innovation but demanding constant adaptation to stay ahead. And then there's the human side of scaling: attracting and retaining top talent, maintaining organizational culture as teams grow, and aligning diverse stakeholders with a shared purpose.

Take, for instance, the story of a once-promising tech startup that grew too quickly. Flush with funding and early success, its leadership prioritized rapid expansion over deliberate strategy. Teams were hired en masse, but systems lagged behind. Communication fractured, product quality suffered, and customer trust eroded. Within two years, the company filed for bankruptcy—not because it lacked potential, but because its leaders relied on traditional methods to navigate a landscape that demanded agility and foresight.

This is not an uncommon story. Many organizations fall into the same trap: chasing growth without a clear compass, mistaking speed for progress, and underestimating the complexities of scaling in a world defined by constant change. These failures remind us of a crucial truth: the strategies that got you here won't get you there.

But not all stories end in failure. Consider the leaders who adapted—those who viewed challenges as opportunities to innovate, who grounded their strategies in purpose, and who built organizations that thrived amidst uncertainty. The difference wasn't just in their decisions; it was in their mindset. They understood that scaling isn't just about expanding—it's about evolving.

For leaders of scale-ups, the stakes have never been higher. Growth requires more than ambition; it demands clarity, resilience, and the courage to rethink how we lead. The question isn't whether the challenges will come—they will. The real question is: how will you face them? Will you cling to outdated playbooks, or will you embrace a new paradigm of transformative leadership?

Unstoppable Growth: A New Paradigm for Transformative Leadership

Growth, in its most traditional sense, has often been measured by speed, size, and profitability. Many leaders focus on scaling as quickly as possible—hiring faster, expanding markets, and outpacing competitors. But what happens when the foundations can't support the weight of that growth? History is littered with examples of businesses that sprinted toward success only to crumble under their own momentum. Traditional growth models often sacrifice purpose, adaptability, and long-term vision for short-term wins. This is where the concept of *unstoppable growth* offers a new path.

Unstoppable growth is not about speed; it's about sustainability.

It's a paradigm of leadership that prioritizes purpose over scale, adaptability over rigidity, and resilience over immediate results. It acknowledges that true growth happens when organizations align with their core values, embrace change, and build systems capable of weathering complexity. In this model, growth isn't something leaders chase—it's something they cultivate.

Consider the story of a thriving bamboo grove. Bamboo is remarkable for its growth, but its strength lies in its roots. Before a bamboo shoot emerges above ground, it spends years developing a deep and expansive root system. When it finally breaks through, it grows rapidly, often towering over other plants. But its growth isn't a fluke—it's the result of patient, intentional preparation.

Now contrast this with a monoculture crop planted for a quick yield. Its initial growth may be impressive, but without diversity or strong roots, it's vulnerable to disease, environmental shifts, and overuse of resources. The difference between the two is the difference between traditional growth models and unstoppable growth. One seeks immediate returns, often at the expense of long-term viability. The other invests in a foundation that ensures lasting success, even in the face of disruption.

In today's world, where market dynamics shift rapidly, and the expectations of employees and customers continue to evolve, the need for unstoppable growth is more pressing than ever. Purpose-driven organizations not only survive uncertainty but thrive within it. Leaders who adopt this paradigm see challenges not as obstacles but as opportunities to align more deeply with their mission, adapt to change, and build resilience.

This book is your guide to achieving unstoppable growth. Through case studies, frameworks, and reflective exercises, we'll unpack the principles of this paradigm and explore how leaders can implement them in their own organizations. Whether it's navigating a volatile market, building scalable systems, or leading with authenticity, each chapter will equip you with actionable tools to grow sustainably, impactfully, and meaningfully.

Because in the end, growth isn't just about getting bigger—it's about becoming better. And that's the foundation of unstoppable growth.

Why This Book Matters: Grounded in Evidence, Built for Action

Leadership is both an art and a science, and this book is crafted to honour both. In an era of constant disruption, leaders of scale-ups and growth-focused organizations face unique challenges: navigating market volatility, building systems that scale without compromising culture, and leading with purpose in an ever-changing world. *Unstoppable Growth* offers a comprehensive roadmap to meet these challenges head-on, rooted in evidence, frameworks, and hard-earned expertise.

Research-Driven Insights

The principles in this book are built on a foundation of rigorous research. Studies consistently highlight that purpose-driven companies outperform their peers in areas like employee engagement, customer loyalty, and long-term profitability. For instance, a Harvard Business Review analysis revealed that organizations with clear, articulated missions saw 20% higher financial performance over a decade. McKinsey's work on scaling businesses emphasizes the importance of adaptable systems, while research from Deloitte underscores that resilience is the defining trait of successful leaders in turbulent times. These findings inform every chapter, ensuring that the insights presented are not only inspiring but proven.

Practical Frameworks for Real Results

This book introduces actionable frameworks designed to transform theory into practice. From the **FOCUS Framework** for aligning resources with strategic priorities to the **GAIN Framework** for achieving quick wins, these tools are tailored for leaders navigating growth. Each framework is accompanied by real-world applications, ensuring that you can immediately apply the concepts to your own organization. The emphasis is not just on what to do but *how* to do it—step by step.

A Decade of Expertise and Hands-On Leadership

As the author, I bring over three decades of experience working with scale-ups, leading turnarounds, and guiding organizations through periods of rapid growth. Having successfully navigated multiple exits, consulted for diverse industries, and coached countless leaders, I understand the complexities of scaling first-hand. This book distills those lessons, combining them with insights from psychology, systems thinking, and leadership development to provide a holistic approach to growth.

What You Can Expect from This Book

Unstoppable Growth is more than a collection of ideas—it's a toolkit for transformative leadership. Each chapter is packed with:

- **Case Studies:** Real-world examples of leaders and organizations that have successfully navigated the challenges of growth.
- **Research-Based Insights:** Evidence-backed findings that illuminate the why behind effective strategies.
- **Actionable Tools:** Frameworks, exercises, and practical steps to implement the concepts immediately.
- **Reflective Prompts:** Questions and scenarios that challenge you to think deeply about your leadership approach.

Your Trusted Guide to Growth

This book isn't about generic advice or one-size-fits-all solutions. It's a personalized guide for leaders ready to embrace complexity and lead with vision. Whether you're refining your systems, redefining your purpose, or rallying your team for the next stage of growth, this book offers the clarity, tools, and inspiration you need.

In the pages ahead, you'll discover not only how to lead but how to grow—your business, your impact, and yourself. Because leadership isn't just about managing what's in front of you; it's about creating what's ahead. With *Unstoppable Growth*, you'll have the insights, frameworks, and support to do just that.

Your Invitation to Lead Boldly and Grow Purposefully

Leadership is rarely a straight path. It's filled with moments of doubt, hard decisions, and unforeseen challenges that can test even the strongest resolve. If you're reading this, it's because you already know the weight of those moments. You've built something worth fighting for—a business, a vision, a dream—and now, you're ready to take it to the next level. But let's be honest: scaling isn't easy. It demands more of you, your team, and your organization than you've likely ever faced before.

This book is here to remind you of something important: you're not alone. The challenges you face, while daunting, are also the opportunities that will define your growth—both as a leader and as a creator of lasting impact. In these pages, you'll find tools to navigate complexity, stories to spark new ideas, and insights to reimagine how growth can look and feel. But more than that, you'll find a companion—a guide to walk with you as you take your next steps.

The journey ahead isn't just about scaling your organization; it's about scaling your thinking, your systems, and your purpose. You are not merely a passenger on this path; you're a co-creator of something extraordinary. Your decisions, your resilience, and your courage will shape the outcomes—and the legacy—you leave behind.

So, as you stand at the threshold of this journey, I ask you: **What kind of leader will you choose to become?** Will you lead with intention, curiosity, and purpose? Will you take the steps to grow not just your business but also your ability to inspire and empower others?

The chapters ahead offer more than strategies—they offer a way to transform how you lead and grow. Together, we'll explore what it takes to embrace change, align with purpose, and build something that matters.

Are you ready to create unstoppable growth—growth that transforms not only your organization but also the people, communities, and world it touches? Let's begin.

Chapter 1

Setting the Stage for Unstoppable Growth

> *"Growth isn't just about numbers. It's about meaning. It's about resilience. It's about building something that lasts—something that matters."*

Growth is thrilling, isn't it? It's that spark of possibility that gets you out of bed in the morning, the adrenaline rush of seeing your vision come to life. But let's be honest—growth is also terrifying. It's messy, uncomfortable, and often full of moments where you question whether you're truly ready for what's next. Leading a growing organization can feel like juggling flaming torches while riding a unicycle. The stakes are high, and the margin for error feels impossibly thin.

A few years ago, I had a conversation with the founder of a social enterprise. She was in the middle of scaling her business after years of building it from scratch. On paper, everything looked perfect—revenue was climbing, new markets were opening, and investors were taking notice. But when we sat down, her first words were, "I feel like I'm holding this thing together with duct tape and sheer willpower. How do I grow without breaking everything?"

Her vulnerability struck a chord because it's something so many leaders feel but rarely admit. Growth is often romanticized as this upward, unstoppable trajectory, but the reality is far more complex. Growth asks us to stretch beyond what feels safe, to operate in a space where uncertainty is the norm. It's not just about moving forward; it's about holding everything together—your vision, your team, your values—while navigating terrain you've never crossed before.

This chapter is about what it takes to build a foundation strong enough to carry that growth. It's about understanding that growth isn't just a set of outcomes; it's a process that requires intention, alignment, and a willingness to confront the hard stuff. We'll explore what makes growth sustainable—not just from a business perspective, but from a human one. How do you, as a leader, create the systems, the culture, and the inner resilience needed to thrive through the challenges that growth inevitably brings?

Before we dive in, I want to ask you a question: What does "unstoppable growth" mean to you? Is it hitting milestones and scaling fast? Or is it about something deeper building something that lasts, something that matters? As you think about this, remember that growth isn't just about what you accomplish; it's about how you show up in the process. Let's explore how to create a foundation for growth that doesn't just elevate your business but strengthens everything it's built upon.

The Challenges of Leadership Today

Scaling an organization is often portrayed as the ultimate achievement—a time of upward momentum, market wins, and undeniable growth. But ask any leader who has walked this path, and they'll tell you it's rarely as seamless as it looks from the outside. Beneath the surface lies a maze of complexities: navigating unpredictable markets, managing the evolving needs of a diverse workforce, and balancing innovation with stability. These challenges don't just test strategy; they test the very core of leadership.

Consider the relentless pace of technological disruption. The tools and platforms that gave your organization a competitive edge just five years ago may now be obsolete. A study by Deloitte found that 87% of executives consider digital transformation a priority, yet only 30% feel they are prepared to adapt quickly enough to keep pace. For scale-up leaders, this gap can mean the difference between thriving and losing relevance in a hyper-competitive landscape.

Then there's the challenge of cultural erosion. As organizations grow, the tightly knit, mission-driven teams that characterized the startup phase can start to fray. Layers of management, competing priorities, and the pressure to deliver results can dilute the very culture that made the business successful in the first place. Leaders often find themselves wondering: *How do I scale without losing the essence of what makes us unique?*

Market volatility adds another layer of complexity. The global economy is more interconnected than ever, making businesses vulnerable to geopolitical shifts, supply chain disruptions, and fluctuating consumer demands. In this environment, the traditional growth playbook—focused on rapid expansion and short-term wins—

often falls short. Organizations that rely too heavily on rigid strategies can find themselves paralyzed when the unexpected occurs.

A Counterexample: When Growth Becomes the Enemy

Consider the cautionary tale of Blockbuster. At its peak, Blockbuster was the undisputed leader in home entertainment, with over 9,000 stores worldwide. Yet, its leadership clung to an outdated growth model—focused on physical locations and late fees—while ignoring the rising tide of digital streaming. Despite opportunities to pivot, including the chance to acquire Netflix in its infancy, Blockbuster's leadership underestimated the pace of change and overestimated the strength of its existing model. By the time they attempted to adapt, it was too late. The company declared bankruptcy in 2010, a stark reminder of how failing to align growth with adaptability can lead to irrelevance.

The Stakes of Leadership Today

The challenges leaders face aren't just operational—they're existential. The decisions made during a scale-up phase can determine whether an organization becomes a lasting force for good or a forgotten name in the marketplace. Leaders must grapple with questions like: *How do I foster innovation without losing focus? How do I maintain alignment across a rapidly growing team? How do I embrace change without compromising the core of my mission?*

These are not easy questions, but they are necessary ones. The complexities of today's leadership landscape demand a shift away from outdated models of growth. Leaders must embrace a new paradigm—one that balances purpose with adaptability, resilience with innovation, and short-term wins with long-term impact.

In this chapter, we'll explore how to navigate these challenges with clarity, courage, and a commitment to sustainable growth. The journey won't be simple, but as the failures of the past have shown us, staying static in a dynamic world is no longer an option. Let's dive into the tools and mindsets that can transform these challenges into opportunities.

Defining Unstoppable Growth

Unstoppable growth isn't just about bigger numbers, faster timelines, or expanding into every available market. It's a new paradigm for leadership—one that prioritizes purpose, adaptability, and resilience over the superficial markers of success. At its core, unstoppable growth is about creating something that lasts, something that impacts not just the bottom line but the people, communities, and environments touched by the organization.

Unlike traditional growth models, which often chase speed and scale above all else, unstoppable growth is intentional. It's a commitment to aligning every step of expansion with a clear purpose, remaining flexible enough to adapt when challenges arise, and fostering the resilience needed to withstand disruptions. This isn't about chasing growth for growth's sake; it's about building something meaningful, sustainable, and transformative.

The Core Principles of Unstoppable Growth

1. Purpose-Driven Action: Purpose is the compass that guides decision-making, ensuring that growth serves a greater mission. Whether it's improving lives, advancing innovation, or contributing to social equity, purpose provides the "why" behind the work. Companies like Patagonia exemplify this

principle, scaling responsibly while remaining steadfast in their commitment to environmental stewardship.

2. Adaptability to Change: Markets evolve, technologies disrupt, and challenges emerge without warning. Unstoppable growth requires leaders to see change not as a threat but as an opportunity for reinvention. Netflix, for example, transitioned from a DVD rental service to a global streaming powerhouse by embracing change rather than resisting it.

3. Resilience in the Face of Challenges: Growth inevitably comes with setbacks—unexpected competition, resource constraints, or even global crises. Resilient organizations not only recover from these challenges but emerge stronger. They cultivate cultures that encourage learning, experimentation, and persistence.

Building a Garden That Thrives

Imagine building a garden. The traditional approach to growth might involve planting as many seeds as possible, as quickly as possible, with little attention to soil quality or the ecosystem that supports the plants. For a while, the garden may flourish—but eventually, the soil is depleted, pests arrive, and the plants wither.

Now consider an intentional gardener. They plant with purpose, choosing seeds that align with the climate and soil. They adapt as the seasons change, introducing new methods or planting diverse crops to protect the ecosystem. And when storms inevitably come, the garden survives because its roots are deep and its systems are resilient. Over time, this garden doesn't just grow—it thrives, providing nourishment and beauty for years to come.

This is the essence of unstoppable growth. It's about tending to the roots while reaching for the sky, balancing short-term wins with long-term sustainability. It's about understanding that growth isn't just a destination; it's a journey of continuous alignment, adaptation, and resilience.

Why Traditional Growth Models Fall Short

Traditional growth models often focus on rapid expansion—maximizing market share, increasing output, or scaling operations without regard for sustainability. While these approaches can yield impressive short-term results, they frequently lead to burnout, mission drift, or vulnerabilities when market conditions shift.

Take the case of WeWork. Once valued as a high-growth disruptor in the real estate industry, its rapid expansion masked deep flaws in its business model. The pursuit of growth at all costs led to unsustainable operations and a dramatic downfall. In contrast, organizations that adopt an unstoppable growth mindset recognize that sustainable success requires alignment with purpose, thoughtful adaptation, and the capacity to weather setbacks.

Unstoppable Growth in Action

This book will serve as your guide to embracing unstoppable growth, breaking down each of its principles into actionable strategies. Together, we'll explore how purpose can anchor your decisions, how adaptability can keep you ahead of the curve, and how resilience can turn challenges into catalysts for transformation.

Unstoppable growth isn't just a leadership philosophy—it's a way to reimagine success, ensuring that your organization doesn't just grow, but grows in a way that matters.

Why Purpose is the North Star

In the journey of unstoppable growth, purpose is the North Star. It's the unchanging guide that keeps an organization grounded, focused, and aligned, even when market conditions shift or challenges arise. Purpose doesn't just inspire—it informs. It's the foundation upon which strategy is built, decisions are made, and cultures are shaped.

The Power of Purpose: Insights from Research

Studies consistently show that purpose-driven companies outperform their peers. Research by Harvard Business Review found that organizations with a clear sense of purpose experienced higher levels of innovation, employee engagement, and long-term profitability. Similarly, Deloitte's *2020 Global Marketing Trends* report revealed that 82% of companies that prioritized purpose over profits achieved strong business results and built greater customer trust.

Purpose-driven companies are also more resilient. McKinsey's research highlights that during economic downturns, organizations with a well-defined purpose retain employees at higher rates and recover faster than competitors who lack a guiding mission. Purpose acts as both a rallying cry during difficult times and a lens through which tough decisions can be evaluated.

Case Study: Patagonia's Purpose in Action

Patagonia, the outdoor apparel company, is a textbook example of purpose-driven leadership. From its inception, the company has aligned its growth with a commitment to environmental sustainability. Patagonia's purpose, encapsulated in its mission statement—"We're in business to save our home planet"—drives every decision, from the materials used in its products to its advocacy for climate policies.

One pivotal moment came in 2011, when Patagonia launched its now-famous "Don't Buy This Jacket" campaign. The advertisement, paradoxically, discouraged unnecessary consumerism, urging customers to consider the environmental impact of their purchases. The bold move reinforced Patagonia's purpose and resonated deeply with environmentally conscious consumers, strengthening brand loyalty and driving long-term growth.

Patagonia's commitment to purpose has also fostered employee engagement. A Gallup survey found that organizations with strong purpose statements see 68% higher engagement among employees—a trend evident in Patagonia's passionate workforce. By staying true to its mission, the company has proven that profitability and purpose are not mutually exclusive but mutually reinforcing.

Reflective Questions: Anchoring Your Organization in Purpose

Purpose-driven growth isn't reserved for companies like Patagonia; it's accessible to every leader willing to align their mission with their strategy. As you reflect on your own leadership, consider these questions:

1. What is the core purpose of your organization, beyond financial goals?
2. How do your decisions reflect and reinforce this purpose?
3. Does your team understand and connect with your mission? If not, how can you bridge that gap?
4. In what ways can purpose guide you through challenges and opportunities in your growth journey?

Purpose isn't just an inspiring idea—it's a tangible driver of sustainable growth. When leaders anchor their organizations in purpose, they

create a foundation that can weather storms, inspire loy
the way for transformation.

Building Resilience Through Adaptability

In an era defined by rapid change, adaptability is no longer a nice-to-have quality—it's a survival imperative. For organizations striving to scale, the ability to pivot in the face of disruption can mean the difference between thriving and becoming obsolete. Adaptability is not just a reactive measure; it's a proactive mindset that builds resilience into the very fabric of an organization.

The Case for Adaptability: Netflix's Evolution

Few companies embody adaptability better than Netflix. Founded in 1997 as a DVD rental service, Netflix initially thrived on a mail-based delivery model. However, as broadband internet became more widespread, the leadership at Netflix recognized a critical shift in consumer behavior: the demand for on-demand content. Rather than clinging to its successful DVD rental business, Netflix boldly pivoted to streaming. This transition required not only technological innovation but also a complete reimagining of its business model.

Today, Netflix is a global streaming giant, with over 238 million subscribers as of 2024, credited with reshaping the entertainment industry. Its adaptability didn't end there—Netflix continued to evolve by investing in original content, harnessing data analytics to personalize user experiences, and expanding globally to reach untapped markets. Each decision reinforced its resilience, ensuring relevance in an ever-changing landscape.

When Adaptability Fails: The Fall of Kodak

In stark contrast, Kodak's story illustrates the perils of failing to adapt. A pioneer in photography, Kodak was once synonymous with innovation. However, despite inventing the first digital camera in 1975, Kodak clung to its traditional film business, fearing that embracing digital technology would cannibalize its core revenue. Competitors, including Sony and Canon, capitalized on the digital revolution, leaving Kodak scrambling to catch up. By the time Kodak attempted to pivot, its dominance had eroded, culminating in bankruptcy in 2012.

Lessons from Adaptability: Actionable Insights for Leaders

1. **Monitor Market Shifts Proactively**: Regularly assess trends, customer behaviors, and technological advancements. Organizations that anticipate change are better positioned to respond effectively.

2. **Foster a Culture of Experimentation**: Encourage teams to test new ideas without fear of failure. Innovation thrives in environments where experimentation is celebrated.

3. **Develop Agile Systems**: Build processes that allow for rapid decision-making and resource allocation. Agile systems are critical for responding to disruptions with speed and precision.

4. **Empower Your Workforce**: Equip teams with the skills and autonomy to adapt to new challenges. Adaptive organizations are built on adaptive people.

Framework for Cultivating Adaptability: The PIVOT Model

To embed adaptability into your organization, consider the PIVOT model:

- **Predict**: Use data and trends to anticipate shifts before they occur.
- **Innovate**: Experiment with creative solutions to emerging challenges.
- **Validate**: Test new strategies on a small scale before wider implementation.
- **Organize**: Align teams and resources to act quickly and cohesively.
- **Transform**: Embrace the changes that drive sustainable growth.

Adaptability as a Path to Resilience

Adaptability isn't just about reacting to the unexpected; it's about building resilience so that challenges become opportunities for reinvention. Netflix's evolution shows that adaptability can fuel long-term success, while Kodak's decline underscores the risks of clinging to the status quo. By cultivating adaptability within teams and systems, leaders ensure their organizations are not only prepared for change but also capable of thriving in its midst.

How adaptable is your organization? As you move through this book, consider how you can integrate adaptability into your leadership, making it a cornerstone of unstoppable growth.

The Balance of Short-Term Wins and Long-Term Vision

Leadership is often a balancing act, especially when scaling an organization. The pressure to deliver short-term wins—quick sales, operational efficiencies, or immediate market impact—can sometimes overshadow the importance of staying aligned with a long-term vision. Yet, the most successful leaders understand that sustainable growth requires harmonizing these two priorities, creating a path where immediate achievements pave the way for enduring success.

Case Study: Amazon's Relentless Long-Term Focus

Amazon offers a masterclass in balancing short-term execution with long-term ambition. In its early days, the company prioritized customer acquisition and rapid expansion over immediate profitability. Jeff Bezos famously reinvested profits back into the business, focusing on infrastructure, technology, and customer-centric innovations like Amazon Prime. This strategy often drew criticism from investors seeking quicker returns. However, Bezos maintained that "long-term thinking is both a survival requirement and a competitive advantage."

At the same time, Amazon achieved short-term wins by focusing on incremental improvements in logistics, pricing, and product selection—each enhancing the customer experience. These small victories reinforced the company's long-term strategy of becoming the "everything store." Today, Amazon's dominance is a testament to how short-term wins, aligned with an overarching vision, can drive unstoppable growth.

The Pitfalls of Overemphasizing the Short-Term

Contrast Amazon's story with that of WeWork, a company that skyrocketed in valuation but struggled to balance short-term expansion with sustainable practices. Fueled by aggressive growth, WeWork rapidly scaled its co-working spaces worldwide, prioritizing market share over financial stability. The absence of a clear, long-term strategy combined with questionable decision-making led to a failed IPO and significant reputational damage. Leaders learned the hard way that growth without alignment to values or vision is unsustainable.

Guidelines for Balancing Short-Term and Long-Term Goals

1. Define the Big Picture: Clearly articulate your organization's long-term vision, ensuring every team member understands its importance.

2. Set Milestone Wins: Identify short-term goals that directly contribute to your long-term strategy, creating a sense of progress without deviating from the mission.

3. Prioritize Alignment: Evaluate each decision for its impact on both immediate results and the broader vision. Avoid short-term gains that compromise foundational values.

4. Communicate the Balance: Transparently share how short-term wins connect to the bigger picture, reinforcing alignment across teams and stakeholders.

Maintaining Focus in the Growth Journey

Balancing short-term and long-term priorities requires discipline, clarity, and intentionality. Leaders must resist the urge to chase quick wins at the expense of strategic direction while ensuring that the pursuit of long-term goals doesn't paralyze short-term action. By maintaining this balance, organizations can scale sustainably, ensuring that each achievement strengthens the foundation for future growth.

As you reflect on your leadership journey, consider:

- Are your short-term wins aligned with your long-term vision?

- How do your daily decisions reflect your organization's mission and values?
- What mechanisms do you have in place to ensure balance during periods of rapid growth?

The key to unstoppable growth lies in mastering this duality—executing today with tomorrow in mind. By finding harmony between immediate results and enduring purpose, leaders create organizations that don't just grow—they thrive.

An Invitation to the Journey

Growth isn't just a destination—it's a journey, a continuous unfolding of potential, purpose, and possibility. The path to unstoppable growth isn't paved with shortcuts or temporary fixes; it's carved by the leaders who dare to embrace adaptability, resilience, and vision in equal measure. It's a mindset, a strategy, and most importantly, a way of being.

As you stand on the threshold of this journey, consider what growth means to you—not just for your organization, but for the people you lead, the communities you touch, and the legacy you aim to create. This book isn't a prescription; it's an invitation to co-create your own path, to explore new frameworks, and to challenge old ways of thinking.

This isn't a journey you walk alone. The insights and stories within these pages are your companions, offering guidance, reflection, and practical tools to navigate the complexities ahead. Each chapter is designed to build upon the last, equipping you to lead with clarity, courage, and purpose.

Take a moment to imagine what's possible if you fully embrace the principles of unstoppable growth. Picture the kind of leader you'll become—the one who doesn't just respond to change but shapes it, the one who inspires teams to achieve the extraordinary, the one who builds not just a successful organization but one that leaves an indelible mark.

So, as we transition into the next chapter, ask yourself:

- What does unstoppable growth mean for me and my organization?
- Am I ready to embrace the challenges, the learning, and the transformation this journey will bring?

With these questions in mind, let's move forward together. Chapter 2 awaits, ready to explore the mindset that underpins every great leader's journey: the growth mindset. Your path to unstoppable growth begins here.

Chapter 2

The Growth Mindset: From Survival to Scaling

> *Scaling successfully isn't just about strategies or tactics—it's about how leaders think. Imagine growth not as a ladder to climb, but as a field to cultivate. What seeds are you planting today that will sustain your organization tomorrow? Growth begins with a mindset rooted in resilience, possibility, and the ability to turn challenges into opportunities.*

Leadership is a word that carries weight. It's inspiring, powerful, and full of potential. But it's also heavy. For those in the thick of it, leadership can feel like a constant balancing act—one foot planted firmly in the present, managing day-to-day demands, and the other stepping into the future, navigating unknown terrain. At its best, leadership transforms not just businesses, but people. At its hardest, it can leave you wondering if you're making the kind of impact you dreamed of when you first stepped into this role.

I once spoke with the founder of a rapidly growing creative agency. Her team adored her, her clients trusted her, and her business was thriving. Yet, she admitted something that surprised me. "I'm leading, but I don't know if I'm actually making a difference," she said. "I'm running from one fire to the next, and while we're hitting our goals, I don't feel like I'm moving the needle where it matters."

Her honesty stopped me in my tracks because it revealed a truth that so many leaders experience but rarely articulate. Leadership isn't just about steering the ship—it's about creating ripples of impact that reach beyond the immediate horizon. It's about shaping the culture, the people, and the trajectory of the organization in ways that endure long after you've left the room.

This chapter is about what I call *The Leadership Effect*—the ripple effect that leaders have on their teams, their organizations, and even the broader communities they serve. Great leadership isn't just about achieving results; it's about building trust, inspiring purpose, and fostering a culture where people can thrive. It's about understanding that every decision you make, every word you speak, and every value you model sends ripples outward, shaping everything and everyone around you.

But here's the catch: The Leadership Effect doesn't happen by accident. It requires intention. It requires clarity about what kind of impact you want to have and how you're going to show up to create it. In this chapter, we'll explore the qualities and practices that define transformative leadership. We'll look at how trust, vision, and emotional intelligence combine to create the conditions for meaningful, lasting impact.

So, let me ask you: What kind of ripple effect do you want to create? Is your leadership leaving behind just metrics and milestones, or is it building something deeper—something people will remember and carry forward? As we journey through this chapter, we'll uncover how you can cultivate the kind of leadership that doesn't just guide—it transforms.

Understanding the Survival Mentality

In the early days of any business, survival is the name of the game. It's a phase of hustle and urgency, where leaders focus on immediate needs: securing funding, attracting customers, and putting out fires before they spread. This mindset is characterized by scrappiness and ingenuity—qualities that can turn a vision into reality against all odds. However, the same survival mentality that fuels early success can become a roadblock as businesses begin to scale.

Consider a startup founder juggling multiple roles, wearing every hat from marketer to operations manager. Each decision is reactive, aimed at addressing today's challenge rather than planning for tomorrow's opportunities. While this approach is often necessary to navigate the uncertainty of starting up, it fosters a pattern of short-term problem-solving. The result? A business designed to survive the moment, not thrive in the long run.

This survival mentality, though valuable in its time, carries hidden costs when carried into the scaling phase. Leaders accustomed to tight control may struggle to delegate effectively, preventing their teams from taking ownership and driving innovation. Prioritizing immediate wins can lead to underinvestment in systems, processes, and culture—the very elements that sustain growth. Over time, a reactive approach can leave the organization brittle, unable to adapt to shifting markets or seize transformative opportunities.

Research supports this shift in leadership focus. A study by the Harvard Business Review found that organizations stuck in a survival mindset during growth periods were 40% more likely to experience operational bottlenecks, employee burnout, and diminished innovation. Conversely, companies that embraced long-term thinking—prioritizing investments in systems, culture, and strategic goals—demonstrated greater resilience and adaptability in volatile markets.

An example of this misstep is Kodak, which, despite its initial dominance in photography, clung to short-term revenue streams from film sales rather than embracing digital technology early. The company's survival-oriented decisions made it resistant to innovation, ultimately leading to its decline. Kodak's inability to shift from a survival mindset to a growth mindset highlights a cautionary tale for leaders of scaling businesses.

Recognizing when to move beyond survival mode is pivotal. It begins with a mindset shift—seeing challenges not as barriers to overcome but as opportunities to learn and evolve. Leaders must step back, reassess their focus, and shift their attention from daily firefighting to building a resilient foundation for the future.

Ask yourself: Are your decisions driven by short-term pressures, or are you creating the space to think exponentially? Scaling isn't just about doing more; it's about doing better, smarter, and with a vision for lasting impact. The survival mentality may have brought your business this far, but letting it go is the first step toward unstoppable growth.

Defining the Growth Mindset

The growth mindset is more than just a leadership strategy; it's a fundamental shift in how we view challenges, innovation, and the potential for growth. Coined by psychologist Carol Dweck, the concept of a growth mindset focuses on the belief that abilities, intelligence, and potential are not fixed but can be developed through effort, learning, and persistence. For leaders of scaling organizations, this mindset is essential—not just for their personal development, but for the success of their teams and businesses.

At its core, the growth mindset is about seeing opportunity in obstacles. It thrives on a simple yet transformative idea: setbacks are not failures; they're stepping stones. Leaders with a growth mindset don't just react to challenges; they actively seek them out as opportunities to innovate, learn, and adapt. This mindset is contagious, fostering a culture where teams feel empowered to experiment, take risks, and pursue continuous improvement.

Research consistently underscores the power of this mindset in driving organizational success. A study by Stanford University found that individuals with a growth mindset were more likely to embrace challenges, persist through difficulties, and achieve higher levels of mastery. These qualities translate directly into organizational outcomes. Companies led by growth-minded executives often report higher employee engagement, greater innovation, and stronger financial performance compared to their peers. A Deloitte survey found that organizations with a culture of continuous learning—rooted in growth mindset principles—were 92% more likely to innovate effectively.

One compelling example of the growth mindset in action is Satya Nadella's transformation of Microsoft. When Nadella became CEO in 2014, the company was facing stagnation. Its culture had grown rigid, marked by internal silos and resistance to change. Nadella brought with him a clear vision for a growth-oriented culture. He introduced the mantra of a "learn-it-all" mentality, replacing the company's previous fixation on being "know-it-alls." By embracing curiosity and learning, Nadella encouraged innovation and collaboration across teams.

Under his leadership, Microsoft reinvented itself, pivoting toward cloud-based services and open-source technologies. Nadella's growth mindset not only revitalized Microsoft's culture but also drove substantial financial success, with the company's market value tripling during his tenure. His leadership exemplifies how embracing challenges and fostering a culture of continuous learning can turn stagnation into momentum.

For leaders of scale-ups, adopting a growth mindset isn't just an option—it's a necessity. Scaling demands adaptability, resilience, and a willingness to evolve. The challenges of today's volatile markets require leaders who can inspire their teams to see obstacles as opportunities and commit to learning as a path to innovation.

Reflect on this: How do you view challenges within your organization? Are they roadblocks to avoid or opportunities to grow? Embracing a growth mindset means seeing every hurdle as a chance to build resilience and adaptability—qualities that are foundational to unstoppable growth.

Transforming Challenges into Catalysts for Development

Challenges are inevitable in the journey of scaling a business, but how leaders respond to them can make all the difference. Adopting a growth mindset transforms these moments of adversity into opportunities for innovation, learning, and long-term success. Instead of viewing setbacks as insurmountable roadblocks, growth-minded leaders see them as the raw material for breakthroughs.

Take the example of Slack, the workplace communication platform that now boasts millions of daily users. Before becoming a household name, Slack began as a gaming company called Tiny Speck. The team poured time and resources into developing their game, *Glitch*, only to see it fail to gain traction. For many, this failure might have marked the end of the journey. But the founders, led by Stewart Butterfield, adopted a growth mindset.

Instead of closing shop, they analysed what had worked during the project. One key insight stood out: the internal communication tool they had built for their team was highly effective and could address a pressing market need. With this realization, they pivoted away from gaming and developed Slack as a standalone product. What could have been a devastating failure became the foundation for one of the most successful SaaS companies in the world.

This ability to reframe challenges is at the heart of a growth mindset. It requires leaders to ask, *What can we learn from this? What opportunities does this reveal?* By doing so, they can unlock pathways to innovation and resilience that would otherwise remain hidden.

Reframing Challenges: A Framework for Turning Obstacles into Opportunities

- Pause and Reflect: When faced with a challenge, resist the urge to react immediately. Take a step back to assess the situation with clarity.
- Identify the Root Cause: Look beyond the surface symptoms to understand the deeper issues at play.
- Seek Insights: Engage your team, analyse data, and explore feedback to uncover lessons and opportunities within the challenge.
- Experiment and Adapt: Test potential solutions, remaining open to iteration and new approaches.
- Celebrate Learning: Recognize the growth and insights gained, even if the challenge hasn't been fully resolved.

This framework equips leaders to navigate adversity with purpose and composure. It shifts the narrative from *Why is this happening to us?* to *What can we do with this?*—a subtle but transformative shift that drives progress.

Reflective Pause

Think of a recent challenge your organization faced. What lessons emerged, and how could they be applied to new opportunities?

How does your leadership team approach obstacles—reactively or proactively?

What systems or processes could you implement to encourage a culture of experimentation and learning?

The journey of scaling is rarely linear. Challenges are the crucibles in which resilience, creativity, and innovation are forged. By adopting a growth mindset, leaders can transform obstacles into stepping stones, laying the groundwork for sustainable and unstoppable growth.

Cultivating the Growth Mindset Within Teams

The growth mindset isn't just a personal philosophy; it's a cultural foundation that leaders can instill across their teams. A growth-oriented culture empowers teams to take calculated risks, learn from failures, and continuously improve. By cultivating this mindset, leaders create an environment where innovation thrives and resilience becomes second nature.

The Power of Culture: Pixar's Commitment to Creativity and Growth

Pixar, the renowned animation studio, provides an exemplary model of fostering a growth mindset within teams. Under the leadership of Ed Catmull, Pixar cultivated a culture that celebrated creativity, collaboration, and continuous learning. One of its defining practices is the "Braintrust," a feedback mechanism where filmmakers present their work in progress to a group of peers. This isn't just a critique session; it's a safe space where ideas are challenged constructively, and solutions are collaboratively explored.

What sets Pixar apart is its emphasis on effort and learning over perfection. Teams are encouraged to experiment, take risks, and embrace the iterative process of storytelling. Catmull famously said, *"Mistakes aren't a necessary evil. They aren't evil at all. They are an inevitable consequence of doing something new, and should be seen as valuable."* This mindset has driven Pixar to produce one groundbreaking film after another, from *Toy Story* to *Inside Out*.

The Role of Resilience in Scaling

Scaling a business is never a straight path—it's a winding journey filled with peaks of opportunity and valleys of disruption. Resilience, the ability to recover and thrive in the face of adversity, is the cornerstone of sustainable growth. For leaders, building resilience isn't just about weathering storms; it's about using them as catalysts for transformation.

Case Study: Netflix—Reinventing Resilience in the Face of Disruption

In the early 2000s, Netflix faced a defining challenge. Its original DVD rental model was under threat as digital streaming emerged, but the technology and consumer readiness weren't fully there yet. Rather than clinging to its existing business model, Netflix demonstrated resilience by preparing for the inevitable. It invested heavily in streaming technology, even as its core DVD rental business remained profitable.

When streaming became viable, Netflix pivoted swiftly, fully committing to the new model. The move came with challenges—reshaping its supply chain, licensing content, and creating original programming—but resilience enabled Netflix to adapt and lead the industry. Today, Netflix is a global leader, not just because it survived disruption but because it embraced it as an opportunity to innovate.

A Cautionary Tale: Blockbuster's Collapse

In stark contrast, Blockbuster, once the king of video rentals, failed to demonstrate resilience. Despite opportunities to adapt to the changing landscape, it stuck to its traditional model, dismissing the streaming trend as a niche. By the time Blockbuster attempted to pivot, it was too late. The company's inability to adapt under pressure turned a once-thriving business into a cautionary tale.

Building Resilience Within Teams and Systems

Resilience isn't just a word we admire from a distance—it's a capability that leaders can embed into the DNA of their organizations. It's about creating environments where challenges aren't roadblocks but stepping stones, and where teams emerge from setbacks stronger, wiser, and more unified. Building resilience within teams and systems requires a deliberate approach, blending culture, communication, and adaptability into the very foundation of how an organization operates.

Let me share a story. A mid-sized tech company I worked with had just experienced a major product failure. Deadlines had been missed, customers were frustrated, and morale was at an all-time low. The leadership team could have reacted with blame or panic, but instead, they chose a different path. They sat down with their teams to deconstruct what had happened—not to point fingers, but to uncover lessons. Out of those conversations came a new understanding: resilience isn't about avoiding failure; it's about using failure as a tool for growth.

That company emerged from the setback not only with a better product but with a stronger culture. Employees felt heard, they felt valued, and they felt equipped to face future challenges with confidence. That's the power of building resilience into your teams and systems. Here's how leaders can do it.

Foster a Culture of Adaptability

Resilience thrives in teams that see change not as a threat but as an opportunity. Leaders can cultivate this mindset by encouraging flexibility while maintaining focus on long-term objectives. For example, regular scenario-planning exercises can help teams practice responding to hypothetical disruptions, building their capacity to pivot without losing sight of the bigger picture. When adaptability is part of the culture, teams become less afraid of change and more energized by it.

Build Psychological Safety

Resilience can't exist without trust. When employees feel safe to voice concerns, share ideas, and admit mistakes, they're more willing to take risks and innovate. Psychological safety creates a space where growth happens, even in the face of setbacks. Leaders can reinforce this by holding "failure-sharing" sessions—safe spaces where teams openly discuss what went wrong, extract valuable lessons, and normalize the idea that mistakes are stepping stones to success.

Invest in Continuous Learning

The most resilient teams are those equipped with the tools to navigate the unexpected. Continuous learning isn't just about skills development; it's about cultivating the confidence to face uncertainty. Leaders can provide opportunities for employees to develop not just technical expertise but also problem-solving and emotional intelligence. This isn't just about preparing for challenges—it's about empowering teams to thrive through them.

Reinforce Mission and Purpose

When the going gets tough, purpose becomes the anchor that keeps teams grounded. Organizations that regularly communicate the "why" behind their work inspire teams to push through adversity with determination. Leaders should take time to connect daily activities to the organization's mission, showing employees how their efforts contribute to something bigger. Purpose provides the fuel that keeps resilience alive, even in the most turbulent times.

Design Flexible Systems

Resilience isn't just about people—it's about the systems that support them. Rigid processes can crack under pressure, while flexible systems allow teams to adapt quickly to shifting demands. Agile project management is one way to embed this flexibility, enabling workflows to be reconfigured as circumstances change. When systems are designed with adaptability in mind, organizations are better positioned to weather storms and seize opportunities.

Building resilience isn't about eliminating challenges—it's about preparing teams and systems to face them with courage, clarity, and confidence. As you think about your organization, ask yourself: Are your teams empowered to adapt? Do your systems bend without breaking? And perhaps most importantly, are you cultivating a culture where setbacks fuel growth rather than derail it? The answers to these questions will determine not just how your organization survives, but how it thrives.

Embracing the Unknown

Uncertainty is the space where growth happens. It's in the uncharted territories of innovation, new markets, and bold decisions that leaders unlock transformative possibilities. Yet, for many, uncertainty triggers fear—fear of failure, fear of making the wrong move, or fear of losing control. To embrace the unknown is to shift from seeing uncertainty as a threat to viewing it as a canvas for discovery.

The Pioneer's Path: A Narrative of Bold Exploration

Imagine a young entrepreneur venturing into a new market. Their product—a groundbreaking health app—had proven wildly successful in its home country, but international expansion presented unfamiliar cultural norms and regulatory hurdles. With every meeting, this leader faced unanswered questions: Would their business model translate? Would consumers trust their platform?

Rather than retreat into what was familiar, the entrepreneur chose to embrace curiosity. They immersed themselves in the local culture, learning from focus groups and community feedback. They reimagined their product with features tailored to the new audience and partnered with local healthcare providers to build credibility. This willingness to step into ambiguity paid off—the app not only gained traction but became a case study in how businesses can grow by adapting to the unknown.

Contrast this with a once-dominant global retailer that resisted e-commerce. Leaders clung to the predictability of brick-and-mortar stores, doubting the viability of online shopping. By the time they attempted to catch up, their competitors had already claimed the digital frontier, leaving the company struggling to survive. Fear of stepping into the unknown sealed their fate.

The Growth Mindset in Uncertainty

Uncertainty is often painted as the villain in the story of leadership, but for those with a growth mindset, it's an untapped well of opportunity. Leaders who embrace uncertainty don't see it as a threat; they see it as a playground for discovery, a chance to innovate in ways they never imagined. Instead of asking, "What could go wrong?" they ask, "What could we learn?" This mindset doesn't just change how leaders approach challenges—it transforms how their teams respond to volatility.

I once worked with a design firm that found itself at a crossroads. A major client, accounting for nearly 40% of their revenue, suddenly canceled its contract. For weeks, the office was a mix of shock and panic. But the founder, a leader who had long championed curiosity and experimentation, stood before the team and asked one simple question: "What could this make possible?"

At first, the question felt counterintuitive. How could losing their biggest client be anything but a disaster? But slowly, the team began to brainstorm. Freed from the constraints of their previous commitments, they explored new markets, revisited shelved ideas, and tested a handful of bold concepts they'd been hesitant to pursue. Within a year, the company had diversified its client base, developed a new service line, and emerged stronger than before.

This is the power of a growth mindset in uncertainty. It doesn't ignore the risks or the discomfort of ambiguity—it embraces them as catalysts for growth. Here's how leaders can foster this mindset within their teams and organizations.

Foster a Culture of Curiosity

Curiosity is the foundation of innovation, especially in times of uncertainty. Leaders who encourage their teams to ask "What if?" and "Why not?" open the door to creative solutions that might otherwise remain hidden. Consider hosting regular "curiosity sessions" where employees tackle ambiguous challenges without worrying about feasibility. By creating space for exploration, you send a powerful message: Uncertainty is not something to fear; it's something to explore.

Redefine Failure as Learning

In organizations with a fixed mindset, failure is seen as the end of the road. In those with a growth mindset, failure is just a fork in the path—an opportunity to learn, pivot, and grow. Leaders can reinforce this perspective by normalizing conversations about failure. For example, implementing a "lessons learned" initiative allows teams to document and share insights from projects that didn't go as planned. This not only reframes failure but also builds resilience and collective wisdom.

Pilot New Ideas in Low-Risk Settings

Uncertainty doesn't mean jumping into the deep end without a life jacket. Leaders with a growth mindset create environments where it's safe to test new ideas incrementally. Running micro-experiments—whether in target markets or within limited audiences—provides valuable data without the fear of committing to unproven strategies. These small wins build confidence, both in the team and in the ideas themselves.

Model Comfort with Uncertainty as a Leader

Leadership during uncertain times is as much about what you do as it is about how you show up. Teams look to their leaders for cues on how to navigate ambiguity. When leaders openly share their own experiences with uncertainty—including the missteps and lessons learned—they foster trust and encourage their teams to do the same. Vulnerability, far from being a weakness, becomes a bridge that connects teams during challenging times.

Uncertainty is inevitable, but how you approach it is a choice. Leaders with a growth mindset don't just survive uncertainty—they thrive in it, turning volatility into an engine for innovation and growth. As you think about your own leadership, ask yourself: How do I respond to the unknown? Am I modeling curiosity, resilience, and a willingness to learn? And most importantly, am I creating a culture where uncertainty feels less like a threat and more like an invitation to explore? Because in the end, it's not about erasing uncertainty—it's about learning to grow within it.

Framework: The Expansion Cycle

Use the The Expansion Cycle to navigate ambiguity:

1. Explore: Approach challenges with a beginner's mindset, asking, "What don't we know yet?"
2. Test: Run small experiments to validate assumptions.
3. Reflect: Evaluate outcomes and refine strategies.
4. Expand: Scale what works, using insights gained along the way.

Reflective Questions for Leaders

- When was the last time you stepped out of your comfort zone? What did you learn?

- How does your organization respond to uncertainty? Are teams paralyzed by fear, or do they embrace ambiguity as a chance to innovate?

- What micro-experiments could you launch today to explore new possibilities?

Embracing the unknown isn't about reckless leaps; it's about stepping forward with curiosity and a willingness to learn. Leaders who lean into uncertainty inspire their teams to do the same, unlocking potential that lies just beyond the boundaries of the familiar. The growth mindset thrives not despite uncertainty but because of it, turning challenges into stepping stones and the unknown into a wellspring of possibility.

Growth is more than a destination; it's a way of being. Adopting a growth mindset isn't simply about navigating the challenges of scaling—it's about embracing life as an ever-evolving journey of learning, resilience, and possibility. Every leader faces moments where the path forward feels uncertain or overwhelming. It's in these moments that the growth mindset shines, transforming what might seem like an obstacle into an opportunity to expand your perspective, your skills, and your impact.

Think back to a challenge you've recently faced. Did it feel insurmountable at the time? What could have changed if you had approached it with curiosity rather than fear, with a question of *"What can I learn?"* rather than *"What might I lose?"* This is the essence of the growth mindset—a commitment to seeing beyond the immediate and striving for what's possible, even in the face of setbacks.

As a leader, your mindset doesn't just shape your own journey; it sets the tone for those you lead. A growth mindset is contagious. When you embrace learning and resilience, you empower your teams to do the same, cultivating a culture that thrives on adaptability and innovation.

An Invitation to Grow

The path to scaling with purpose and impact begins here. It begins with the decision to leave behind survival thinking and embrace the possibilities of exponential growth. What would it look like for you to lead with resilience and adaptability? What would it mean to your organization, your team, and your vision for the future?

This chapter has laid the groundwork for rethinking challenges, reframing setbacks, and cultivating a mindset of endless potential. As we move into Chapter 3, we'll explore the foundation that supports this mindset—rediscovering and realigning with your core purpose. Because growth, at its most transformative, starts with knowing your "why."

So, I ask you: What does growth mean to you? How will you use this moment to set the stage for the next chapter of your leadership journey? Let's step into the next phase together, with curiosity, courage, and a commitment to unstoppable growth.

Chapter 3

Rediscovering Core Purpose for Lasting Impact

"Purpose is the North Star that keeps a business steady, especially when growth brings complex challenges and competing priorities."

For many leaders, uncertainty feels like standing at the edge of a vast, uncharted ocean. The waves rise and fall unpredictably, and the horizon seems just out of reach. It's tempting to wait for the waters to calm before setting sail, to search for absolute certainty before moving forward. But here's the truth: in the world of leadership, calm seas are rare, and the leaders who thrive are the ones who learn to navigate the waves with courage and adaptability.

I recently spoke with the CEO of a mid-sized manufacturing company who found himself grappling with a sudden disruption in his supply chain. "I kept asking myself," he admitted, "'How do I make decisions when I don't have all the answers?'" The uncertainty was paralyzing at first. But then, he realized that waiting for perfect clarity would cost him the momentum his company desperately needed. Instead, he focused on making small, deliberate decisions, testing assumptions, and learning as he went.

This story is not unique. Every scale-up leader faces moments when the path forward is unclear—moments when the fear of making the wrong choice can feel overwhelming. Yet, it is in these very moments that the opportunity for growth and innovation lies. The most effective leaders don't just accept uncertainty; they embrace it as a catalyst for creative problem-solving, strategic thinking, and transformation.

This chapter is about equipping you to lead in the unknown. It's about shifting your mindset from fear to possibility and developing the skills to make decisions with confidence, even when the answers aren't clear. Through research, frameworks, and real-world examples, we'll explore how leaders can turn ambiguity into an ally and uncertainty into an advantage.

Because here's the paradox: uncertainty, when met with resilience and vision, becomes less of a barrier and more of a bridge—a bridge to new opportunities, new ways of thinking, and ultimately, new levels of success. So, as you read this chapter, I invite you to consider: What could embracing the unknown make possible for you and your organization? And what new horizons might come into view if you learned to navigate the waves, rather than waiting for them to settle?

The Erosion of Purpose During Growth

Growth, while exhilarating, can sometimes act like a powerful river—reshaping the land it flows through. For organizations, this current of expansion can erode the foundational purpose that once gave them clarity and direction. What begins as a single, clear mission can become diluted under the weight of new priorities, market demands, or the relentless pursuit of short-term goals. Over time, the alignment that fuelled early success may give way to fragmentation, leaving teams and customers disconnected from the organization's original vision.

This phenomenon, often referred to as *mission drift*, is a common challenge for scaling businesses. A study by Deloitte found that 60% of employees felt their organizations lost sight of their purpose during periods of rapid growth. Without clear alignment, employee engagement and loyalty falter, and customers sense a loss of authenticity. What was once a shared vision can devolve into competing agendas, diminishing the organization's ability to sustain its impact.

Consider the cautionary tale of a global retail chain that started with a mission to offer affordable, sustainable clothing. In its early years, the company's commitment to ethical practices won it widespread acclaim. But as it expanded aggressively into new markets, pressures to cut costs and meet shareholder demands took precedence. The company outsourced production to lower-cost suppliers, compromising its sustainability standards. Loyal customers began to notice, and its reputation eroded. Employee surveys revealed declining morale, with many citing a disconnect between the company's values and its actions. Once a market leader in purpose-driven retail, the brand struggled to regain its footing.

The stakes of losing sight of purpose are clear: a disengaged workforce, disillusioned customers, and diminished long-term value. Yet, not all companies succumb to this erosion. Organizations like Patagonia offer a compelling counterexample. Even as they've scaled globally, they've remained steadfast in their commitment to environmental sustainability, embedding purpose into every decision and communicating it transparently to employees and customers alike.

For leaders, the lesson is urgent: purpose must be actively preserved and re-examined as the organization grows. It's not a relic of the past, but a guiding force for the future. Reconnecting with your core mission isn't just about reflecting on where you started—it's about aligning every decision, every team, and every action with the impact you aim to create. This is the antidote to drift and the foundation for lasting growth.

The Dynamic Nature of Purpose

Purpose, much like a living organism, isn't fixed—it evolves in response to its environment. While the core essence of an organization's mission remains steadfast, its expression must adapt to external changes such as market dynamics, societal expectations, and organizational growth. A static purpose, no matter how noble, risks becoming irrelevant if it doesn't evolve alongside the organization it anchors.

Research supports this notion. A study by *Harvard Business Review* found that companies able to adapt their purpose to shifting cultural and market contexts are 1.6 times more likely to experience sustained growth and employee engagement. Leaders who treat purpose as a dynamic force, rather than a rigid statement, empower their organizations to remain authentic while staying relevant.

Take Unilever as a case in point. For decades, the global consumer goods giant was known for its iconic brands. But by the early 2000s, changing consumer priorities and growing environmental concerns posed challenges to its market position. Recognizing the need to adapt, then-CEO Paul Polman led a transformation grounded in purpose. The company introduced the Unilever Sustainable Living Plan, committing to ambitious goals like halving its environmental footprint and enhancing the livelihoods of millions.

This evolution didn't abandon Unilever's core mission—to improve lives through everyday products—but expanded it to meet the needs of a more sustainability-conscious world. By embedding these commitments into every aspect of its operations, from sourcing to marketing, Unilever not only stayed relevant but also strengthened customer loyalty and attracted purpose-driven talent. Its dynamic approach to purpose turned societal challenges into opportunities for growth, positioning the company as a leader in both business and sustainability.

Reflecting on your own organization, consider:

- Does your current purpose resonate with the realities of today's market and societal landscape?
- Have you expanded your mission to reflect new opportunities for impact while staying true to your core values?
- How do your employees and customers perceive your purpose today, and what might need realignment to maintain authenticity?

Purpose is not a relic of your organization's founding—it is a compass that must be recalibrated as you grow. The ability to evolve while staying true to your essence isn't just a strategy; it's the hallmark of leadership that inspires lasting impact.

Aligning Purpose with Action

Purpose, no matter how compelling, remains inert unless it's translated into daily actions and strategic priorities. The challenge for leaders isn't just to articulate a purpose but to weave it into the fabric of their organization—into systems, processes, and culture—so that it guides every decision, from the boardroom to the frontlines.

Organizations that succeed in embedding purpose into their operations become more than businesses; they become movements. Take Patagonia, for example. Its purpose—"We're in business to save our home planet"—isn't just a tagline but a driving force behind its operations. From sourcing sustainable materials to committing 1% of its sales to environmental causes, Patagonia ensures that purpose is baked into its products and policies. When the company made the bold decision to stop producing certain high-volume products that contradicted its sustainability goals, it sent a clear message: values over profit.

Warby Parker offers another example. The eyewear company's mission—"to inspire and impact the world with vision, purpose, and style"—drives both its business and philanthropic efforts. For every pair of glasses sold, Warby Parker donates a pair to someone in need. This alignment not only resonates with customers but also motivates employees, fostering a culture of accountability and impact.

Purpose is more than a statement on a website or a mantra spoken in meetings—it's the heartbeat of an organization. Yet, for many leaders, the challenge lies in operationalizing purpose, turning lofty ideals into tangible actions that resonate throughout the organization. It's not enough to believe in purpose; it must be woven into the very fabric of how the organization operates, grows, and interacts with the world.

Take the story of a rapidly scaling e-commerce company that wanted to embed sustainability at its core. The leadership team believed in minimizing their environmental footprint, but their actions weren't yet aligned with their ambitions. Packaging decisions prioritized cost over eco-friendliness, and supply chain practices lacked transparency. Recognizing the gap between intent and execution, the CEO rallied the team with a clear challenge: "If purpose is what sets us apart, then every decision we make should reflect it." What followed was a complete reevaluation of their strategy, systems, and culture—a transformation that not only aligned the organization with its values but also strengthened its connection with consumers and employees.

To operationalize purpose, leaders can take deliberate steps to ensure it's not just a guiding star but a daily reality:

Integrating Purpose into Strategy

Purpose must serve as the foundation for strategic decision-making. Every goal, initiative, or expansion plan should be evaluated against the organization's mission. For example, when considering entering new markets, ask: *Does this align with our purpose? How will it create value beyond profit?* Purpose-driven leaders prioritize partnerships, products, and innovations that reflect their core values from day one. This alignment ensures that growth enhances—not detracts from—the organization's mission.

Embedding Purpose in Systems and Processes

Purpose becomes actionable when it's embedded in the systems and processes that define how an organization operates. Patagonia exemplifies this approach with environmental audits that ensure products meet strict sustainability criteria. Warby Parker's buy-one-give-one model seamlessly integrates social impact into its supply chain. These organizations don't treat purpose as an afterthought; they design their operations to live out their values.

Cultivating a Purpose-Driven Culture

Purpose thrives when it's embraced at every level of the organization. Leaders must go beyond one-time initiatives and ensure employees feel a deep connection to the mission. Practices like "Mission Moments," where teams share stories of purpose-driven impact, help bridge the gap between organizational goals and individual contributions. When employees understand how their daily work drives a greater mission, purpose becomes personal—and powerful.

Measuring What Matters: Metrics for Purpose Alignment

"What gets measured gets managed." This principle applies as much to purpose as it does to financial outcomes. Organizations that track purpose-related metrics alongside traditional KPIs send a clear message: purpose matters. For instance, a company committed to sustainability might report progress on carbon emissions reductions with the same rigor as it tracks revenue growth. These metrics ensure accountability and reinforce purpose as a key driver of success.

Leaders looking to align purpose with action can take practical steps to ensure it's more than a guiding ideal:

- Conduct a Purpose Audit: Identify where strategies, systems, or processes are misaligned with the organization's mission.
- Set Purpose-Driven Goals: Embed purpose into every level of the organization, ensuring alignment from executives to individual contributors.
- Highlight Purpose in Action: Incorporate storytelling into team meetings, sharing examples of how the mission is lived out.

- Recognize Purpose-Driven Behaviors: Reward individuals and teams who embody the company's values, reinforcing a culture of authenticity.

In today's world, where consumers and employees demand authenticity, aligning purpose with action isn't just a leadership strategy—it's a necessity. By operationalizing purpose, organizations cultivate sustainable growth, build lasting trust, and create a legacy that goes far beyond profits. As you reflect on your organization, ask: *How well does our daily decision-making align with our purpose? What actions can we take today to bridge the gap between vision and reality?*

The Business Case for Purpose

In an era of increasing competition, volatile markets, and ever-evolving consumer expectations, purpose is no longer a "nice-to-have"—it's a strategic advantage. The idea that businesses must choose between purpose and profit is an outdated notion. In fact, purpose-driven organizations consistently outperform their peers across multiple dimensions: financial performance, customer loyalty, and innovation.

The Evidence Is Clear

A landmark study by Deloitte revealed that purpose-driven companies report 30% higher levels of innovation and 40% higher employee retention compared to their less purpose-oriented counterparts. Meanwhile, research published in *Harvard Business Review* demonstrated that organizations with clearly defined and well-communicated purpose saw stock price growth 12 times faster than the S&P 500 average over a 10-year period.

Why does purpose drive such exceptional outcomes? Because it creates a magnetic alignment between what the company stands for and what stakeholders—employees, customers, and investors—seek. When purpose is clear, employees feel connected to something bigger than themselves, leading to higher engagement and productivity. Customers are drawn to brands that reflect their values, deepening loyalty and advocacy. Investors increasingly look to purpose-driven organizations as long-term, stable opportunities in a turbulent economic landscape.

Purpose in Action: Tangible Benefits

Take Unilever as a case in point. Under the guidance of former CEO Paul Polman, the company launched the Unilever Sustainable Living Plan, embedding sustainability into its core operations. Critics initially doubted whether purpose and profit could coexist at scale. But Unilever proved otherwise: its purpose-driven brands, such as Dove and Ben & Jerry's, grew 69% faster than the rest of its portfolio, accounting for 75% of the company's growth. Purpose didn't just inspire; it delivered measurable financial results.

Similarly, Microsoft's transformation under Satya Nadella illustrates the power of purpose to reignite a stagnant organization. By embedding a growth mindset and emphasizing a mission "to empower every person and every organization on the planet to achieve more," Microsoft shifted from being perceived as a legacy tech company to a leader in cloud computing and innovation. Its market value soared from $300 billion to over $2 trillion during Nadella's tenure—proof that purpose, when lived out, drives enduring success.

Addressing the Sceptics

For leaders sceptical about prioritizing purpose, consider this: according to a 2021 PwC survey, 79% of business leaders believe that purpose is central to success, yet only 34% say their company's purpose drives decision-making. The disconnect between belief and action is where opportunity lies. Aligning purpose with operations not only builds resilience but also attracts the right customers, employees, and investors—those who see shared value as the foundation for long-term relationships.

Moreover, purpose isn't just a moral imperative; it's a hedge against disruption. In times of crisis, companies with a strong sense of purpose fare better because their stakeholders rally around a shared mission. For example, during the COVID-19 pandemic, businesses with purpose-aligned responses, such as retooling operations to produce essential goods, saw increased trust and loyalty, while others struggled to stay relevant.

Practical Takeaways

1. Embed Purpose into Strategy: Purpose must influence product development, market expansion, and customer experience. When it becomes a filter for decisions, it delivers both tangible and intangible returns.

2. Communicate with Authenticity: Share purpose-driven stories that resonate with stakeholders, fostering emotional connections and long-term loyalty.

3. Measure What Matters: Track purpose-aligned metrics—like employee engagement, customer loyalty, or sustainability milestones—alongside traditional KPIs to ensure accountability.

The Transformative Power of Purpose

Purpose-driven organizations prove that success doesn't have to come at the cost of values. Instead, they show us a more sustainable, inspiring path: one where businesses thrive by solving problems that matter to society. For leaders willing to embrace this paradigm, purpose becomes not just a compass but a powerful engine for growth.

Reflection: How can your organization's purpose be leveraged to build trust, drive innovation, and outperform competitors? What barriers must you overcome to align purpose with profit?

Leading with Purpose During Uncertainty

Uncertainty tests the core of any organization. In moments of crisis, market volatility, or disruptive change, leaders face a deluge of decisions, each with high stakes. In such times, purpose acts as an anchor—a steadying force that clarifies priorities, guides actions, and rallies teams around a shared mission. Without a clearly defined purpose, organizations risk drifting into reactive decision-making, sacrificing long-term impact for short-term fixes.

Purpose as a North Star: The Airbnb Story

During the pandemic, Airbnb faced an existential crisis. Global travel ground to a halt, and the company's revenue plummeted by nearly 80% overnight. The natural response might have been to retreat, cut costs indiscriminately, and focus solely on survival. Instead, Airbnb's leadership turned to their core purpose: creating a world where anyone can belong anywhere. This guiding principle shaped their response to the crisis.

Airbnb made tough but intentional decisions, such as streamlining their operations by focusing solely on core offerings like home-sharing while pausing other ventures. They also upheld their values by prioritizing host and guest support, even creating a $250 million relief fund to help struggling hosts. By staying aligned with their mission, Airbnb not only weathered the storm but emerged stronger, eventually executing a highly successful IPO in December 2020. Their ability to lean into their purpose during a time of uncertainty preserved their brand integrity and trust with stakeholders.

The Cost of Losing Clarity: Kodak's Downfall

In stark contrast, consider Kodak's failure to adapt during the rise of digital photography. Despite being a pioneer in the space, Kodak's leadership clung to their profitable but fading film business, losing sight of their broader purpose: to help people capture and share memories. Instead of leveraging their innovation to lead the digital photography revolution, they resisted change, prioritizing short-term profits over long-term vision. Without a clear anchor to guide them through disruption, Kodak ultimately declared bankruptcy in 2012—a cautionary tale of what happens when purpose is neglected.

Purpose as a Decision-Making Tool

When faced with uncertainty, purpose provides a framework for making tough choices without losing direction. It helps leaders ask critical questions:

- Does this decision align with our mission?
- How will this impact our stakeholders in the long term?
- What trade-offs are we willing to accept to stay true to our values?

For example, during supply chain disruptions in 2021, Patagonia prioritized sourcing sustainable materials over opting for cheaper, faster alternatives. Though this decision increased costs temporarily, it reinforced their commitment to environmental responsibility, strengthening customer loyalty and preserving their reputation.

Actionable Strategies for Leading with Purpose During Uncertainty

1. Revisit Your Mission: Use times of volatility as opportunities to reaffirm your organization's core purpose. Ensure all decisions flow from this foundation.
2. Communicate Transparently: During crises, consistent communication rooted in purpose builds trust with employees, customers, and stakeholders.
3. Empower Purpose-Driven Teams: Encourage teams to propose solutions that align with the organization's mission, fostering a sense of ownership and alignment.
4. Balance Immediate Needs with Long-Term Goals: Address pressing challenges while ensuring short-term actions don't compromise the organization's overarching vision.

Reflection: The Resilience Purpose Brings

Purpose is more than an inspiring idea—it's a practical tool for navigating complexity. When markets shift or crises arise, it offers clarity and focus, helping leaders prioritize what truly matters.

> **Reflection:** In moments of uncertainty, how does your organization's purpose inform your decisions? How might leaning into your mission during a crisis strengthen trust and resilience for the future?

Case Reflection: Grameen Bank – Scaling Purpose-Driven Impact through Microcredit

Grameen Bank's story is a shining example of how purpose-driven leadership can create transformative, scalable impact. Founded in Bangladesh by Nobel laureate Muhammad Yunus in 1976, the bank began as a bold experiment in addressing poverty through microcredit. Yunus believed that small loans, provided without collateral, could empower marginalized communities—particularly women—to become financially self-sufficient. Starting in a single village, the concept grew into a global movement that has transformed millions of lives.

The bank's foundational principle was radical at the time: trust in people's innate ability to succeed when given an opportunity. Grameen rejected the traditional banking model, which often excluded the poor, and instead focused on building trust-based relationships with its borrowers. By organizing borrowers into peer groups, Grameen encouraged accountability and collaboration, fostering a sense of shared purpose.

As Grameen Bank scaled its operations, it faced challenges common to growth: maintaining its mission while adapting to diverse cultural and economic contexts. To address these challenges, the bank innovated its loan structures and repayment models to meet the needs of different communities. For example, Grameen introduced flexible repayment plans and expanded its offerings to include education and housing loans, ensuring its services remained relevant without straying from its core mission of poverty alleviation.

Grameen's growth is a testament to the power of purpose-driven leadership. Even as it expanded globally, it remained deeply committed to empowering women—who make up over 90% of its borrowers—and promoting financial inclusion. This unwavering focus on social impact has not only improved lives but also demonstrated that sustainable business practices can coexist with profitability.

Today, Grameen Bank is a globally recognized model for social entrepreneurship, inspiring countless organizations to adopt similar purpose-driven approaches. Its success underscores that scaling does not mean compromising on values—it means finding innovative ways to amplify them.

Measurable Outcomes

- **Global Reach:** By 2023, Grameen Bank had provided microloans to over 100 million borrowers worldwide, lifting millions out of poverty.

- **Women's Empowerment:** Studies revealed that Grameen's programs significantly increased household income and improved access to education for children in borrower families, particularly girls.

- **Sustainability:** The bank achieved a repayment rate exceeding 97%, demonstrating that mission-driven initiatives could also be financially viable.

Lessons Learned

- Align Growth with Mission: Grameen Bank exemplifies how purpose-driven growth can achieve both social and financial impact, proving that profitability and values are not mutually exclusive.
- Focus on Community Empowerment: By prioritizing borrower empowerment, Grameen fostered trust, accountability, and a shared sense of purpose that strengthened its impact.
- Innovate Without Losing Sight of Purpose: Grameen's ability to adapt its loan structures and services while staying true to its mission showcases the importance of innovation rooted in core values.

- Unstoppable Growth Requires Purpose: Grameen's expansion demonstrates that true scale happens when growth is guided by a clear, unwavering purpose—creating lasting, meaningful impact.

Grameen Bank's story is a reminder that rediscovering and realigning with purpose is not just an exercise in reflection—it's a strategic imperative for growth and impact. Leaders should regularly revisit their organization's mission, ensuring it remains both authentic and adaptable to new challenges.

> **Reflection:** What steps can you take to ensure your organization's growth is deeply aligned with its core purpose? How might realignment with your mission amplify your impact on the people and communities you serve?

The Expansion Cycle Applied to Purpose

Purpose isn't static. It's not a set of words etched in a mission statement or something we reference when it's convenient. Purpose is alive, evolving as our world changes and as we change. Rediscovering and amplifying purpose requires intentionality—a willingness to ask hard questions, embrace discomfort, and commit to action. It's in this space of exploration and growth that the **Expansion Cycle**—Explore, Test, Reflect, Expand—comes alive.

This framework isn't about perfection or quick fixes. It's about creating a rhythm of discovery and alignment, ensuring that purpose isn't just an aspiration but the heartbeat of everything we do.

Step 1: Explore—Reconnecting with the Why

The first step in any journey is to pause and ask: Why did we start this in the first place? What was the spark that lit the fire? Exploring purpose begins with revisiting these origins, not to live in the past but to understand how far we've come and where we need to go.

Consider a clean energy company that began with a mission to make solar power affordable for underserved communities. Over the years, they achieved this goal in countless ways, but as they listened to their customers, a new need emerged. People wanted not just access to clean energy but also education about sustainability—how to make long-term changes in their lives and communities.

Actionable Insight: Hold **"Purpose Reflection Sessions"** where diverse stakeholders—employees, customers, and partners—are invited to share their perspectives. Ask questions like, "What does our purpose mean to you today?" and "What needs are we uniquely positioned to meet now?"

Step 2: Test—Bringing Purpose to Life in Small Ways

Once you've reconnected with your purpose, the next step is to experiment. Testing isn't about massive overhauls or sweeping declarations; it's about small, intentional actions that bring purpose into focus.

The clean energy company decided to pilot a community-based initiative: combining solar installations with sustainability workshops. They didn't roll this out nationwide or assume they'd get it right the first time. Instead, they treated it as an experiment, listening carefully to feedback and learning as they went.

Actionable Insight: Use key performance indicators (KPIs) to measure the impact of purpose-driven pilots. For example, track engagement, community feedback, or team alignment to understand how well the initiative aligns with your purpose.

Step 3: Reflect—Learning with Courage and Curiosity

Testing isn't the end of the story—it's just the beginning. Reflection is where growth happens. It's where leaders ask, "What worked? What didn't? And what does this teach us about who we are and where we're headed?"

For the clean energy company, feedback revealed a surprising challenge: while workshops were impactful, they weren't scalable. This wasn't a failure; it was an opportunity to adapt. They explored digital education models to reach more people while maintaining the heart of their mission.

Actionable Insight: Schedule regular "Purpose Check-Ins" to analyze data, gather feedback, and make adjustments. This creates a culture of learning and resilience, where purpose isn't fixed but responsive.

Step 4: Expand—Scaling Purpose Across the Organization

The final step is about embedding purpose so deeply into the organization that it becomes second nature. It's not just what you say; it's what you do, how you hire, how you market, how you lead.

For the clean energy company, this meant integrating sustainability education into their standard offerings. It wasn't a side project; it was part of their DNA. Marketing campaigns celebrated their dual mission of affordability and advocacy, while team trainings reinforced the role of purpose in every decision.

Actionable Insight: Develop a **"Purpose Playbook"** to document stories, strategies, and best practices. Share this across teams to ensure consistency and inspire collective ownership of the mission.

A Story of Transformation: Purpose in Action

When Satya Nadella took the reins at Microsoft, the company was struggling to find its footing. Using a process much like the Expansion Cycle, Nadella helped the organization reconnect with its purpose. He started by exploring cultural pain points, such as a rigid, know-it-all mindset that stifled innovation. Through small tests—like employee empowerment programs—he began shifting the culture toward curiosity and empathy.

Reflection became a cornerstone of the process, with leaders examining what changes resonated and why. Over time, Nadella scaled this mindset across the company, embedding purpose into every facet of Microsoft's operations. Today, the "learn-it-all" culture he championed is credited with revitalizing the company's growth and innovation.

Living Your Purpose Every Day

Purpose isn't a box you check or a banner you hang in the office. It's a living, breathing force that requires constant attention and care. The Expansion Cycle offers a roadmap, but the real work comes in committing to the journey—in being willing to explore, test, reflect, and expand over and over again.

As you think about your organization, ask yourself:

- What does purpose mean to us right now?
- How can we take the first step toward realignment?

Remember, purpose isn't just about what you do—it's about why you do it and who you serve along the way.

An Invitation to Reflect

Rediscovering purpose is not just an exercise in looking back—it's a powerful step forward. In the ever-evolving journey of leadership, purpose is the anchor that holds steady amidst the chaos and the wind that propels growth. It's the reason behind the choices you make, the vision you champion, and the impact you strive to create. Purpose transforms growth from a series of milestones into a meaningful legacy.

As you reflect on your organization's core mission, consider this: Does your purpose shine as brightly today as it did in the beginning? Or has it dimmed under the weight of growth pressures and competing priorities? Realigning with purpose isn't just about rediscovering what once was—it's about uncovering what's possible.

Take a moment to ask yourself and your team:

- How does our purpose guide our daily actions and strategic decisions?
- Have we allowed growth to dilute our mission, or are we using growth to amplify it?
- What steps can we take today to ensure that our purpose evolves alongside us, staying authentic and relevant?

Leaders who embrace this journey find themselves building not just organizations, but movements—communities of employees, customers, and partners who are united by a shared mission. By committing to rediscover and realign with purpose, you position yourself and your organization to create impact that lasts far beyond quarterly profits or market share.

Thought to Carry Forward: *What would your organization look like if every decision, every initiative, every milestone was deeply rooted in purpose?*

In the next chapter, we'll dive into the systems and processes that transform purpose into scalable action. Because purpose, no matter how profound, must be operationalized to drive sustainable growth. Let's explore how to bridge the gap between vision and execution.

Chapter 4

Building Scalable Systems and Processes for Seamless Expansion

> *"Growth is only sustainable when the systems that support it are resilient, reliable, and built to evolve."*

Growth is exhilarating—but it can also be overwhelming. For leaders of scale-up organizations, the excitement of reaching new heights often comes with an undercurrent of unease. You've built something extraordinary, but as success accelerates, so does the complexity. Suddenly, what used to feel manageable begins to strain under the pressure: communication slows, errors creep in, and the very systems that supported your success start to falter.

Take the story of a thriving design company. For years, their close-knit team operated like clockwork—collaborative, creative, and effective. Then, a string of high-profile client wins tripled their workload overnight. Projects were delayed, quality standards slipped, and their once-energetic team felt exhausted and disconnected. The issue wasn't lack of talent or commitment; it was the absence of scalable systems to support their growth.

Scaling a business isn't just about adding more resources or replicating what already works. It's about designing processes that can adapt to growth while preserving what makes your organization unique. Scalable systems aren't just logistical necessities—they're a reflection of your leadership. They tell your team, "I see where we're going, and I'm building a foundation that will carry us there together."

In this chapter, we'll explore the frameworks and strategies that help leaders turn complexity into clarity. We'll unpack how scalable systems create the structure your organization needs to grow without losing its soul. Along the way, you'll hear stories of leaders who've navigated the growing pains of expansion, transforming challenges into opportunities to strengthen their organizations.

Because here's the truth: growth without systems isn't sustainable. It's a short sprint instead of a marathon. And as a leader, your role isn't just to keep up with growth—it's to ensure your systems enable it. Let's dive into how you can create a foundation that fuels your organization's long-term success, resilience, and impact.

The Hidden Costs of Missing Systems

In the early stages of growth, improvisation is often a strength. A scrappy team can solve problems quickly, pivot as needed, and thrive on creativity. But as the organization grows, this lack of structure can create hidden costs. Misaligned teams, inconsistent delivery, and burnout become familiar struggles. Like the lighthouse keeper, leaders must decide: Will they scale their systems to match their growing demands, or will they risk everything on the hope that they can keep improvising indefinitely?

Take the story of a fast-growing tech startup. Early on, its informal culture of "getting things done" was celebrated. Everyone wore multiple hats, and communication flowed freely. But as the team expanded, cracks began to show. Deadlines were missed because no one knew who was responsible for what. Customers grew frustrated with inconsistent service. Employees, once motivated by the fast pace, began to feel burned out by the lack of clarity. Without systems to support its growth, the startup was on the brink of collapse—despite its innovative product and passionate team.

Why Systems and Processes Matter

Scalable systems and processes aren't about stifling creativity or imposing bureaucracy; they're about creating a foundation that allows creativity to thrive. When systems are clear and aligned with the organization's purpose, they act as enablers, freeing leaders and teams to focus on what matters most.

Charles Handy once described good systems as "the scaffolding of freedom"—structures that provide support and stability while allowing the organization to build upward. Without them, even the most brilliant leaders can find themselves bogged down in operational chaos. With them, organizations can grow seamlessly, balancing efficiency with adaptability.

For leaders of scale-up organizations, building these systems is not optional; it's essential. It's the difference between sustainable growth and burnout, between leading with intention and being consumed by the demands of the moment.

A Roadmap for Scalable Growth

In this chapter, we'll explore how to build systems and processes that support seamless expansion. We'll begin by examining research-backed insights into the role of scalable systems in high-growth organizations. Then, we'll introduce practical frameworks like the FOCUS Framework to help you align your resources and streamline your operations. You'll see these concepts come to life through real-world examples of organizations that transformed chaos into clarity. And finally, we'll challenge you to reflect on your own systems, asking how they can evolve to support your growth.

As you read, keep the lighthouse keeper in mind. Scaling isn't about working harder; it's about working smarter. It's about designing a foundation that shines brightly, no matter how many ships depend on it. So, are you ready to build a system that not only supports your growth but inspires it? Let's get started.

The Case for Scalable Systems

Growth without scalable systems is like building a skyscraper on shifting sands. Research consistently shows that as organizations scale, their ability to establish clear, repeatable processes becomes one of the most critical determinants of success. Without these systems, growth-stage companies face inefficiencies, misalignment, and an ever-increasing risk of burnout and stagnation.

According to a McKinsey study, companies without scalable processes experience operational inefficiencies that can cost them up to 20-30% of their annual revenue. This isn't just about dollars lost; it's about opportunities missed. When processes aren't aligned with growth, leaders spend more time firefighting than innovating, employees grapple with confusion and frustration, and customers feel the brunt of inconsistent service.

One vivid example comes from a high-growth retail brand that expanded its footprint rapidly. Initially celebrated for its unique product and customer-first culture, the company struggled to maintain its standards as it grew. Inventory management relied on manual processes, leading to frequent stockouts and frustrated customers. Employee training varied from store to store, resulting in an uneven customer experience. By the time the leadership team recognized the need for scalable systems, customer loyalty had begun to erode, and the brand's reputation was at risk.

This is the paradox of growth: the very success that propels a company forward can also overwhelm it without the systems to sustain it.

Why Scalable Systems Matter: Research-Backed Benefits

Studies from Harvard Business Review underscore the importance of scalable systems in driving alignment, efficiency, and long-term success. A 2020 analysis revealed that companies with well-structured processes experience 40% faster decision-making and are twice as likely to meet their growth targets compared to those operating without them.

Key benefits of scalable systems include:

1. Efficiency: Repeatable processes reduce friction and free up resources for innovation.
2. Alignment: Clear systems ensure everyone is rowing in the same direction, minimizing confusion and duplication of efforts.

3. Consistency: Customers receive a predictable, high-quality experience, reinforcing trust and loyalty.

Consider the example of **Canva**, the design platform that scaled from a scrappy startup to a global powerhouse. Early on, the company prioritized building systems that could grow with its expanding user base. Automated onboarding processes ensured consistent experiences for millions of new users, while clear internal workflows allowed teams to launch updates and features at a breakneck pace. These systems weren't about stifling creativity—they were about enabling it at scale.

The Bottleneck Effect: A Warning for Leaders

Leadership bottlenecks are a common challenge for organizations without scalable systems. When processes are overly reliant on individual leaders, decision-making slows, and teams become disengaged. Research by Gallup found that companies with poorly defined systems have **23% lower employee engagement**, as team members struggle to navigate unclear priorities and expectations.

A striking case comes from a fast-growing tech firm that relied heavily on its founder for approvals and strategic decisions. Initially, this hands-on approach worked, but as the company grew, the founder became a bottleneck, delaying projects and demoralizing teams. The lesson? Systems aren't just operational tools; they're a way to distribute leadership and empower teams to act independently.

Scaling as a Leadership Imperative

As Charles Handy once wrote, "Growth requires leaving behind the structures that brought you this far and embracing the ones that will take you forward." Leaders of scale-up organizations must recognize that systems are not bureaucratic roadblocks but enablers of freedom and focus. When systems are thoughtfully designed, they allow leaders to step back, empowering their teams while maintaining the organization's trajectory.

The research is clear: scalable systems are a strategic imperative for growth-stage organizations. They create the stability needed to handle complexity, the alignment needed to move as one, and the freedom needed to focus on the future.

Reflection for Leaders

Where are the bottlenecks in your organization today? Are there areas where a lack of systems is causing friction, slowing decisions, or undermining consistency? Building scalable systems isn't just about efficiency—it's about unlocking the full potential of your team and ensuring that growth doesn't come at the cost of sustainability. The data is compelling, but the next step is yours. How will you use these insights to set your organization on a path to seamless expansion?

Turning Complexity into Clarity

The word "scaling" often evokes both excitement and unease for leaders. Growth opens new doors but can just as easily unleash a whirlwind of complexities. Systems that once served you well begin to strain under the weight of new demands. Processes buckle, priorities blur, and the pace of decision-making slows to a crawl. Yet, at the heart of every successful scale-up lies the ability to cut through this chaos and create systems that align with the organization's ambitions.

This clarity doesn't arrive by chance—it's cultivated. Leaders must embrace frameworks that transform complexity into manageable, actionable steps. The FOCUS framework—**Filter, Optimize, Commit, Unify, Streamline**—provides a practical roadmap to help organizations not only survive growth but thrive within it.

Filter: Prioritizing What Matters Most

Growth often tempts organizations to take on everything at once, but true scalability demands ruthless prioritization. Filtering helps leaders focus on what directly advances their goals while shedding distractions.

Take the story of a mid-sized e-commerce company at a crossroads. As demand soared, their team found itself juggling initiatives—from expanding inventory to refining packaging designs—only to see delivery timelines slip. By pausing to filter, the leadership team identified their core priority: improving shipping speed. Non-essential projects were paused, and resources were redirected to streamline logistics. Within months, customer satisfaction rebounded, and delivery times improved.

Reflective Insight: Where in your organization are you expending energy without clear returns? What would happen if you paused to refocus on what truly matters?

Optimize: Building Efficiency into Core Processes

Clarity without efficiency can only take you so far. The second step is about creating workflows that deliver maximum value with minimal waste.

Consider a SaaS company grappling with onboarding bottlenecks. As new clients signed on, inconsistent handoffs between sales and customer success teams delayed implementation. By optimizing their onboarding process—introducing shared dashboards, automated follow-ups, and standardized templates—the company reduced onboarding time by 30%, boosting both team morale and client satisfaction.

Reflective Insight: Which of your processes feels clunky or inconsistent? What small refinements could make a significant difference?

Commit: Aligning Resources and Ownership

Great systems falter without dedicated support. The Commit step ensures that the right people, tools, and time are allocated to sustain each process.

A fast-growing consultancy learned this the hard way. Without project managers, client experiences varied wildly. By committing to hire and train a team of dedicated project managers, the organization created consistency in delivery, reduced strain on consultants, and improved client outcomes.

Reflective Insight: Who owns the success of your most critical processes? Are resources adequately aligned to the outcomes you're striving for?

Unify: Creating Alignment Across Teams

As teams grow, silos often emerge. Misalignment doesn't just slow you down—it can erode trust and derail progress.

A health tech startup scaling into multiple regions faced this challenge. Each regional team had developed its own approach to customer support, creating uneven experiences for users. By unifying these processes under a single playbook, they created consistency while leaving room for localized nuances. The result was a seamless customer journey and stronger internal cohesion.

Reflective Insight: Where might silos be creating friction in your organization? What steps could you take to foster alignment across teams?

Streamline: Simplifying for Scalability

Finally, scaling isn't just about adding layers—it's about shedding what no longer serves you. Streamlining ensures that your systems stay lean and adaptive.

For an international nonprofit, the grant application process had become a quagmire of redundant paperwork. By digitizing submissions and reducing unnecessary steps, they doubled their applicant pool and cut review times in half, freeing up resources to focus on their mission.

Reflective Insight: How might your current systems collapse under the strain of future growth? What could you simplify today to make room for tomorrow?

Bringing It All Together

The FOCUS framework transforms the abstract concept of scalability into a concrete, actionable process. By filtering out distractions, optimizing workflows, committing resources, unifying teams, and streamlining operations, leaders create systems that empower their organizations to thrive.

As you consider how these principles apply to your journey, pause and reflect:

- What systems in your organization feel stretched or misaligned?
- Where could greater clarity or collaboration unlock new levels of performance?
- What's one small adjustment you could make this week to set your team up for sustainable growth?

In the next section, we'll dive into real-world examples of organizations that have embraced these principles, demonstrating how the FOCUS framework can turn growing pains into a foundation for lasting success.

Turning Chaos into Seamless Expansion

Case Study 1: Amazon – Scaling Through Systematic Precision

In the mid-1990s, Amazon was a scrappy startup with a simple mission: to be the "Earth's biggest bookstore." With a handful of employees working out of Jeff Bezos's garage, the company thrived on hustle and adaptability. But as customer orders grew exponentially, so did the cracks in its operational systems. Packages were delayed, inventory management faltered, and the pressure on employees to keep up became unsustainable. Bezos knew that without scalable systems, Amazon's ambition to grow beyond books would be impossible.

The turning point came when Amazon introduced its Fulfilment Centres—a network of warehouses powered by cutting-edge technology and optimized processes. Each fulfilment centre was designed with scalability in mind, incorporating robotics, data-driven inventory management, and streamlined workflows. These centres became the backbone of Amazon's operations, enabling the company to offer faster delivery times while maintaining cost efficiency.

To ensure alignment across the rapidly growing organization, Bezos instituted the "two-pizza team" rule—ensuring that no team was larger than what could be fed with two pizzas. This structure created clear accountability while empowering teams to innovate within their areas of focus.

The Results:

- Amazon transitioned from chaos to a finely tuned operation capable of delivering millions of products daily.

- With systems in place, Amazon expanded its offerings far beyond books, eventually becoming a global e-commerce giant with $500 billion in annual revenue.

- Today, Amazon's operational systems are a gold standard in scalability, allowing the company to introduce services like Prime delivery and AWS without disrupting its core business.

Scalable systems aren't just operational tools; they're enablers of growth and innovation. By investing in processes that reduce complexity, Amazon created the freedom to explore new markets while maintaining a seamless customer experience.

Case Study 2: Canva – Democratizing Design with Seamless Systems

When Canva launched in 2013, its vision was bold: to democratize design by making professional-quality tools accessible to everyone. Early success brought rapid growth, but with it came a host of challenges. User onboarding was inconsistent, customer support struggled to keep up, and feature development slowed as teams navigated competing priorities.

Melanie Perkins, Canva's co-founder, recognized that the company's systems weren't built to handle the scale it was rapidly achieving. Without a foundation of scalable processes, the very creativity Canva aimed to empower could be stifled.

The solution lay in two key systems:

1. Automated Onboarding: Canva introduced a guided onboarding experience that adapted to user needs, whether they were creating a social media post or designing a business presentation. This system not only improved the user experience but also reduced the burden on customer support teams.

2. Cross-Functional Alignment: Perkins implemented OKRs (Objectives and Key Results) across the organization, ensuring that every team's efforts aligned with Canva's overarching goals. This system created clarity and cohesion, allowing teams to prioritize effectively.

The Results:

- Canva scaled to 135 million monthly active users across 190 countries, all while maintaining a user experience that felt personal and intuitive.
- Automated systems allowed Canva to support its growing user base without exponentially increasing its team size.
- By 2021, Canva was valued at $40 billion, becoming a model of how scalable systems can amplify a company's impact.

Scalability isn't just about handling growth; it's about enhancing the user experience at every step. By building systems that adapt to user needs and align teams, Canva turned complexity into opportunity.

Reflection: Scaling with Intention

Both Amazon and Canva faced the same core challenge: success outpacing their systems. Their ability to overcome this challenge wasn't about adding more resources but about designing systems that could grow with them. Amazon's fulfilment centres and team structures created operational precision, while Canva's automated onboarding and alignment processes fostered a seamless user experience.

As you think about your organization, consider these questions:

- Are your systems built to handle the growth you envision, or are they a bottleneck?
- How can you ensure alignment across teams to avoid miscommunication and inefficiency?
- What processes could you automate to free up resources for innovation?

Scalable systems don't just solve today's problems—they lay the foundation for tomorrow's possibilities. The choice isn't whether to build them but how intentional you'll be in designing them.

Expert Spotlight: Indra Nooyi – Scaling with Vision and Purpose

When Indra Nooyi became CEO of PepsiCo in 2006, she faced a daunting challenge: how to scale a global powerhouse while aligning it with the shifting priorities of the 21st century. The world was changing, and so were consumer expectations. Healthier products, sustainable practices, and a purpose-driven brand were no longer optional—they were essential. Scaling PepsiCo's operations to meet these demands required more than incremental improvements. It required a bold reimagining of systems and processes.

Nooyi's approach was rooted in her philosophy of Performance with Purpose—the idea that businesses thrive when they balance financial growth with societal impact. This vision became the guiding framework for every decision she made, ensuring that PepsiCo's systems could scale sustainably while staying true to its mission.

Redesigning Systems for Sustainable Growth

Under Nooyi's leadership, PepsiCo underwent a significant transformation. Recognizing that the company's existing systems were optimized for short-term gains rather than long-term sustainability, she spearheaded efforts to build systems that could scale in alignment with consumer demands and global challenges.

1. Data-Driven Decision-Making:

Nooyi introduced advanced data analytics to PepsiCo's operations, ensuring that decisions were backed by real-time insights. From supply chain optimization to product innovation, these systems allowed PepsiCo to scale efficiently while minimizing waste.

2. R&D Investments:

To meet the growing demand for healthier products, Nooyi invested heavily in research and development. This meant creating systems that could support rapid innovation, from developing new product lines to reformulating existing ones.

3. Supply Chain Sustainability:

Nooyi also reengineered PepsiCo's supply chain to prioritize sustainability. By implementing scalable systems that reduced water usage and carbon emissions, she ensured that PepsiCo could grow responsibly while addressing environmental concerns.

Leading with Empathy and Vision

What set Nooyi apart wasn't just her ability to design scalable systems but the way she connected them to a larger purpose. She understood that systems don't operate in a vacuum—they're powered by people.

Nooyi's leadership style was marked by empathy and inclusion, ensuring that employees felt connected to the company's mission.

One of her most famous practices was writing personalized letters to the parents of her executives, thanking them for their contributions to PepsiCo. This gesture underscored her belief that scaling an organization isn't just about systems—it's about inspiring people to bring their best to the table.

The Results: Transforming PepsiCo's Legacy

By the end of her tenure in 2018, Nooyi had transformed PepsiCo into a global leader in both performance and purpose:

- Revenue Growth: PepsiCo's revenue grew from $35 billion to $63 billion under her leadership.

- Sustainability Leadership: The company reduced water usage by 26% per unit of production and became a global leader in sustainable packaging.

- Innovation: Healthier product lines like Quaker Oats and Tropicana became cornerstones of PepsiCo's portfolio, aligning with shifting consumer trends.

Nooyi's ability to connect scalable systems with purpose-driven leadership offers a profound lesson for today's leaders: growth and impact aren't mutually exclusive—they thrive together when supported by intentional systems.

Indra Nooyi's story challenges leaders to think beyond efficiency and profitability. As you consider your own approach to scaling, ask yourself:

- Are your systems aligned with your organization's purpose?

- How can you ensure that your processes not only support growth but also contribute to a greater good?
- Are you inspiring your people to see their role in something larger than themselves?

Nooyi's legacy is a testament to what's possible when systems are designed with both precision and purpose. It's not just about building a bigger organization—it's about building a better one.

Leadership Perspectives: The Fork in the Road

Imagine this: a tech startup is celebrating its meteoric rise. Its founders are hailed as visionaries, its product is a market darling, and investors can't stop talking about its potential. On the surface, everything looks golden. But beneath the shine lies a brewing storm.

The startup's team, once a tight-knit group driven by passion, is now buckling under the weight of rapid growth. Deadlines are slipping. Customers are complaining. And the founders—exhausted from juggling day-to-day firefighting and high-stakes decisions—begin to feel the pressure of expectations they're struggling to meet.

This is the fork in the road that many organizations face during growth: scale quickly to meet rising demand, or slow down to build the systems that will sustain that growth. One path promises immediate returns but risks long-term chaos. The other requires patience, investment, and a willingness to pause—but lays the groundwork for seamless expansion.

Scaling Too Quickly: The Risks of Rushed Growth

Take the first path: scaling quickly. The startup founders decide to hire aggressively, onboard new customers as fast as possible, and push forward with minimal process. They reason that they can "build the plane while flying it," trusting their team's resilience to keep up.

For a while, this works. Revenue climbs, headlines sing their praises, and the organization feels unstoppable. But soon, cracks begin to show:

- New employees, overwhelmed by unclear expectations, struggle to deliver.
- Teams work in silos, duplicating efforts and creating inefficiencies.
- Customers start to notice inconsistencies in service, leading to eroded trust.

Without systems to support their growth, the startup finds itself in a vicious cycle of reacting to problems rather than proactively solving them. The momentum that once drove them forward begins to stall.

Growing Sustainably: The Rewards of Thoughtful Systems

Now imagine they took the second path. Instead of chasing immediate growth, the founders decide to invest in scalable systems first. They define clear processes for onboarding new employees, align teams around shared goals, and implement technology to automate repetitive tasks.

The initial months feel slower. Growth doesn't spike overnight, and investors question the pace. But gradually, the benefits of this approach become clear:

- Employees feel empowered by clarity, knowing their roles and how they contribute to the big picture.
- Customers receive consistent, high-quality experiences, building trust and loyalty.
- The founders regain their focus, shifting from firefighting to innovation.

This path isn't without its challenges—it requires discipline and a willingness to delay gratification. But it also lays the foundation for sustained, purposeful growth.

A Tale of Two Choices

Scaling too quickly without systems is like building a house on sand. The structure might look impressive at first, but it can't weather the storms of complexity. Growing sustainably, on the other hand, is like pouring a strong foundation before adding walls and a roof. It may take longer, but it ensures the house stands the test of time.

Reflection for Leaders

As you think about your own organization, ask yourself:

- Are we chasing immediate growth at the expense of long-term sustainability?
- Do we have the systems in place to support the complexity that comes with scaling?
- How can we balance the urgency of today with the vision of tomorrow?

Growth isn't just about speed—it's about intention. The fork in the road is always there, but the choice is yours to make. Which path will you take?

Beyond the Traditional Blueprint

Scaling systems isn't a one-size-fits-all endeavour. While frameworks like FOCUS provide a strong foundation, every organization operates within its unique context. Leaders must remain open to alternative strategies—approaches that challenge conventional thinking, leverage innovation, and adapt to the specific needs of their industry. Whether it's embracing cutting-edge technology, outsourcing non-core tasks, or fostering cross-functional collaboration, these strategies offer diverse pathways to scalability.

Leveraging Technology: Automating for Agility

Imagine a nonprofit organization that has grown from serving a single community to operating nationwide. Its operations, once managed with spreadsheets and manual processes, are now buckling under the weight of expansion. Enter technology. By adopting a cloud-based project management platform, the nonprofit not only streamlined its workflows but also gained real-time visibility into project timelines and resource allocation.

Why It Works: Technology doesn't just automate tasks; it enhances decision-making by providing actionable insights. For organizations struggling with inefficiency, tools like customer relationship management (CRM) systems or artificial intelligence (AI)-powered analytics can transform chaos into clarity.

Applications Across Industries:

- In healthcare, AI-driven scheduling systems reduce patient wait times and optimize staff availability.
- In retail, inventory management software ensures that shelves stay stocked while minimizing waste.

For leaders, the question isn't whether to adopt technology but how to integrate it in a way that complements existing systems and supports long-term goals.

Outsourcing: Scaling with Strategic Partners

When a scale-up reaches its growth threshold, leaders often face a dilemma: should they hire in-house talent to manage growing demands, or should they look outward? Outsourcing can be a powerful alternative. By partnering with specialists for tasks like IT support, payroll management, or even customer service, organizations free up internal resources to focus on their core competencies.

Example: A fast-growing e-commerce brand struggled with managing its logistics as order volumes surged. Instead of building an internal logistics team, they partnered with a third-party provider specializing in supply chain management. This allowed the brand to maintain its focus on product development and marketing while ensuring seamless delivery experiences for customers.

Why It Works: Outsourcing non-core tasks reduces operational complexity, enables access to specialized expertise, and allows organizations to scale without overstretching their teams.

Are there aspects of your operations that could be handled more efficiently by external partners? What would outsourcing free your team to achieve?

Cross-Functional Collaboration: Breaking Down Silos

Growth often brings silos. Departments become insular, focusing on their own priorities at the expense of broader organizational goals. Cross-functional collaboration is a strategy that ensures scalability doesn't come at the cost of alignment.

When Spotify began its international expansion, it relied on cross-functional teams to integrate local market insights with global product strategies. Engineers, marketers, and customer service teams worked together to tailor the platform's offerings for diverse audiences while maintaining a unified brand experience.

Why It Works: Collaboration fosters innovation by bringing diverse perspectives to the table. It also ensures that as organizations scale, they remain cohesive, with every department contributing to a shared vision.

How Leaders Can Encourage Collaboration:

- Create cross-departmental task forces to tackle growth-related challenges.
- Use collaborative tools like shared dashboards to ensure visibility across teams.
- Build a culture that values open communication and collective problem-solving.

Adapting Strategies for Different Contexts

While these strategies offer universal insights, their application will vary depending on an organization's industry, size, and stage of growth. A small tech startup might lean heavily on automation to streamline operations, while a global manufacturing firm might focus on fostering cross-functional alignment to manage complexity.

The Key Is Intentionality: Each alternative strategy should align with the organization's broader goals and values. Leaders must approach these decisions with clarity, asking not just what systems they need but why they need them and how they'll serve the organization's mission.

Reflection: Exploring Your Possibilities

As you consider your own organization's path to scalability, think about these alternative strategies:

- Are there technologies that could free your team from repetitive tasks and unlock innovation?
- Could outsourcing non-core activities provide the bandwidth needed to focus on growth?

- How might collaboration across teams bring fresh energy and alignment to your efforts?

Scalability isn't just about following a single framework—it's about exploring the possibilities that best serve your vision. By staying open to diverse strategies, you create the flexibility and resilience needed to thrive in an ever-changing landscape. Growth doesn't have to mean more complexity; it can mean smarter, more intentional choices. Which possibility will you pursue?

Building the Foundation for Enduring Growth

Scaling an organization is like tending a lighthouse in an ever-growing storm. The light must shine brighter, reach farther, and remain steady no matter how chaotic the waters become. Throughout this chapter, we've explored how scalable systems and processes serve as the foundation for that light—ensuring your organization can navigate the complexities of growth without faltering.

Key Insights: The Power of Systems

We began by understanding why systems matter: they transform the chaos of growth into clarity, empowering teams and leaders to focus on what truly drives success. Through research-backed insights, we saw the tangible benefits of scalable systems, from increased efficiency to enhanced alignment and innovation.

The **FOCUS Framework** offered a practical approach for designing systems that filter distractions, optimize processes, and unify teams. Real-world examples from Amazon and Canva brought these principles to life, demonstrating how thoughtful systems unlock extraordinary potential. And through reflective scenarios and alternative strategies, we explored the nuances of scaling—balancing speed with sustainability, and tradition with innovation.

The Bigger Picture: Scaling with Intention

At its core, building scalable systems is about more than efficiency or growth. It's about leading with intention, creating structures that serve not just today's needs but tomorrow's aspirations. Charles Handy likened systems to scaffolding, providing the support that allows an organization to rise higher while maintaining its stability.

For leaders, the challenge is to design systems that reflect their vision, values, and purpose. It's not just about building processes; it's about building trust, enabling creativity, and fostering resilience. It's about ensuring that as your organization grows, it stays true to what made it great in the first place.

A Call to Action

As you step back and reflect on this chapter, ask yourself:

- Are your systems supporting growth or standing in its way?
- Are you building for today or laying a foundation for the future?
- How can you create processes that empower your people to shine as brightly as your vision?

Scaling isn't about working harder; it's about working smarter, with clarity and purpose. The systems you build today will define the organization you lead tomorrow. They are the bridge between chaos and clarity, between vision and execution, between growth and sustainability.

Looking Ahead

In the next chapter, we'll explore the role of communication in scaling organizations. Just as systems provide the structure for growth, communication ensures alignment, inspiration, and connection across your expanding team. Together, systems and communication form the twin pillars of successful leadership—steadying your organization while guiding it toward a brighter future.

As you prepare to dive into this next chapter, remember this: the lighthouse's beam shines brightest not because of the keeper's hard work but because of the systems that amplify its reach. What light will your systems help you shine? Let's find out.

Reflect and Refocus: Designing Systems That Reflect Your Vision

As you close this chapter, take a moment to pause and reflect. Systems and processes may sound technical, even impersonal, but at their heart, they are deeply human. They represent your organization's way of translating vision into action, aligning diverse efforts, and ensuring that growth doesn't come at the cost of chaos.

Think about your leadership journey. Have you built systems that empower your team, or are you relying on ad hoc fixes to keep the wheels turning? Are your processes serving your growth, or are they becoming roadblocks to progress?

Imagine standing at a crossroads, much like the lighthouse keeper we met at the beginning of this chapter. You can continue working harder, spinning more plates, and putting out fires—or you can pause, design systems that align with your vision, and create the clarity that allows your light to shine brighter.

Reflective Prompts for Leaders

1. **Assess Your Foundation:**
   - What processes in your organization feel like a source of friction?
   - Are there areas where your team struggles to align, leading to inefficiencies or missed opportunities?

2. **Evaluate Your Growth Readiness:**
   - If your organization doubled in size tomorrow, what would break first?
   - Are there systems you've outgrown that need to be reimagined?

3. **Align with Your Purpose:**
   - Do your systems reflect your organization's values and mission?
   - Are they designed to empower creativity and innovation, or do they stifle it?

4. **Commit to Action:**
   - What is one process you could improve this month to reduce bottlenecks or increase alignment?
   - Who on your team could you empower to take ownership of streamlining or refining key systems?

A Personal Leadership Check-In

As Charles Handy wrote, "The key to growth is the introduction of higher dimensions of consciousness into our awareness." Systems are not just about efficiency—they're about cultivating awareness, clarity, and alignment across your organization.

Ask yourself:

- Am I leading with intention when it comes to systems, or am I letting growth happen to me?

- How can I show up as a leader who builds not just for today's needs but for the organization I dream of leading tomorrow?

Take a moment to identify one area of your organization that feels tangled or unclear. Commit to untangling it—not by doing more, but by creating a system that works smarter. Share this commitment with your team, inviting them into the process of building something that serves everyone.

Growth is a journey, not a destination, and the systems you create today will shape the path you walk tomorrow. So, how will you design your organization's foundation for the future? The answers lie in your ability to reflect, refocus, and lead with purpose.

Chapter 5

Leadership in Turbulent Times: Thriving Through Change

"In times of turbulence, leadership isn't just about managing change—it's about grounding your team in clarity, resilience, and shared purpose."

There's a moment in every leader's journey when the storm rolls in. It's not a question of *if*—only *when*. The winds of market disruption, the waves of organizational upheaval, or the sudden jolt of an external crisis can shake even the most confident among us. In these moments, leadership isn't about having all the answers. It's about who you *become* when the answers aren't clear.

For one scale-up CEO, it came during a global supply chain crisis. Overnight, shipments stalled, customer complaints poured in, and the company's reputation hung in the balance. As she faced her team, she had a choice: hide behind a veneer of certainty or lean into vulnerability, acknowledging the challenge while rallying her people around shared resolve. She chose the latter, and in doing so, she modeled the kind of resilience and adaptability that inspired her team to navigate the crisis together.

Turbulence doesn't just test leaders; it transforms them. The ability to thrive in uncertainty isn't born from technical expertise alone. It's rooted in emotional intelligence, clear communication, and a deep commitment to the people and purpose that anchor an organization through the storm.

This chapter explores the art of leading through change. It's about stepping into the discomfort of the unknown and finding clarity amid chaos. Together, we'll unpack research-backed insights, practical strategies, and real-world examples of leaders who not only survived turbulent times but emerged stronger.

At its core, this chapter is an invitation—to embrace uncertainty not as a threat but as a catalyst for growth. What if, instead of resisting the storm, we learned to sail with it? Let's dive in.

The Leadership Imperative in Times of Change

Change, whether anticipated or sudden, is one of the greatest tests of leadership. According to research from **Harvard Business Review**, 70% of change initiatives fail, not because of flawed strategies, but due to leadership that struggles to navigate the uncertainty and resistance that accompany transformation. For scale-up leaders, who are often balancing the demands of rapid growth with external market shifts, this insight is especially pertinent: thriving through change requires not just strategy, but a leadership approach grounded in resilience, clarity, and adaptability.

The Cost of Reactive Leadership

A **McKinsey study** found that organizations lacking proactive leadership during times of change are three times more likely to experience employee disengagement, operational inefficiencies, and customer attrition. Reactive leadership—characterized by a short-term focus, fragmented communication, and ad-hoc decision-making—exacerbates the turbulence of change, amplifying its negative effects.

Take the example of a fast-growing tech company that entered a new market during a global economic downturn. Leadership responded to the initial signs of financial strain by cutting costs indiscriminately, including scaling back critical customer support functions. This reactive approach created a ripple effect: customer complaints surged, employees felt undervalued, and the brand's reputation suffered long after the downturn had passed. The lesson? Leading through turbulence requires more than quick fixes; it demands intentionality and foresight.

What the Research Tells Us About Thriving Through Change

The ability to thrive in turbulent times hinges on specific leadership behaviours that build trust, foster alignment, and encourage adaptability. Here's what the data reveals:

1. Clarity and Communication Are Non-Negotiable
    - According to a Gallup survey, employees are four times more likely to be engaged when leaders communicate clearly during periods of change. Ambiguity creates anxiety, while transparency fosters trust.
    - Effective leaders don't just share facts; they provide context, framing challenges as opportunities and articulating a vision for the future.

Example: During the 2020 pandemic, the CEO of a global logistics firm held weekly town halls to address employees' concerns, provide updates on company performance, and answer questions candidly. This consistent communication reassured employees, driving a 15% increase in engagement despite industry-wide uncertainty.

2. Empathy Strengthens Organizational Resilience

    - Research from MIT Sloan Management Review highlights that empathetic leadership improves employee retention and performance during periods of disruption. Leaders who acknowledge and validate the emotions of their teams create psychological safety, a critical component of resilience.

    - Empathy is not about having all the answers; it's about listening, responding authentically, and fostering a sense of shared humanity.

Example: A mid-sized manufacturing company facing supply chain delays due to geopolitical shifts took the time to meet with employees across all levels, listening to their frustrations and involving them in problem-solving efforts. This approach not only strengthened morale but also led to innovative solutions that mitigated the impact of delays.

3. **Adaptability Drives Sustainable Growth**

    - A **PwC report** found that 86% of CEOs cite adaptability as one of the most important traits for navigating disruption. Leaders who are open to recalibrating strategies and empowering their teams to innovate are more likely to seize opportunities within the chaos.

Example: When a leading beverage company faced declining sales due to changing consumer preferences, leadership pivoted quickly, investing in healthier product lines while ramping up digital marketing efforts. This adaptability turned a potential downturn into a 12% growth in market share over three years.

The Relevance for Scale-Up Leaders

Scale-up leaders are particularly vulnerable during times of change. Their organizations often lack the established systems and resources of larger firms, meaning that leadership plays an outsized role in steering through turbulence. The behaviors highlighted in the research—clear communication, empathetic leadership, and adaptability—are not just ideal; they are essential.

For a leader overseeing rapid growth, these insights translate into practical imperatives:

- Communicate frequently and transparently to align teams and reduce uncertainty.

- Foster empathy to build trust and resilience within your workforce.

- Remain flexible, willing to pivot strategies in response to changing conditions.

Transitioning to Practical Strategies

While these insights offer a foundation for thriving in turbulent times, they raise an important question: how can leaders translate these behaviours into actionable strategies? What tools and frameworks can guide decision-making, foster adaptability, and strengthen resilience in the face of uncertainty?

In the next section, we'll explore frameworks designed to help leaders navigate change with intention, ensuring their organizations don't just survive turbulence, but emerge stronger on the other side.

Tools for Leading Through Turbulence

Thriving through change requires more than intuition—it demands intentional strategies that empower leaders to navigate complexity while maintaining clarity and focus. Frameworks serve as practical tools for guiding decisions, aligning teams, and fostering resilience during turbulent times. One such framework, **LEARN**—Look, Evaluate, Adapt, Refine, Normalize—provides a structured approach to leading through uncertainty, ensuring that leaders can respond with purpose rather than react out of fear.

The LEARN Framework: A Roadmap for Navigating Change

1. **Look: Assess the Landscape**

    The first step is to pause and look. This involves taking a wide-angle view of the situation to understand the forces driving change and their potential impact on the organization.

    Example in Action:

    When a healthcare startup faced regulatory changes that threatened its core product offering, leadership conducted a thorough assessment of the new rules. They identified gaps in their compliance strategy and mapped out the potential risks and opportunities. This step provided clarity, helping them move forward with confidence rather than panic.

Key Insight: Looking isn't just about gathering data; it's about creating a shared understanding among your leadership team to align perspectives before taking action.

2. **Evaluate: Prioritize the Response**

Once the landscape is clear, leaders must evaluate their options and prioritize the actions that will deliver the greatest impact. This step is about focusing resources on what matters most.

Example in Action:

A mid-sized retail chain experiencing supply chain disruptions during a global crisis evaluated its priorities. Instead of reacting to every logistical hiccup, the leadership team focused on securing inventory for their highest-margin products, ensuring profitability while addressing customer needs.

Key Insight: Evaluation prevents overwhelm. It helps leaders distinguish between urgent distractions and strategic priorities, ensuring efforts are aligned with long-term goals.

3. **Adapt: Pivot with Purpose**

Change often requires adaptation—pivoting strategies, reallocating resources, or shifting focus. This step emphasizes flexibility while staying rooted in the organization's core mission.

Example in Action:

When a SaaS company saw a sudden drop in demand from its traditional customer base during an economic downturn, it adapted by repurposing its product for remote workforces. This quick pivot allowed the company to capture a new market segment and recover lost revenue.

Key Insight: Adaptation isn't about abandoning your vision; it's about finding new pathways to achieve it.

4. **Refine: Test and Improve**

Adaptation is rarely perfect on the first try. Leaders must continuously refine their strategies based on feedback and evolving conditions. This iterative process ensures that changes are effective and sustainable.

Example in Action:

A nonprofit organization responding to a sudden funding shortfall launched a digital fundraising campaign but saw limited initial success. By analyzing donor feedback and tweaking their messaging, they improved engagement and exceeded their funding goals within two months.

Key Insight: Refinement is where resilience is built. It transforms initial missteps into opportunities for growth and learning.

5. **Normalize: Embed Resilience**

The final step is to normalize. Once effective strategies are in place, leaders should integrate them into the organization's standard practices to ensure long-term stability.

Example in Action:

After successfully navigating a major merger, a financial services firm normalized its crisis communication strategies, embedding them into its leadership training programs to prepare for future disruptions.

Key Insight: Normalizing isn't about returning to "business as usual." It's about creating a new baseline that equips the organization for ongoing change.

Table: The LEARN Framework in Practice

Step	Key Action	Real-World Example
Look	Assess the external and internal landscape.	Healthcare startup maps regulatory risks and opportunities.
Evaluate	Prioritize actions based on strategic value.	Retail chain focuses on high-margin inventory during supply chain disruptions.
Adapt	Pivot strategies to align with new realities.	SaaS company targets remote workforce with retooled product offerings.
Refine	Test, gather feedback, and improve strategies.	Nonprofit adjusts digital campaign messaging to exceed fundraising goals.
Normalize	Embed effective strategies into organizational practices.	Financial firm integrates crisis communication into leadership training.

Why LEARN Matters for Scale-Up Leaders

For leaders in fast-growing organizations, the LEARN framework provides structure in moments of uncertainty. It emphasizes the importance of clarity, prioritization, and adaptability while reinforcing the value of continuous improvement. Most importantly, it transforms change from a reactive challenge into an intentional process that drives resilience and growth.

Setting the Stage for Action

The LEARN framework lays the groundwork for navigating turbulence with confidence, but how does it look when applied on a larger scale? In the next section, we'll explore real-world examples of organizations that embodied these principles, turning disruption into opportunity. Through their stories, you'll see how thoughtful frameworks can inspire remarkable outcomes—even in the face of profound uncertainty.

Real-World Applications: Thriving Through Turbulence

Case Study 1: Starbucks – A Masterclass in Adaptation

In 2008, Starbucks was facing what many considered an existential crisis. After years of rapid expansion, the company found itself overextended, with declining sales, frustrated employees, and a waning brand reputation. The very growth that had propelled Starbucks to global prominence was now threatening its survival. Faced with turbulence, CEO Howard Schultz returned to lead the company, determined to steer it back to stability and renewed success.

Schultz's approach was a textbook example of the **LEARN Framework** in action. His first step was to **look**—to assess the true state of the company. Schultz spent weeks traveling to Starbucks locations, speaking with employees, and listening to customers. What he discovered was sobering: the brand's identity had been diluted, operations were inefficient, and the customer experience had lost its magic.

With a clear understanding of the challenges, Schultz moved to **evaluate** the company's priorities. He chose to focus on two critical areas: restoring the quality of Starbucks coffee and reigniting its connection with customers. To achieve this, he made a bold decision—closing all U.S. stores for an afternoon to retrain baristas on the fundamentals of making espresso. It was a costly move, but one that signalled to employees and customers alike that Starbucks was serious about returning to its roots.

The company then began to **adapt**, making changes that balanced efficiency with authenticity. Starbucks simplified its menu to streamline operations and refocused on sourcing premium coffee beans to elevate quality. At the same time, Schultz invested in technology to improve customer convenience, such as launching the Starbucks Rewards program and mobile ordering.

The journey wasn't without missteps. Initial attempts to introduce healthier food options were met with lukewarm reception, and some investors questioned Schultz's decision to slow expansion. But by embracing the **refine** phase, Starbucks iterated on its strategies, fine-tuning its product offerings and customer engagement efforts.

Finally, Starbucks worked to **normalize** its renewed approach. The company embedded its customer-centric philosophy into its operations, ensuring that every decision—from store design to product innovation—aligned with its core mission: creating a sense of connection over coffee.

By 2010, Starbucks had turned its fortunes around. Revenue rebounded, employee engagement soared, and the brand regained its status as a cultural icon. Schultz's leadership through turbulence wasn't just about weathering the storm; it was about emerging stronger and more focused on the company's values.

Case Study 2: Airbnb – Navigating the Pandemic's Disruption

In early 2020, Airbnb was poised for its most successful year yet. Then the pandemic hit, and overnight, the company's bookings plummeted by 80%. As countries locked down and travel ceased, Airbnb faced a crisis unlike anything it had encountered before. The company's survival depended on its ability to adapt—and quickly.

Co-founder and CEO Brian Chesky turned first to **look**, gathering data on how the pandemic was reshaping travel. He spoke with hosts and guests, gaining insight into their fears, frustrations, and emerging needs. Chesky realized that while traditional travel was on hold, there was a growing demand for local, longer-term stays and unique accommodations.

Next, Chesky and his team **evaluated** their priorities. They made the difficult decision to lay off 25% of their workforce to reduce costs, but they did so with empathy and transparency, offering generous severance packages and ongoing support. At the same time, they prioritized initiatives that aligned with their new focus, such as promoting rural stays and introducing features for remote workers.

In the **adapt** phase, Airbnb overhauled its platform to reflect the shifting landscape. It updated its search functionality to highlight nearby getaways, implemented enhanced cleaning protocols, and rolled out flexible booking options to ease traveler uncertainty.

Chesky and his team continued to **refine** these changes based on user feedback. For example, they introduced a "Work from Anywhere" category to cater to the rising number of remote workers seeking temporary relocation options.

By 2021, Airbnb began to **normalize** its new strategies, embedding flexibility and innovation into its long-term vision. The company redefined its identity, not as a traditional travel platform, but as an enabler of connection and discovery, even in uncertain times.

The Results:

Despite the initial devastation, Airbnb made a remarkable recovery. The company went public in December 2020, with its stock valuation exceeding expectations. Chesky's leadership through turbulence demonstrated the power of adaptability, empathy, and a clear focus on long-term vision.

Tying It All Together

Both Starbucks and Airbnb faced different kinds of turbulence—one born of internal misalignment, the other driven by external forces. Yet their leaders shared a common approach: they assessed the landscape, prioritized with intention, and adapted their strategies to align with evolving realities. They didn't just survive the storm—they emerged stronger, with clearer purpose and renewed resilience.

For scale-up leaders, these stories illustrate that turbulence isn't just a challenge; it's an opportunity to reaffirm your organization's values, innovate with purpose, and strengthen the bonds of trust with your team and customers.

As we move forward, we'll explore how you can adopt these lessons in your own leadership journey, using practical strategies to guide your team through times of uncertainty and toward sustainable growth.

Jacinda Ardern – Leading with Empathy and Clarity in Turbulent Times

When Jacinda Ardern became the Prime Minister of New Zealand in 2017, few could have anticipated the challenges she would face during her tenure. From the Christchurch mosque attacks in 2019 to the global COVID-19 pandemic, Ardern's leadership was tested by crises of unprecedented scale and complexity. Yet, throughout these turbulent times, she emerged as a global example of empathetic, decisive leadership, showing how clarity, connection, and adaptability can guide teams and nations through uncertainty.

A Leadership Style Rooted in Empathy

One of the hallmarks of Ardern's leadership is her ability to connect with people on a deeply human level. During the aftermath of the Christchurch mosque attacks, in which 51 people lost their lives, Ardern's response was immediate and compassionate. Wearing a hijab as a gesture of solidarity, she visited grieving families, embraced survivors, and publicly declared, "They are us," reinforcing the country's shared identity in the face of hate.

This act of empathy wasn't just symbolic—it was transformative. It set the tone for the country's healing process and inspired unity during a deeply divisive moment. Ardern's leadership demonstrated that in times of crisis, empathy isn't a soft skill; it's a powerful tool for building trust and resilience.

Clarity and Communication During the COVID-19 Pandemic

When the pandemic hit in 2020, New Zealand faced the same uncertainty as the rest of the world. Ardern's leadership stood out for its emphasis on clarity and proactive communication. She held daily press briefings, often addressing the nation directly on social media. Her messaging was consistent, transparent, and accessible, ensuring that people understood not only the "what" of the government's actions but also the "why."

Under Ardern's leadership, New Zealand implemented one of the world's strictest lockdowns early on, aiming to eliminate the virus rather than simply contain it. The strategy required significant sacrifices, but her clear communication fostered widespread public buy-in. She framed the effort as a collective mission, famously saying, "Stay home, save lives."

The results were remarkable: New Zealand kept its COVID-19 cases and deaths among the lowest globally, allowing the country to return to relative normalcy much earlier than many others.

Reinforcing the Lessons of Leadership Through Change

Ardern's approach to turbulence aligns seamlessly with the key themes of this chapter:

1. **Empathy as a Strength:** Ardern's ability to lead with empathy created trust and unity, reminding leaders that emotional connection is as critical as strategic decision-making.
2. **Clarity in the Chaos:** Her transparent and consistent communication ensured alignment and minimized fear, demonstrating the importance of clarity during uncertainty.

3. **Adaptability with Purpose:** From managing lockdowns to responding to economic challenges, Ardern remained flexible, pivoting strategies as conditions evolved while staying grounded in her overarching vision.

Lessons for Scale-Up Leaders

Jacinda Ardern's leadership offers invaluable insights for leaders navigating turbulence within their organizations:

- **Make it Human:** In times of uncertainty, people look to leaders not just for direction but for connection. Show them you understand their fears and aspirations.

- **Communicate Early and Often:** Even when the path forward isn't fully clear, consistent communication reassures your team and builds trust.

- **Stay Grounded in Purpose:** Adaptability doesn't mean losing focus. Align every decision with your organization's values and mission to ensure your team moves forward with clarity.

Inspiration for the Journey Ahead

Ardern's leadership reminds us that thriving through change isn't about knowing every answer in advance—it's about showing up with empathy, communicating with clarity, and leading with purpose. Whether you're guiding a nation or a scale-up team, these principles serve as an enduring compass in turbulent times.

As you reflect on your own leadership, consider this: How can you create trust and connection within your organization, even when the path ahead feels uncertain? The lessons Ardern leaves behind are clear: when we lead with heart, clarity, and purpose, we empower others to face change with resilience and hope.

The Two Roads of Leadership in Turbulence

Imagine two leaders standing at a crossroads as turbulence sweeps through their organizations. Both face the same external pressures—disruptions to their markets, fear among their teams, and uncertainty about the future. The difference lies in how they choose to navigate the storm.

Leader 1: The Reactive Path

The first leader acts quickly, driven by the urgency of the moment. Meetings are hastily called, and decisions are made without fully understanding the ripple effects. Communication becomes fragmented, with updates coming sporadically and often too late to align the team.

Initially, this reactive approach seems effective. Problems are addressed rapidly, and the leader appears decisive. But as weeks turn into months, cracks begin to show. Teams grow frustrated with the lack of clarity and direction. Decisions made in haste create new challenges, compounding the pressure on already strained resources.

When a key client voices dissatisfaction with the company's response to the disruption, the leader responds with defensiveness, blaming the circumstances rather than acknowledging the gaps in the organization's preparedness. Trust erodes, and morale sinks. The turbulence has been weathered, but the organization is left battered, its resilience diminished.

Leader 2: The Intentional Path

The second leader approaches the same turbulence differently. Before taking action, they pause to understand the landscape, gathering input from their team and external advisors. They communicate early and openly, acknowledging the uncertainty while outlining a clear plan for the immediate steps ahead.

Instead of trying to solve every problem at once, the leader focuses on high-impact priorities, empowering their team to address less critical issues. They remain adaptable, willing to pivot strategies as new information emerges, but always rooted in the organization's core values and mission.

This intentional approach fosters trust and cohesion. Teams feel supported, not overwhelmed. Customers appreciate the leader's transparency and proactive efforts, deepening their loyalty. When the turbulence passes, the organization emerges stronger—not because it avoided the storm, but because it navigated through it with purpose and unity.

The Dilemma: Reacting vs. Responding

Both leaders faced the same storm, but their choices led to vastly different outcomes. The dilemma they highlight is one all leaders face:

- **Do you react to turbulence with speed and urgency, risking fragmentation and short-term thinking?**
- **Or do you respond with intentionality, balancing clarity and adaptability while staying anchored in your values?**

In the heat of the moment, the reactive path can feel tempting. It provides a sense of control and immediate action, but its costs—misalignment, eroded trust, and diminished resilience—often outweigh the benefits. The intentional path, though slower and more measured, creates the foundation for long-term growth and strength.

Reflection for Leaders

As you reflect on this contrast, consider your own leadership approach:

- When turbulence arises, do you find yourself reacting impulsively, or do you take the time to assess and prioritize?
- How do your actions during uncertainty affect the trust and alignment within your team?
- Are you anchoring your decisions in your organization's values, or are you letting the urgency of the moment dictate your choices?

Leadership in turbulent times isn't about avoiding the storm—it's about navigating it with intention. The choices you make, the way you communicate, and the values you uphold will shape not just how your organization survives but how it thrives on the other side.

What kind of leader do you want to be when the waters are rough? The answer lies in how you choose to respond when faced with the storm.

Beyond the Familiar Approaches

When navigating turbulent times, it's tempting to lean solely on established frameworks and strategies. They provide clarity, structure, and a sense of control amid chaos. But turbulence often requires us to think beyond the familiar, exploring alternative approaches that challenge traditional leadership paradigms. These complementary strategies not only broaden your toolkit but also open new doors for innovation and resilience.

Cultivating Shared Leadership

In times of uncertainty, the traditional model of a single, decisive leader at the helm can become a bottleneck. Turbulence demands fast decisions and diverse perspectives, and no single leader can hold all the answers. Shared leadership—distributing decision-making authority across the team—offers an alternative that fosters agility and engagement.

Imagine a mid-sized tech company grappling with market disruptions. Instead of centralizing control, the CEO creates a "turbulence task force" made up of cross-functional leaders. Each member is empowered to take ownership of specific challenges, such as supply chain issues or customer retention. This shared approach ensures that no single individual is overwhelmed while also leveraging the unique insights of each team member.

The result? Faster decisions, more innovative solutions, and a team that feels deeply invested in the organization's success. Shared leadership isn't about relinquishing control; it's about multiplying capacity and strengthening alignment.

Building Adaptive Networks

Leaders often think of their organization as a standalone entity, but in turbulent times, strength comes from connection. Adaptive networks—partnerships and collaborations with external stakeholders—can provide resources, insights, and resilience that no single organization can achieve alone.

Consider the story of a small beverage company during the early days of the pandemic. Faced with declining sales as restaurants and bars closed, the company partnered with local food delivery platforms to offer bundled meal and drink options. By building an adaptive network, the company not only maintained revenue but also expanded its customer base to include individuals ordering from home.

This strategy isn't limited to partnerships with other businesses. Engaging with customers, suppliers, and even competitors to share resources or align on common goals can turn turbulence into an opportunity for collective growth. Adaptive networks remind leaders that resilience isn't built in isolation—it's a collaborative effort.

Embracing Scenario Thinking

While many leaders focus on responding to the immediate challenges of turbulence, scenario thinking offers a proactive approach to navigating uncertainty. This strategy involves envisioning multiple possible futures and preparing flexible plans for each.

Picture a regional healthcare provider bracing for fluctuating patient volumes due to an unpredictable flu season. Instead of committing to a single forecast, leadership develops three scenarios: low, moderate, and high patient demand. For each scenario, they identify key actions—adjusting staffing levels, coordinating with nearby hospitals, and stockpiling essential supplies.

When the flu season hits harder than expected, the organization isn't caught off guard. Their scenario thinking has prepared them to pivot quickly, ensuring continuity of care without overwhelming their resources.

Scenario thinking shifts the focus from predicting the future to preparing for it, enabling leaders to act with confidence regardless of the uncertainties they face.

Reframing Challenges as Opportunities

At the heart of all these strategies is a shift in mindset. Turbulence isn't just a challenge to overcome; it's an opportunity to innovate, build trust, and strengthen the bonds within your organization.

A global nonprofit organization facing donor fatigue reframed its fundraising challenges as an opportunity to engage supporters more meaningfully. Instead of relying on traditional appeals, they launched a campaign centered on storytelling, sharing the personal impact of their work on communities worldwide. The result was not only a successful fundraising effort but also a deeper emotional connection with their donor base.

Reframing challenges allows leaders to approach turbulence with curiosity and optimism, unlocking possibilities that might otherwise remain hidden.

The Bigger Picture

These alternative strategies—shared leadership, adaptive networks, scenario thinking, and reframing challenges—remind us that there is no one-size-fits-all approach to leading through turbulence. Each context demands its own combination of tools, perspectives, and innovations.

As you consider your own leadership journey, ask yourself:

- Are you leaning too heavily on familiar strategies, or are you exploring the full range of possibilities?
- How can you engage others—both inside and outside your organization—to create resilience through collaboration?

- What opportunities for growth and innovation might be hiding within the turbulence you're facing?

Leadership in turbulent times is an invitation to think expansively, to challenge assumptions, and to embrace the unexpected. The strategies you adopt now will not only define how your organization navigates the storm but also how it thrives in the calm that follows.

Thriving Through the Storm

Leadership in turbulent times is much like crossing a rushing river. The waters are unpredictable, the path is unclear, and every step carries risk. But as we've seen throughout this chapter, the right approach—grounded in empathy, clarity, and adaptability—can transform even the most daunting challenges into opportunities for growth and renewal.

Key Insights for Leading Through Change

At the heart of thriving in turbulence lies a simple truth: leadership is less about having all the answers and more about how you respond to uncertainty. We explored how frameworks like **LEARN** provide structure, offering practical steps to look, evaluate, adapt, refine, and normalize in the face of change. Through stories of Starbucks and Airbnb, we saw that intentional leadership isn't about avoiding the storm—it's about navigating through it with purpose.

Jacinda Ardern's empathetic, clear, and adaptive leadership style reinforced the idea that connecting with people is as vital as crafting strategy. And we challenged ourselves to consider the difference between reacting impulsively and responding intentionally, a choice that defines not only the leader but the organization they guide.

Finally, we broadened the horizon with alternative strategies—shared leadership, adaptive networks, scenario thinking, and reframing challenges—that encourage leaders to think beyond the familiar and embrace the full spectrum of possibilities.

A Call to Action

Now, it's your turn to step into the current. Reflect on your own leadership during times of turbulence:

- Are you creating clarity and connection for your team, or are you unintentionally adding to the noise?
- Do your decisions reflect adaptability and purpose, or are they reactions to immediate pressures?
- How are you preparing your organization not just to survive turbulence, but to thrive because of it?

Leadership in uncertainty isn't a solo journey. It's a collaborative effort, built on trust, communication, and the shared resilience of a team aligned with its values. As you face the inevitable storms ahead, remember that every challenge is an opportunity to strengthen the bonds within your organization, reaffirm its mission, and innovate with courage.

Looking Ahead

In the next chapter, we'll delve into the art of communication during turbulent times—a skill as vital as any framework or strategy. Just as a steady hand guides a ship through rough waters, clear and authentic communication keeps your team aligned, inspired, and focused on the journey ahead.

The river will always flow, and the storm will inevitably come. The question is: how will you lead through it? With clarity, empathy, and adaptability, the answer is yours to define. Let's take the next step together.

Leading Through the Waters of Change

As we close this chapter, take a moment to step back and reflect. Leadership in turbulent times is not defined by the absence of challenges but by the choices you make in the face of them. How you navigate uncertainty shapes not only your organization but also your legacy as a leader.

Think of the river we've journeyed through in this chapter. It's a powerful metaphor for the ever-changing currents of growth, disruption, and opportunity. Are you standing on the edge, hesitant to step forward? Are you rushing into the waters without a clear plan? Or are you leading your team with purpose, charting a path that balances courage with caution?

Your Leadership Lens

Begin by reflecting on your approach to turbulence:

- **Empathy:** How do you connect with your team during times of uncertainty? Are you creating space for their concerns, or are you so focused on solutions that their voices are getting lost?
- **Clarity:** When the path ahead feels unclear, how do you communicate your vision? Are you providing enough context and consistency to build trust, or are your messages reactive and fragmented?

- **Adaptability:** In moments of change, are you clinging to old strategies that no longer serve you, or are you willing to pivot and explore new possibilities?

Revisiting the Framework

Consider how the **LEARN Framework** might guide your next steps:

- Are you taking the time to look and assess the full landscape before making decisions?

- When evaluating priorities, are you focusing on actions that align with your organization's values and goals?

- How have you adapted your leadership style to meet the unique demands of turbulence?

Your Organization's Resilience

Beyond your personal leadership, think about your organization as a whole:

- Do your systems and processes support clarity and flexibility, or do they add friction during times of change?

- How well does your team collaborate under pressure? Are there silos that need breaking or new opportunities for shared leadership?

- Are you building networks and partnerships that strengthen your ability to adapt and thrive?

A Moment of Introspection

As you pause to reflect, let this chapter's lessons settle into your leadership journey. Consider the challenges you're currently facing and the opportunities they might hold. Ask yourself:

- What is one change I can make today to lead with more intention?

- How can I create trust and alignment within my team, even when the path forward feels unclear?

- What does resilience mean to me, and how am I fostering it in myself and those around me?

Looking Forward

Turbulence is inevitable, but how you respond is within your control. Take what you've learned in this chapter and carry it forward—not as a rigid blueprint but as a guide to help you navigate the uncertainties that lie ahead.

The river may be unpredictable, but you are not without tools, wisdom, and a team ready to follow your lead. How will you step into the current? The choice is yours.

Chapter 6

Effective Communication in a Noisy World

"Effective communication cuts through noise, creates clarity, and inspires action. For leaders, it's the skill that enables connection, trust, and resilience."

It's a feeling we've all experienced: standing in a crowded room, trying to share something important, only to realize your voice is getting lost in the noise. The world of leadership often feels like that crowded room. In the constant clamor of emails, meetings, market updates, and opinions flying from every direction, even the clearest message can go unheard.

One founder of a rapidly scaling tech company recalls a turning point when her team seemed paralyzed by misalignment. "We were all talking," she said, "but no one was hearing each other. Decisions stalled, morale dipped, and the pace we prided ourselves on began to falter. I realized then—it wasn't a strategy problem. It was a communication problem."

Effective communication isn't just about transmitting information; it's about creating connection. It's the bridge between vision and action, between intention and impact. And in a world saturated with noise, clarity, empathy, and authenticity aren't just nice-to-haves—they're leadership superpowers.

This chapter is about reclaiming that superpower. Whether you're leading a boardroom, rallying your team, or crafting a message for stakeholders, your ability to cut through the noise and reach people where they are defines your leadership impact.

We'll dive into the psychology of communication, exploring what makes messages stick and why some leaders resonate while others fade into the background. We'll uncover frameworks to help you sharpen your voice, and we'll look at leaders who've mastered the art of meaningful connection—even in the most complex environments.

But this isn't just about technique; it's about trust. The way we communicate isn't just a reflection of what we think—it's a reflection of who we are. Are we willing to listen as much as we speak? To meet people with curiosity instead of judgment? To use words not as weapons but as tools for understanding?

Communication, at its best, is an act of generosity. It's an opportunity to cut through the fog of busyness and say, "This matters. You matter." And when leaders embrace that opportunity, they don't just deliver messages; they inspire movements.

Let's explore what it takes to communicate with clarity and heart, even in the noisiest of worlds.

The Science of Communication in a Noisy World

In a world brimming with messages, mastering communication is no longer optional for leaders—it's essential. Research underscores the critical role that effective communication plays in shaping organizational success, particularly in scale-ups where growth amplifies complexity. The data is clear: how leaders communicate can determine whether their teams thrive amid the noise or get lost in it.

Clarity is the Anchor

A **Harvard Business Review study** found that employees are 23% more likely to be engaged when their leaders communicate clear goals and expectations. Yet, clarity often becomes a casualty in fast-paced environments where information flows relentlessly and priorities shift. Without a clear anchor, teams drift, wasting time and energy on misaligned efforts.

Example: A growing fintech company struggling to scale its operations discovered through an internal survey that 40% of its employees were unclear about their individual roles in achieving the company's strategic goals. Leadership responded by overhauling their communication practices, introducing monthly town halls and concise, targeted updates from managers. The result? A measurable increase in productivity and a significant reduction in project delays.

Clarity isn't just about eliminating confusion; it's about creating alignment. For scale-up leaders, it means ensuring that every message reinforces the "why" behind the organization's actions, connecting day-to-day efforts with the bigger picture.

Empathy Builds Bridges

According to a **McKinsey report**, empathy in leadership directly correlates with higher employee satisfaction and retention. This insight is especially relevant for scale-ups, where rapid growth often leads to stress, uncertainty, and change fatigue. Leaders who fail to acknowledge these emotions risk alienating their teams, while those who communicate with empathy foster trust and resilience.

Example: Consider a software development firm that implemented a major shift to remote work during the pandemic. While many leaders defaulted to task-oriented updates, one team lead began each meeting by asking, "How are you really doing?" This simple act of empathy not only strengthened morale but also improved team collaboration, as employees felt valued and supported.

Empathy isn't just a soft skill; it's a strategic advantage. Leaders who listen actively, validate concerns, and adapt their communication to the emotional state of their teams create stronger, more engaged organizations.

Consistency is Trust's Foundation

The **Edelman Trust Barometer** reveals that 59% of employees believe their leaders need to communicate consistently to build trust during times of uncertainty. Inconsistent messaging—whether in tone, frequency, or content—creates confusion and erodes confidence, particularly in growth-stage organizations where trust is a cornerstone of collaboration.

Example: A consumer goods start-up learned this lesson the hard way when its leadership team sent mixed messages about a new product launch. While the CEO emphasized speed, the COO focused on quality, leaving teams uncertain about priorities. After recognizing the disconnect, the leadership aligned on a unified message and established a cadence of weekly updates, restoring trust and improving execution.

Consistency ensures that communication feels reliable and predictable, even in unpredictable times. For scale-up leaders, it's the difference between inspiring confidence and sowing doubt.

Adaptability Cuts Through Noise

In a world where one-size-fits-all communication no longer works, adaptability is a critical skill. Research from **PwC** highlights that 76% of employees believe organizations that tailor their messaging to different audiences are more effective in achieving their goals. Leaders who can adapt their tone, content, and delivery method to suit various stakeholders—from investors to frontline teams—are better positioned to drive alignment and action.

Example: When a global ed-tech company launched a new product line, its leadership team adapted their messaging for each audience. For employees, they focused on the mission of empowering learners; for investors, they emphasized growth projections; and for customers, they highlighted features that addressed specific pain points. This tailored approach ensured each group felt engaged and understood, leading to a successful launch.

Adaptability in communication isn't about changing the message; it's about changing the way it's delivered to resonate with diverse audiences.

The Cost of Getting It Wrong

While the benefits of effective communication are evident, the risks of poor communication are equally significant. A study by **The Holmes Report** estimated that miscommunication costs companies $37 billion annually in lost productivity. For scale-ups, these costs manifest in delayed decisions, fractured teams, and missed opportunities—all avoidable with intentional communication strategies.

From Insights to Action

The research makes a compelling case: clarity, empathy, consistency, and adaptability are the cornerstones of effective communication. But how do leaders put these principles into practice? What tools and frameworks can guide them in crafting messages that inspire trust, alignment, and action?

In the next section, we'll explore practical frameworks designed to help leaders navigate the noise, ensuring their messages not only reach their audience but resonate deeply. Let's turn insight into action.

Frameworks in Action: Navigating the Noise

Effective communication isn't a matter of luck; it's an intentional practice that bridges clarity with connection and turns words into a catalyst for action. In today's noisy world, where every message competes for attention, leaders need more than instinct—they need a strategy. That's where the **VOICE Framework** comes in: a thoughtful, structured approach to crafting communication that resonates deeply and inspires change.

The VOICE Framework doesn't just tell you what to say; it guides you on how to say it in a way that cuts through complexity and builds trust. Each element of the framework—**Value, Organize, Interact, Customize, Empower**—works together to ensure your words create meaningful impact.

Start with the "Why"

At the heart of powerful communication lies purpose. When leaders begin with the "why," they draw people in with a shared sense of meaning. Why does this matter? What's the bigger picture? Anchoring your message in purpose not only captures attention but also builds trust, helping people connect emotionally before they engage intellectually.

Think about a renewable energy start-up navigating a company-wide restructuring. Employees, initially resistant, worried about uncertainty and change. The CEO didn't start with technical details. Instead, she began with the "why." She painted a vision of the company's role in leading the emerging green hydrogen market and how restructuring would ensure they stayed ahead of competitors. By aligning the changes with the company's mission of driving sustainability, she transformed hesitation into alignment.

Ask Yourself:

- Have I articulated why this matters in a way that connects emotionally with my audience?

Structure Your Message for Clarity

In a world saturated with information, scattered messages are like whispers in a storm—they disappear before they reach their destination. Clarity is the antidote. Effective communication follows a clear, intentional structure:

- Opening: Capture attention with a compelling start.
- Middle: Share focused and concise key details.
- Closing: Reinforce the takeaway and desired outcome.

Take the example of a healthcare scale-up launching a new app for patient care. Their announcement followed this structure:

- Opening: They painted a vivid picture of the challenges patients face in fragmented healthcare systems.

- Middle: They positioned their app as the solution, explaining its key features and impact on patient outcomes.
- Closing: They invited stakeholders to a live demo, connecting the message to action.

This clarity ensured that stakeholders not only understood the message but were inspired to engage.

Ask Yourself:

- Is my message clear and structured enough for my audience to follow effortlessly?

Foster Dialogue and Engagement

Communication is most powerful when it's a two-way street. Leaders who invite dialogue foster trust, surface fresh ideas, and deepen their connection with their audience. It's not just about delivering a message—it's about creating space for people to respond and engage.

When a tech company introduced a major policy change around remote work, the leadership team didn't stop at making an announcement. They hosted town halls where employees could voice concerns, ask questions, and suggest improvements. By leaning into interaction, the leaders didn't just share a decision—they strengthened relationships and refined the policy to better serve everyone.

Ask Yourself:

- How can I create space for my audience to contribute to the conversation?

Tailor Your Message to Your Audience

No two audiences are the same. Customizing your communication ensures that your message lands where it's intended. It's not about changing your values or goals but adapting how you present them based on what matters most to the people you're speaking to.

Consider a manufacturing company transitioning to automation. Leadership didn't rely on a one-size-fits-all message. Instead:

- For employees, the focus was on upskilling opportunities and job security.
- For investors, the message highlighted cost efficiency and innovation.
- For customers, they emphasized improved product quality and reliability.

By tailoring their message to each audience, they ensured that every stakeholder felt seen, understood, and valued.

Ask Yourself:

- Am I meeting my audience where they are, in language they'll understand and care about?

Inspire Action with Empowering Closures

Words have the power to move people—but only if they're pointed in the right direction. Every message should close with a call to action that's clear, empowering, and actionable.

Think of a nonprofit tackling food insecurity. Instead of a vague appeal, they ended their donor campaign with this: "Join us in feeding 1,000 families this holiday season. Every $10 you give puts a meal on the table." The specificity of this ask created an immediate connection between action and impact, driving a 30% increase in donations compared to the previous year.

Ask Yourself:

- Have I ended with an invitation that inspires my audience to take the next step?

Bringing It All Together

The VOICE Framework offers a way to turn communication into a tool for leadership—one that bridges purpose with action, clarity with connection. By starting with value, structuring your message, fostering dialogue, customizing for your audience, and ending with empowerment, you create communication that not only informs but inspires.

As you consider your next leadership message, pause and reflect:

- What's the deeper purpose driving what I want to say?
- How can I organize my thoughts to create clarity and engagement?
- Am I inviting dialogue, adapting to my audience, and inspiring action?

The words you choose have the power to shape trust, align teams, and drive change. In the next section, we'll explore real-world leaders who have mastered this art, showing how the VOICE Framework can create lasting impact in even the noisiest of worlds.

From Framework to Action

The VOICE Framework provides leaders with a roadmap for crafting messages that are clear, engaging, and impactful. By focusing on value, structure, interaction, customization, and empowerment, scale-up leaders can ensure their communication resonates deeply, even in the noisiest environments.

In the next section, we'll explore how these principles play out in real-world scenarios, highlighting organizations that have mastered the art of effective communication to drive alignment and inspire action.

Communication That Breaks Through the Noise

Case Study 1: Airbnb – Redefining Connection During Crisis

In March 2020, as the world shut down in response to the COVID-19 pandemic, Airbnb faced a devastating reality. Overnight, the platform saw bookings plummet by 80%, and its core business—facilitating travel—seemed obsolete in a locked-down world. Employees, hosts, and guests alike were anxious, unsure of what the future held.

CEO Brian Chesky recognized that clear, empathetic, and adaptive communication would be critical to navigating the crisis. He leaned on principles that mirrored the **VOICE Framework**, crafting messages that addressed immediate concerns while laying a foundation for resilience.

- **Value:** Chesky began by addressing the "why." In a letter to hosts, he acknowledged the profound uncertainty they were facing, expressing gratitude for their role in building Airbnb's community. By centering the message on shared values—trust, connection, and mutual support—he reinforced Airbnb's mission even in turbulent times.

- **Organize:** His communication was structured to provide clarity in a chaotic moment. Chesky outlined the company's immediate steps, including refund policies for guests and financial relief programs for hosts. The message was concise but comprehensive, ensuring every stakeholder understood the company's plan.

- **Interact:** Airbnb created open forums for hosts to share their concerns, offering virtual town halls and direct channels for feedback. This two-way communication fostered trust, allowing the company to refine its strategies based on real-time input.

- **Customize:** Chesky tailored his messages to each audience. For employees, he communicated layoffs with unprecedented transparency and compassion, outlining how decisions were made and offering support for those affected. For hosts, he emphasized long-term stability, introducing new tools and resources to help them weather the storm.

- **Empower:** Every message ended with a call to action. Chesky encouraged hosts to explore new opportunities within the platform, such as long-term rentals for remote workers. These clear steps helped the Airbnb community feel proactive rather than helpless.

The Results:

Airbnb's communication strategy not only stabilized the company during the crisis but also strengthened its community. By the end of 2020, the company had successfully gone public, with Chesky's leadership and messaging widely praised as a model for navigating uncertainty.

Case Study 2: Starbucks – Clarity and Empathy in a Time of Change

When Starbucks announced the closure of 8,000 stores in 2018 for a company-wide racial bias training day, the decision was met with mixed reactions. While some praised the company's commitment to addressing systemic issues, others questioned the financial impact and the potential backlash from skeptics. Navigating this moment required Starbucks to communicate with clarity, empathy, and consistency, principles that aligned seamlessly with the VOICE Framework.

- **Value:** Starbucks grounded its communication in its core values—creating a welcoming environment for all customers. The company's leadership articulated why the training was essential, framing it as a commitment to its employees and communities rather than a reactive measure.

- **Organize:** Starbucks crafted a clear and consistent narrative, ensuring that all stakeholders—employees, customers, and media—understood the purpose and logistics of the closure. The messaging was simple: one day of disruption for a future of inclusion.

- **Interact:** The company invited feedback and engaged in dialogue, partnering with experts and community leaders to design the training. This collaborative approach demonstrated humility and a willingness to learn, building credibility with both internal and external audiences.

- **Customize:** Starbucks tailored its message for different stakeholders. For employees, it emphasized professional growth and the importance of their role in fostering inclusion.

For customers, it focused on the bigger picture: creating spaces where everyone feels safe and valued.

- **Empower:** Each communication ended with a call to action, urging employees to bring the lessons from training into their daily interactions and inviting customers to hold Starbucks accountable to its promises.

The Results:

While the decision was bold and polarizing, Starbucks' communication strategy ensured the company maintained its reputation as a values-driven brand. The training day became a turning point, reinforcing Starbucks' commitment to social responsibility while strengthening trust within its community.

Lessons in Action

Both Airbnb and Starbucks faced moments of significant turbulence, where the stakes were high, and the path forward was uncertain. What set them apart was their ability to communicate effectively—not just to inform, but to inspire. By grounding their messages in purpose, structuring them for clarity, fostering dialogue, adapting to their audiences, and empowering action, these companies turned challenges into opportunities for connection and resilience.

As scale-up leaders, these stories remind us that communication isn't just about transmitting information—it's about building trust, aligning efforts, and reinforcing purpose. In the next section, we'll delve deeper into the strategies and styles of thought leaders who exemplify these principles, offering inspiration for how you can refine your own communication approach.

Expert Spotlight: Satya Nadella – Redefining Communication to Transform Culture

When Satya Nadella took the helm as CEO of Microsoft in 2014, the company was facing stagnation. Its once-dominant market position had been challenged by more agile competitors, and its internal culture was often described as siloed and combative. Nadella understood that Microsoft didn't just need a new strategy—it needed a cultural transformation. At the heart of this shift was communication, wielded not as a tool for control but as a means to inspire trust, foster collaboration, and create clarity.

The Leadership Philosophy Behind the Message

Nadella's approach to communication was rooted in three core principles: empathy, authenticity, and clarity. He believed that for Microsoft to evolve, its people needed to feel heard, valued, and aligned. From the outset, he made it his mission to listen deeply—to employees, customers, and partners—before making sweeping changes.

One of his first major acts as CEO was to write an internal memo outlining his vision for Microsoft's future. Titled *"Bold Ambition & Our Core,"* the memo articulated not just what the company would do but why it mattered. Nadella emphasized a growth mindset, urging employees to embrace curiosity and continuous learning. His message wasn't just strategic; it was personal, reflecting his own journey as a leader and his vision for a more inclusive, innovative culture.

Empathy as a Catalyst for Change

Nadella's communication style was marked by empathy—a quality often overlooked in corporate leadership. During one of his early employee Q&A sessions, a worker asked about Microsoft's struggles with diversity and inclusion. Instead of deflecting or providing a rehearsed response, Nadella acknowledged the company's shortcomings and expressed a genuine commitment to improvement. He followed this up by launching initiatives aimed at addressing systemic biases, including mandatory training on unconscious bias.

This empathetic approach transformed Microsoft's internal culture. Employees felt seen and heard, fostering trust and engagement at all levels of the organization. As one employee put it, "It felt like we were finally part of a company that cared, not just about results but about people."

Clarity in the Chaos

As Microsoft pivoted toward cloud computing, Nadella used communication to provide clarity during a time of significant disruption. He framed the company's strategy in terms that resonated with both employees and customers: enabling digital transformation and empowering every individual and organization to achieve more. This simple yet profound message became a guiding light, uniting teams across geographies and product lines.

Nadella also embraced transparency in his communication. For example, during earnings calls and investor briefings, he consistently linked Microsoft's financial performance back to its mission and values. This clarity reassured stakeholders and reinforced the company's purpose, even as it ventured into new, uncertain markets.

Authenticity That Resonates

Perhaps the most striking aspect of Nadella's communication style is its authenticity. In his book, *Hit Refresh*, Nadella shares personal stories that shaped his leadership philosophy, including how raising a son with special needs taught him the importance of empathy and resilience. This vulnerability not only humanized him as a leader but also inspired others within Microsoft to lead with authenticity.

By modelling this behaviour, Nadella set a new standard for communication at Microsoft. Leaders across the organization began to prioritize transparency, vulnerability, and connection in their interactions, creating a ripple effect that strengthened the company's culture.

Reinforcing the Lessons of Communication

Nadella's leadership demonstrates the transformative power of effective communication:

- Empathy Builds Bridges: By listening deeply and addressing concerns with humility, he fostered trust and collaboration.

- Clarity Creates Focus: His ability to articulate a simple, compelling vision aligned Microsoft's teams and stakeholders.

- Authenticity Inspires Action: By sharing his own stories and values, Nadella made his messages relatable and impactful.

These principles align seamlessly with the themes of this chapter, offering a roadmap for leaders seeking to communicate effectively in a noisy, complex world.

Practical Takeaways for Leaders

Nadella's example provides invaluable lessons for leaders navigating growth and turbulence:

- Start with Empathy: Make space to listen before you speak. Understanding your audience's needs and concerns creates the foundation for trust.

- Simplify Your Vision: In times of complexity, clarity is your most powerful tool. Ensure your message is focused, memorable, and tied to purpose.

- Be Genuine: Authenticity isn't a weakness—it's a strength. Share your story, acknowledge challenges, and lead with vulnerability.

Inspiration for the Road Ahead

Under Nadella's leadership, Microsoft didn't just recover—it thrived, becoming one of the most valuable companies in the world. At the core of this transformation was communication: a steady, empathetic, and authentic voice that guided the organization through uncertainty and into a new era of growth.

As you reflect on your own communication style, consider this: How can you bring empathy, clarity, and authenticity to your messages? The noisy world isn't going to quiet down, but with the right approach, your voice can become a guiding light that inspires others to follow.

Leadership Perspective: The Fork in the Road – Two Paths of Communication

Imagine two leaders, both at the helm of fast-growing organizations. Their teams are talented, their strategies sound, and their industries brimming with potential. Yet, when turbulence strikes—an unexpected market shift, a critical operational failure, or internal discord—their paths diverge, each shaped by the way they choose to communicate.

Leader 1: The Loud Messenger

The first leader faces the crisis with urgency, leaning into frequent updates and directives. Every email, meeting, and announcement is a volley of information designed to assert control and reassure the team. Yet, the messages are hurried, often contradictory, and lack the coherence needed to inspire confidence.

In one email, this leader emphasizes the importance of staying calm and focused. In the next, they outline an ambitious new initiative that demands immediate attention. The team is left scrambling, unsure of what truly matters. Employees grow frustrated, feeling like mere recipients of endless noise rather than collaborators in solving the challenge.

The results are predictable. Productivity wanes as miscommunication breeds confusion. Team members become disengaged, unsure of their roles in the chaos. Trust erodes, not because the leader failed to communicate, but because they failed to communicate with clarity and purpose.

Leader 2: The Intentional Communicator

The second leader takes a different approach. Before addressing the team, they pause to gather their thoughts, seeking input from key stakeholders and assessing the landscape. Their first message is not a flurry of instructions but a calm acknowledgment of the situation: "We're facing a challenge, and I want to be transparent about what we know and what we don't."

Rather than trying to answer every question at once, this leader focuses on the essentials—what the team needs to know now and what will be addressed in the coming days. Their tone is steady, their words clear, and their actions consistent with their message.

In meetings, they invite dialogue, asking open-ended questions like, "What are you seeing that I might be missing?" or "How can we support each other through this?" This creates a sense of shared ownership and collaboration, transforming the team from passive recipients of information into active participants in navigating the challenge.

The outcome is markedly different. While the turbulence remains, the team feels anchored by their leader's clarity and connection. Trust deepens, creativity flourishes, and a collective sense of purpose propels the organization forward.

The Dilemma: Communication as Noise vs. Communication as Connection

Both leaders communicated, yet their choices led to dramatically different outcomes. The first mistook frequency for effectiveness, flooding their team with noise that only added to the confusion. The second understood that communication isn't about volume—it's about intention.

This contrast highlights a dilemma every leader faces:

- Do you react to uncertainty by speaking louder and more often, risking misalignment and overwhelm?
- Or do you respond with thoughtful, intentional communication that cuts through the noise and fosters connection?

In a world overflowing with information, the difference between noise and connection lies in the leader's ability to pause, reflect, and prioritize clarity and empathy over speed and volume.

Reflective Questions for Leaders

As you consider your own communication style, ask yourself:

- When turbulence arises, do you focus on delivering immediate answers, or do you take the time to assess and align your message?

- How often do you invite dialogue and input, rather than defaulting to one-way communication?

- Are your messages consistent with your actions, reinforcing trust and alignment within your team?

The choice between noise and connection isn't a one-time decision; it's a daily practice, shaped by the leader's mindset and commitment to fostering trust.

A Path Forward

The fork in the road is always there, waiting for the leader to choose. Effective communication isn't about avoiding turbulence; it's about becoming the steady presence that guides others through it. The next time you find yourself at this crossroads, remember that clarity, empathy, and intentionality will always lead to deeper connection—and greater impact.

Which path will you take? The answer lies not in how much you say, but in how thoughtfully and purposefully you choose to say it.

Expanding Possibilities: New Frontiers in Communication

While frameworks like VOICE provide structure and clarity, the dynamic nature of communication invites exploration beyond established tools. Leaders who embrace unconventional strategies can uncover fresh ways to connect, inspire, and align their teams, particularly in complex and noisy environments. Let's explore complementary approaches that push the boundaries of what effective communication can achieve.

The Power of Visual Storytelling

In a digital world dominated by words, visuals have emerged as a compelling medium for cutting through noise. Infographics, videos, and even simple sketches can convey complex ideas with clarity and emotional resonance. Leaders who integrate visual elements into their communication create messages that are not only understood but remembered.

Consider This:

A scale-up in the renewable energy sector faced a challenge: explaining the science behind its groundbreaking technology to potential investors unfamiliar with the field. Traditional presentations filled with data and technical jargon had fallen flat, leaving audiences disengaged.

The CEO decided to reimagine their approach, working with a designer to create a short animated video that illustrated their technology's impact in a visually engaging, relatable way. The result was transformative. Investors not only grasped the concept but became excited about the potential, leading to a successful funding round.

Visual storytelling isn't about replacing words—it's about enhancing them. For leaders, it's an invitation to think creatively about how their message can resonate on multiple levels.

Leveraging Micro-Engagements

In the past, leadership communication often relied on big, set-piece moments: the all-hands meeting, the annual report, the keynote speech. But in today's fast-paced world, micro-engagements—short, targeted interactions—can be equally powerful.

Imagine a manager who, instead of waiting for the next team meeting to address a pressing issue, sends a 30-second video message directly to their team. The message is concise, authentic, and delivered in the moment, creating a sense of immediacy and connection.

Micro-engagements don't replace traditional communication; they complement it, allowing leaders to maintain a steady presence without overwhelming their teams. They remind employees that leadership is accessible, responsive, and engaged, even in the midst of turbulence.

Cross-Cultural Adaptability

In an increasingly globalized world, leaders often communicate across diverse cultures, each with its own norms, values, and expectations. What resonates with one audience might alienate another. The ability to adapt communication styles to different cultural contexts is no longer a luxury—it's a necessity.

A Case in Point:

A global logistics company launching a sustainability initiative tailored its messaging for regional audiences. In Europe, where environmental awareness was high, the communication emphasized the company's role in fighting climate change. In Asia, where efficiency and economic growth were priorities, the message highlighted cost savings and operational improvements.

Both approaches were grounded in the same core values, but by adapting the framing to regional contexts, the company ensured its message resonated widely, fostering global alignment without sacrificing local relevance.

The Art of Silence

In a world where leaders are often encouraged to fill every pause with words, silence can be a radical and powerful tool. Strategic silence—pausing before responding, allowing space for reflection, or simply listening without interruption—can amplify a message's impact.

Reflect on This:

During a contentious board meeting, a tech startup CEO presented a bold new strategy that faced significant resistance. Instead of immediately countering objections with a flurry of justifications, the CEO paused, allowing the room to absorb the proposal fully. The silence created a space for reflection and demonstrated confidence in the strategy. When the CEO finally spoke again, their words carried greater weight, shifting the tone of the discussion toward constructive dialogue.

Silence isn't the absence of communication; it's a powerful element within it, offering leaders a chance to listen, observe, and convey thoughtfulness in high-stakes moments.

Integrating Technology for Connection

Finally, technology offers endless possibilities for enhancing communication, but only when used intentionally. AI-driven tools, for example, can analyze sentiment in employee feedback, helping leaders understand the emotional undercurrents of their organizations. Virtual and augmented reality can create immersive storytelling experiences, bringing complex ideas to life in new and engaging ways.

The key is not to adopt technology for its own sake but to leverage it as a means of deepening connection. When used thoughtfully, technology becomes an extension of the leader's voice, amplifying their ability to inspire and align.

A Broader Horizon

These alternative strategies remind us that communication is as much an art as it is a science. Whether through visuals, micro-engagements, cultural adaptability, the intentional use of silence, or innovative technology, leaders have countless ways to refine and elevate their message.

As you reflect on your own communication style, consider where these possibilities might fit into your leadership journey. How might a visual aid bring clarity to a complex idea? Where could a pause create more impact than a word? What untapped opportunities might lie in tailoring your message for a global audience or embracing new tools?

In a noisy world, the greatest communicators are those who dare to think expansively, crafting messages that resonate across boundaries, mediums, and moments. The question isn't whether your voice can rise above the noise—it's how far your message can carry when it does.

Illuminating the Path Forward

Throughout this chapter, we've explored the profound power of communication in a world that often feels deafening. Like the lighthouse guiding ships through stormy seas, effective communication serves as a beacon, cutting through the noise and offering clarity, connection, and direction. For leaders navigating the complexities of growth, this skill is not merely useful—it's transformative.

Key Lessons from the Chapter

We began by acknowledging the challenges of communication in an age of information overload, where the sheer volume of messages risks obscuring what truly matters. Research underscored the importance of clarity, empathy, consistency, and adaptability, reminding us that the most impactful communication doesn't just inform—it inspires trust and action.

The **VOICE Framework** offered practical guidance, showing how leaders can craft messages that resonate deeply by starting with purpose, structuring for clarity, inviting engagement, tailoring to their audience, and ending with a call to action. Through case studies of organizations like Airbnb and Starbucks, we saw these principles in action, demonstrating how intentional communication can foster alignment and resilience even in turbulent times.

We also broadened the horizon, exploring complementary strategies like visual storytelling, micro-engagements, and the strategic use of silence. These approaches challenge us to think creatively about how we convey our messages, ensuring they resonate across cultures, platforms, and contexts.

A Call to Action

Now, the question turns to you: How will you apply these lessons in your leadership journey?

- Are your messages cutting through the noise, or are they getting lost in it?
- When you speak, are you creating clarity and connection, or adding to the overwhelm?
- How can you refine your communication to foster trust, inspire action, and align your team with purpose?

Every interaction you have—whether it's a town hall, a one-on-one conversation, or an email—carries the potential to either illuminate the path forward or leave your team searching for direction. As a leader, you have the power to make every message count.

Looking Ahead

Effective communication is more than a skill; it's a mindset—one that prioritizes intentionality, empathy, and connection in every interaction. But even the clearest message must be accompanied by the right delivery. In the next chapter, we'll delve into how leaders can tailor their communication to diverse audiences, ensuring their messages resonate across a wide spectrum of stakeholders.

The journey ahead will challenge you to think expansively, to step into your role as a beacon of clarity in a noisy world. As you do, remember: the power of communication isn't in the volume of your words, but in their ability to inspire trust, alignment, and action.

The storm may rage on, but your voice—steady, purposeful, and authentic—has the power to guide your team safely to the other side. Let it shine.

Finding Your Voice

As we draw this chapter to a close, take a moment to pause and reflect. Communication is the bridge between intention and impact, and as a leader, your voice has the power to inspire, align, and guide. But in the midst of the noise, how intentional are you about what and how you communicate?

Picture your recent leadership conversations—team meetings, one-on-one check-ins, or even written updates. Were your messages clear and purposeful, or did they add to the noise? Did your words create connection and understanding, or leave room for confusion? Reflection is where growth begins, and in communication, it's where your impact takes shape.

The Questions Worth Asking

Start by looking inward.

- How well do I align my communication with my organization's mission and values?
- Do I take the time to clarify the "why" behind my messages, or do I rush to the "what" and "how"?
- When I speak or write, do I consider my audience's unique needs, perspectives, and emotional states?

Now, shift your focus outward.

- Am I creating space for dialogue, or do I dominate the conversation?
- Do I invite questions, feedback, and ideas that enrich the communication process?
- Are my messages consistent, reinforcing trust and reliability within my team?

Finally, consider the broader landscape of your leadership.

- How do I adapt my communication style for different audiences, from employees to investors to customers?
- What role does technology play in my communication strategy, and am I using it to deepen connection or simply increase volume?
- Where might I be missing opportunities to innovate or expand my communication approach?

Your Communication Legacy

Every leader leaves behind a legacy, not just of what they achieved but of how they made others feel. Communication is central to that legacy.

When people reflect on their interactions with you, will they remember feeling understood, inspired, and aligned? Or will they recall confusion and a lack of connection?

Your voice has the potential to shape the culture of your organization, the trust of your team, and the trajectory of your vision. But realizing that potential requires deliberate practice and a commitment to refining how you communicate—not just in times of calm but especially in moments of turbulence.

A Practical Next Step

As you move forward, consider this: What is one small, intentional change you can make to elevate your communication? Perhaps it's pausing to clarify your message before sending it. Maybe it's asking an open-ended question that sparks dialogue. Or it might be taking a moment of silence before responding to ensure your words carry the weight of thoughtfulness.

Whatever that next step looks like, take it with intention. Let it be a starting point for transforming your communication from a task to a leadership superpower.

Carrying the Reflection Forward

Communication isn't a static skill; it's a living, evolving art that grows with each interaction. As you continue your leadership journey, keep returning to these reflections. Let them guide you toward greater clarity, deeper empathy, and a stronger connection with those you lead.

In the end, your voice is one of your most powerful tools. Use it thoughtfully, and it will carry not only your message but also your vision, your values, and your humanity into the noisy world– and beyond.

Chapter 7

The Power of Multidisciplinary Teams

"When diverse minds come together, they don't just solve problems—they redefine them."

For any leader striving to scale an organization, the realization often comes in waves: no single discipline holds all the answers. The solutions to complex challenges, the kind that make or break a business, often lie in the spaces between expertise—those intersections where diverse perspectives collide, challenge, and complement one another.

I once spoke with a leader who likened his experience to standing at a crossroads during a storm. His organization was on the brink of something extraordinary—a new product launch that could redefine their industry—but the challenges were immense. The engineers focused on functionality, marketing wanted a story, and finance kept asking, "How much will this cost us?" Each team worked tirelessly, yet progress stalled as their perspectives clashed.

It wasn't until he brought them together, intentionally weaving their insights into a shared vision, that things began to shift. What felt like chaos turned into collaboration. The engineers discovered how their designs could elevate the brand narrative. The marketing team began crafting stories around the innovation itself. Finance realized that aligning all efforts early reduced costly missteps later. The result wasn't just a product; it was a breakthrough forged by their collective brilliance.

This is the transformative power of multidisciplinary teams. They don't just solve problems—they expand what's possible.

But here's the thing: fostering this kind of collaboration doesn't happen by chance. It requires a leader who is willing to embrace the tension that arises when people with different perspectives and priorities work together. It takes intentionality to create an environment where respect, curiosity, and shared purpose can thrive.

In this chapter, we'll explore how multidisciplinary teams become the engine of innovation and impact. We'll dive into the frameworks that help leaders harness diverse expertise and navigate the inevitable challenges of collaboration. And, as always, we'll ground our insights in real-world stories—stories of leaders who have seen what happens when you bring together the right mix of people, ideas, and perspectives.

Because when we work at the crossroads, when we stand in the storm and bring others alongside us, we don't just weather it. We discover new paths, new possibilities, and new ways forward.

Research-Based Insights: The Science Behind Multidisciplinary Success

In an era defined by complexity, multidisciplinary teams offer a powerful antidote to linear thinking. Research consistently shows that teams composed of individuals with diverse expertise and perspectives outperform more homogeneous groups, especially when navigating ambiguous or multifaceted challenges. But these benefits aren't automatic. The effectiveness of such teams depends heavily on how they are structured, managed, and led.

Diversity Drives Innovation

A **Harvard Business Review study** found that companies with higher cognitive diversity—teams composed of individuals from varied disciplines, backgrounds, and thinking styles—are significantly more likely to develop innovative solutions. The logic is simple: when people approach problems from different angles, they uncover possibilities that a single-discipline team might overlook.

Example:

Consider a retail scale-up struggling to reduce its carbon footprint. The initial plan, designed by the operations team, focused solely on logistical efficiencies. However, when the company brought in marketing, design, and legal experts, the conversation shifted. The marketing team proposed aligning the initiative with customer engagement campaigns, while the legal team advised on compliance frameworks for environmental claims. The resulting strategy not only reduced emissions but also enhanced the brand's reputation and mitigated regulatory risks.

The lesson here is clear: innovation thrives at the intersection of disciplines, but it requires intentional collaboration to harness this potential.

The Productivity Paradox

Interestingly, multidisciplinary teams often face what researchers call the **productivity paradox**. While they are more likely to generate innovative solutions, they also tend to experience higher levels of friction. A **McKinsey report** highlights that the diversity of thought that makes these teams effective can also lead to misunderstandings, conflicts, and slower decision-making.

Example:
A software company assembled a multidisciplinary team to develop a new product feature. Engineers prioritized functionality, designers emphasized user experience, and marketers focused on competitive differentiation. The initial meetings were contentious, with each group defending its priorities. It wasn't until the team established shared goals and a clear communication framework that progress accelerated.

The paradox is this: without structure and alignment, the same diversity that drives innovation can become a source of inefficiency. Leaders must recognize this tension and implement strategies to minimize friction while maximizing collaboration.

Psychological Safety as a Catalyst

One of the most critical factors in the success of multidisciplinary teams is psychological safety—the shared belief that team members can express themselves without fear of ridicule or retribution. A **Google study on high-performing teams** identified psychological safety as the single most important determinant of team effectiveness, especially in environments where diverse perspectives must converge.

Example: During the development of a breakthrough cancer treatment, a biotech firm faced the challenge of integrating input from scientists, clinicians, and business strategists. Early discussions were fraught with tension, as stakeholders hesitated to challenge ideas outside their domains. Recognizing this, the project lead implemented ground rules for open dialogue and facilitated workshops to build trust. Over time, the team became more willing to voice concerns and propose bold ideas, leading to a faster development timeline and a more effective treatment.

Psychological safety doesn't eliminate disagreements, but it ensures that conflicts are productive rather than destructive. For leaders, fostering this environment is essential for unlocking the potential of multidisciplinary collaboration.

Multidisciplinary Teams in Action

A **Deloitte study** on high-growth companies found that organizations with well-integrated multidisciplinary teams are 1.8 times more likely to achieve above-average revenue growth. The reason? These teams excel at balancing big-picture thinking with operational precision, enabling them to address both strategic and tactical challenges.

Example: An e-commerce scale-up faced declining customer retention rates. By bringing together data scientists, UX designers, and customer service representatives, the company developed an AI-powered chatbot that not only resolved common issues quickly but also offered personalized recommendations. The initiative reversed the retention decline and increased average order values by 15%.

This example illustrates how multidisciplinary teams can transform challenges into opportunities when guided by a shared purpose and clear objectives.

The Leadership Imperative

The research is unequivocal: multidisciplinary teams are a powerful engine for innovation and growth. But their success hinges on effective leadership. Leaders must create environments where diverse perspectives are valued, ensure alignment on goals, and establish processes that facilitate collaboration without stifling creativity.

As we transition to the next section, we'll explore practical frameworks that help leaders navigate the complexities of multidisciplinary teams, transforming them into high-performing, harmonious units. These tools will provide actionable strategies for addressing the challenges outlined here and unlocking the full potential of your team. Let's move from understanding to application.

Frameworks in Action: Unlocking the Potential of Multidisciplinary Teams

The research makes it clear: while multidisciplinary teams hold immense potential, they need thoughtful guidance to thrive. Leaders must navigate the unique challenges these teams present, balancing diverse perspectives while fostering alignment and collaboration. Practical frameworks offer a structured approach to achieving this balance, transforming potential friction into productive synergy.

The ALIGN Framework

The ALIGN Framework provides a step-by-step guide to harness the power of multidisciplinary teams by focusing on shared purpose, structured collaboration, and iterative refinement. Each step ensures that team dynamics are optimized for creativity and efficiency.

- Assess Skills and Strengths
- Lay a Foundation of Trust

- **I**dentify Shared Goals
- **G**overn Collaboratively
- **N**urture Feedback Loops

Let's explore each step in depth, with practical applications.

1. Assess Skills and Strengths

Multidisciplinary teams thrive on the diversity of expertise, but this diversity can only be leveraged if leaders understand the specific skills and perspectives each member brings to the table. This involves mapping out the team's collective capabilities and identifying gaps or overlaps.

Example in Action:

A health-tech startup assembled a team to develop a wearable device for chronic disease management. Before diving into the project, the team lead conducted a skills inventory, uncovering that while they had strong technical and clinical expertise, they lacked deep marketing knowledge. By adding a marketing strategist to the team, they ensured a more holistic approach, avoiding potential blind spots.

2. Lay a Foundation of Trust

Psychological safety is the cornerstone of effective multidisciplinary teams. Leaders must invest time in building trust among team members, fostering an environment where everyone feels comfortable contributing their ideas.

Example: A renewable energy company facing internal conflicts over a new project hosted a two-day retreat to rebuild trust. Using facilitated team-building exercises, they created space for honest dialogue and mutual understanding. The result was a more cohesive team ready to tackle the challenge collaboratively.

3. Identify Shared Goals

Multidisciplinary teams often struggle with misaligned priorities. By establishing shared goals early, leaders ensure that all members are working toward the same vision, even if their approaches differ.

Example in Action:

A fashion scale-up working on a sustainability initiative found that its designers prioritized aesthetics, while the operations team focused on supply chain efficiency. By agreeing on a shared goal—creating eco-friendly products without compromising quality—they aligned their efforts, leading to the successful launch of a sustainable product line.

4. Govern Collaboratively

To prevent friction, leaders must establish clear processes for decision-making and conflict resolution. This might include rotating leadership roles for specific tasks or using consensus-building techniques to balance competing priorities.

Example in Action:

A fintech company introduced a decision-making matrix for its multidisciplinary innovation team. Decisions requiring technical input were led by engineers, while customer-facing strategies were driven by marketing experts. This collaborative governance reduced bottlenecks and empowered team members to lead within their areas of expertise.

5. Nurture Feedback Loops

Continuous improvement requires regular feedback. Leaders should implement systems that allow team members to share insights and adjust their strategies dynamically.

Example in Action:

A global NGO tackling food insecurity held weekly feedback sessions for its multidisciplinary project team. These sessions uncovered bottlenecks in distribution logistics, enabling the team to refine their approach and improve delivery efficiency by 20%.

Moving Forward with ALIGN

The ALIGN Framework equips leaders with a practical roadmap for navigating the complexities of multidisciplinary teams. It ensures that diversity becomes a strength rather than a source of friction, fostering collaboration that drives innovation and resilience.

In the next section, we'll delve into real-world examples of organizations that have successfully implemented strategies like ALIGN, demonstrating the transformative potential of multidisciplinary collaboration. These stories will inspire and illuminate how the principles explored here can be applied in practice.

Real-World Applications: Collaboration in Action

Case Study 1: NASA's Apollo Program – A Symphony of Expertise

In the 1960s, NASA faced what seemed an insurmountable challenge: landing a man on the moon and returning him safely to Earth. The Apollo program wasn't just a technical feat; it was a testament to the power of multidisciplinary collaboration. Engineers, scientists, mathematicians, and even artists worked side by side, each bringing a unique perspective to the table.

Early in the program, NASA encountered a critical issue: how to design a spacecraft that could support human life in the vacuum of space while ensuring a safe return. This problem required input from multiple disciplines. Aerospace engineers focused on propulsion systems, while biologists worked on life-support mechanisms. Psychologists studied the effects of isolation on astronauts, and graphic designers created interfaces that astronauts could use seamlessly under pressure.

Despite their diverse expertise, the team initially struggled with alignment. Engineers wanted more space for fuel, while biologists argued for additional life-support systems. Friction threatened to stall progress until the leadership team implemented a clear framework for collaboration. Shared objectives were established: prioritize astronaut safety while adhering to strict weight limits. Decision-making processes were clarified, and regular feedback loops ensured that every discipline had a voice.

The result was historic. The Apollo 11 mission successfully landed humans on the moon, a feat achieved not by one discipline but by the collective effort of many. The Apollo program became a blueprint for multidisciplinary teamwork, demonstrating how shared goals and structured collaboration could turn ambitious visions into reality.

This story reminds us that even the most daunting challenges can be overcome when diverse perspectives are aligned toward a common purpose.

Case Study 2: Pixar – Creativity Meets Structure

Pixar is celebrated for producing some of the most beloved animated films of all time, from *Toy Story* to *Inside Out*. But behind its creative brilliance lies a carefully orchestrated system of multidisciplinary collaboration. The studio's success is a result of blending art and technology, where animators, writers, engineers, and producers work in harmony.

During the development of *Finding Nemo,* the team faced a unique challenge: how to create underwater scenes that felt realistic yet emotionally resonant. Artists wanted vibrant, stylized visuals, while the technical team insisted on simulations that mimicked real underwater physics. The narrative team, meanwhile, focused on the emotional journey of the characters, requiring the visuals to serve the story.

Pixar addressed these competing priorities through what they call "the Braintrust," a multidisciplinary feedback group that meets regularly throughout the production process. In these sessions, every participant—regardless of rank or discipline—is encouraged to provide candid, constructive feedback. The key is psychological safety: ideas are critiqued, not people, fostering a culture where collaboration thrives.

The outcome was a film that combined cutting-edge technology with heartfelt storytelling, earning critical acclaim and box-office success. Pixar's process illustrates how multidisciplinary teams can balance creative tension by fostering trust, encouraging dialogue, and staying focused on a shared goal.

Lessons in Multidisciplinary Excellence

Both NASA and Pixar demonstrate that the power of multidisciplinary teams lies in their ability to synthesize diverse perspectives into cohesive, groundbreaking solutions. Yet their successes were not without challenges—misaligned priorities, communication barriers, and conflicting goals all surfaced along the way. What set these organizations apart was their commitment to frameworks and practices that nurtured collaboration.

These stories bring the ALIGN Framework to life: NASA assessed skills and built trust through shared objectives, while Pixar nurtured feedback loops and governed collaboratively through the Braintrust. The common thread is the deliberate effort to create environments where multidisciplinary teams could flourish.

Bringing It Back to Your Team

As scale-up leaders, you may not be designing spacecraft or producing animated masterpieces, but the principles remain the same. Whether you're launching a new product, entering a new market, or solving a complex organizational challenge, multidisciplinary teams can be your greatest asset—if you lead them with intention.

In the next section, we'll spotlight a thought leader who exemplifies the art of leading diverse teams, offering insights you can apply to your own leadership journey. Let's dive deeper into the strategies that make multidisciplinary collaboration not just possible, but transformational.

Expert Spotlight: Reed Hastings – Reinventing Collaboration for Global Impact

Reed Hastings, the co-founder and co-CEO of Netflix, is a master of building and leading multidisciplinary teams. Under his leadership, Netflix transformed from a DVD rental service into a global streaming powerhouse, serving over 200 million subscribers in 190 countries. Hastings' ability to foster collaboration among diverse disciplines—spanning technology, content creation, and data analytics—has been a cornerstone of Netflix's meteoric rise.

A Culture of Candid Collaboration

Hastings is known for championing a culture of openness and innovation at Netflix, one that encourages multidisciplinary teams to work together with transparency and accountability. He understood early on that creating world-class entertainment required more than just creative talent; it demanded the seamless integration of technology, data, and storytelling.

For example, when Netflix began developing its original content, such as *House of Cards*, Hastings ensured that the creative and technical teams worked hand in hand. While writers and directors focused on compelling narratives, data scientists analyzed viewing habits to predict audience preferences. Engineers built algorithms to ensure viewers discovered the right content at the right time, while marketing teams crafted campaigns that resonated globally.

The results were groundbreaking. Netflix not only produced hit shows but also redefined how audiences consumed media, leveraging its multidisciplinary approach to dominate the streaming landscape.

Frameworks for Autonomy and Alignment

One of Hastings' key strategies was to empower teams with autonomy while maintaining alignment on overarching goals. Netflix's now-famous "Freedom and Responsibility" culture gave teams the flexibility to innovate within a framework of accountability. Hastings trusted his teams to make decisions, ensuring they had the resources and clarity needed to succeed.

This autonomy extended to cross-functional collaboration. At Netflix, creative directors could challenge engineers, and data analysts could provide feedback to marketing teams. The lack of silos created a dynamic environment where ideas flowed freely, and diverse perspectives were embraced.

Lessons from Hastings' Leadership

Reed Hastings' approach to multidisciplinary teams provides several key insights for leaders:

- Embrace Data and Creativity: Successful collaboration often blends intuition with data-driven insights. Encourage teams to use both to make informed decisions.
- Foster Psychological Safety: When teams feel safe to challenge ideas and take risks, innovation thrives.
- Prioritize Alignment Over Control: Give teams the autonomy to execute while ensuring their efforts align with the organization's goals.

Scaling Collaboration for a Global Vision

As Netflix scaled internationally, Hastings further refined his approach to multidisciplinary collaboration. He understood that expanding into diverse markets required input from regional experts, legal teams, and global marketing strategists. By fostering trust and respect among these groups, Netflix successfully localized its content while maintaining its global brand identity.

Hastings' ability to lead multidisciplinary teams not only solidified Netflix's position as a market leader but also demonstrated how diverse expertise, when aligned and empowered, can achieve extraordinary outcomes.

Inspiration for Leaders

Reed Hastings reminds us that the best ideas come from the convergence of disciplines, where creativity meets analysis, and innovation thrives in collaboration. As you reflect on your own leadership journey, consider how Hastings' strategies might inspire your approach to multidisciplinary teams.

How can you create a culture where diverse perspectives are not just welcomed but essential? How might you empower your teams to innovate while maintaining alignment with your vision? In the next section, we'll explore the challenges and dilemmas leaders face when guiding multidisciplinary teams, offering deeper insights into the art of collaborative leadership.

The Multidisciplinary Dilemma

Imagine this: two leaders, each guiding multidisciplinary teams tasked with solving complex challenges. Both teams have access to the same resources and talent. Yet, their outcomes couldn't be more different. One team delivers innovative, impactful solutions, while the other struggles to make progress, mired in conflict and inefficiency. What separates success from failure?

This scenario highlights a central leadership dilemma: how do you foster collaboration without stifling individuality? How do you align diverse perspectives without erasing the unique contributions each team member brings? The choices leaders make in navigating these tensions can make or break the potential of a multidisciplinary team.

The Case of Diverging Approaches

Let's consider two real-life scenarios that illustrate the impact of leadership choices on multidisciplinary teams.

Scenario 1: The Hierarchical Leader

At a tech scale-up developing a groundbreaking AI product, the CEO believed in centralized decision-making to maintain control. While the team included engineers, data scientists, marketers, and designers, the CEO insisted on approving every major decision. This approach, while well-intentioned, created a bottleneck.

Team members hesitated to propose bold ideas, fearing they would be overruled. The engineers prioritized technical feasibility, while marketers pushed for features that would differentiate the product. Without a clear framework for collaboration, tensions escalated, and deadlines were missed. In the end, the product launched late and failed to meet customer expectations, a reflection of disjointed efforts and unaddressed conflicts.

Scenario 2: The Collaborative Leader

Contrast this with a leader at a renewable energy company tasked with designing a new solar panel. Recognizing the importance of collaboration, the project lead set the tone early by inviting input from every discipline: R&D, manufacturing, sales, and environmental compliance.

Instead of dictating decisions, the leader facilitated open discussions where disagreements were seen as opportunities to innovate. A shared vision—creating the most efficient and eco-friendly panel in the market—anchored the team's efforts. Regular feedback loops ensured that no perspective dominated at the expense of others. The result? A product that exceeded market expectations, boosting both revenue and brand reputation.

These contrasting outcomes underscore the pivotal role of leadership in shaping how multidisciplinary teams function. The hierarchical leader prioritized control over collaboration, inadvertently stifling innovation. The collaborative leader, by fostering trust and alignment, unlocked the team's collective potential.

The Leadership Tensions

Navigating multidisciplinary teams often involves balancing seemingly contradictory demands:

- **Control vs. Autonomy:** How much direction should a leader provide without stifling creativity?
- **Alignment vs. Individuality:** How do you ensure alignment on goals without suppressing unique contributions?
- **Efficiency vs. Exploration:** How do you manage time-sensitive projects without rushing the creative process?

These tensions don't have easy answers. They require leaders to adapt their style based on the team's dynamics, the project's complexity, and the broader organizational context.

Questions for Reflection

Consider your own leadership approach:

- Do you create space for open dialogue, or do you find yourself making decisions unilaterally?
- How do you address conflicts within your team? Are they seen as barriers or opportunities?
- Are your team's efforts guided by a shared vision, or are they fragmented by competing priorities?

A Path to Intentional Leadership

The power of multidisciplinary teams lies in their diversity, but this diversity can only be harnessed through intentional leadership. As a leader, your role isn't to solve every problem or control every decision—it's to create an environment where collaboration can thrive.

When faced with the inevitable tensions of leading multidisciplinary teams, pause and reflect. Consider the choices that will enable your team to move forward with clarity, alignment, and purpose. In the end, the greatest impact comes not from avoiding challenges, but from navigating them with courage and intention.

As we move to the next section, we'll explore alternative strategies for enhancing multidisciplinary collaboration, offering fresh perspectives for leaders who seek to push the boundaries of what their teams can achieve.

New Horizons for Multidisciplinary Teams

The core principles of leading multidisciplinary teams—building trust, aligning on goals, and fostering collaboration—are timeless. But the evolving nature of work demands that leaders go further, embracing new strategies and innovations that push the boundaries of traditional team dynamics. By integrating technology, nurturing cross-cultural collaboration, and reimagining how teams work together, leaders can unlock even greater potential in their multidisciplinary teams.

Integrating Technology for Seamless Collaboration

In a digital-first world, technology is no longer just a tool; it's the connective tissue that binds multidisciplinary teams together. Platforms like Slack, Asana, and Microsoft Teams offer real-time collaboration features that allow team members from different disciplines to share updates, track progress, and address issues quickly. But technology can do more than streamline workflows—it can also deepen collaboration.

Example: A pharmaceutical company developing a new vaccine used virtual reality (VR) to bridge the gap between lab scientists and manufacturing engineers. By creating immersive VR simulations, the scientists could demonstrate molecular interactions in 3D, enabling engineers to design production processes more efficiently. This approach not only accelerated the project but also strengthened the relationship between two traditionally siloed teams.

For scale-up leaders, the lesson is clear: technology isn't just about efficiency; it's about creating shared experiences that enhance understanding and trust across disciplines.

Fostering Cross-Cultural Dynamics

As teams become increasingly global, cultural diversity has emerged as both an asset and a challenge. Cross-cultural dynamics can spark innovation, but they also require leaders to navigate differences in communication styles, decision-making processes, and work ethics.

Example: An automotive company developing an electric vehicle assembled a team that included designers from Europe, engineers from Asia, and marketers from North America. Initially, cultural differences created tension—Asian engineers prioritized precision and reliability, while North American marketers pushed for speed to market. To bridge these divides, the project leader organized cultural sensitivity workshops and created a playbook for cross-cultural collaboration. This effort transformed the team's dynamic, allowing them to leverage their differences as strengths.

Leaders who embrace cultural diversity and provide the tools to navigate it can turn potential friction into a source of creative energy.

Embracing Hybrid Work Models

The rise of hybrid work has reshaped how teams collaborate. While remote work offers flexibility and access to a broader talent pool, it also introduces challenges around cohesion and communication.

Multidisciplinary teams, in particular, require intentional strategies to maintain alignment in a hybrid environment.

Example: A media start-up producing a global streaming series faced the challenge of coordinating writers, directors, and post-production specialists spread across multiple time zones. To foster collaboration, the company adopted a "core hours" model where all team members were online at the same time for critical discussions. They also used asynchronous tools like Loom to share detailed updates, reducing the need for constant meetings. These strategies ensured that the team remained aligned while respecting individual work preferences.

Hybrid work isn't just about flexibility; it's about rethinking how teams collaborate to balance autonomy with connection.

Encouraging Multidisciplinary Rotations

Another innovative strategy is to rotate team members across disciplines, allowing them to gain firsthand experience in areas outside their expertise. This approach fosters empathy, breaks down silos, and equips individuals with a broader understanding of the organization's goals.

Example: A financial services firm addressing customer retention implemented a rotation program where data analysts spent a week shadowing customer service representatives. The analysts gained a deeper appreciation for the challenges of frontline work, leading to more effective data-driven solutions. Meanwhile, customer service reps learned how their feedback informed broader business strategies, enhancing their sense of purpose.

Rotation programs remind us that understanding others' perspectives isn't just valuable—it's transformative.

Integrating External Expertise

Sometimes, the best way to enhance multidisciplinary collaboration is to invite an external perspective. Bringing in consultants, industry experts, or even customers can provide fresh insights and challenge entrenched thinking.

Example: A healthcare scale-up designing a patient engagement platform invited patient advocates to join their project team. These advocates highlighted overlooked pain points and provided real-world context that shaped the platform's design. The result was a product that not only met technical requirements but also resonated deeply with end-users.

Leaders who welcome external voices ensure their teams remain open to new ideas and perspectives, avoiding the pitfalls of groupthink.

The Expanding Landscape of Possibility

These strategies—integrating technology, fostering cross-cultural dynamics, embracing hybrid work, encouraging rotations, and incorporating external expertise—offer leaders a roadmap for taking multidisciplinary collaboration to the next level. Each approach challenges traditional assumptions about how teams should operate, encouraging leaders to think expansively about what's possible.

As you reflect on these possibilities, consider how they might apply to your own organization. Are there opportunities to leverage technology in new ways? How might cultural diversity or hybrid work models enrich your team's dynamic? What untapped insights could external voices bring to the table?

The future of multidisciplinary collaboration isn't limited by what's been done before—it's defined by leaders willing to explore what's next.

Conducting the Symphony of Collaboration

Multidisciplinary teams are like orchestras, each member bringing their unique instrument and expertise to create something extraordinary. As a leader, your role is to act as the conductor, bringing harmony to the diverse voices within your organization. Throughout this chapter, we've explored how to transform the potential of multidisciplinary teams into a powerful force for innovation and growth.

From the metaphor of the orchestra to real-world examples like NASA's Apollo program and Pixar's Braintrust, we've seen that success lies not just in assembling talent but in fostering collaboration through intentional leadership. Research underscores the value of diversity, while frameworks like ALIGN provide practical tools to navigate the challenges that come with it. Complementary strategies, such as integrating technology, nurturing cross-cultural dynamics, and embracing hybrid work models, further expand the possibilities for what your teams can achieve.

The most impactful leaders don't shy away from the complexities of multidisciplinary collaboration—they embrace them. They see disagreements as opportunities for growth, differences as sources of strength, and challenges as invitations to innovate.

As you reflect on this chapter, consider the following:

- Are you fostering an environment where every team member feels valued and empowered to contribute?

- How are you aligning diverse perspectives toward a shared vision?
- What steps can you take to enhance collaboration across boundaries, whether disciplinary, cultural, or geographic?

These questions aren't meant to be answered quickly but to guide your ongoing leadership journey. They challenge you to think expansively, to question assumptions, and to push beyond the familiar.

Looking Ahead

As your organization grows, the challenges you face will only become more complex. Multidisciplinary teams will continue to play a crucial role in navigating this complexity, offering the creativity and adaptability needed to thrive. But their success depends on your ability to lead with intention, empathy, and clarity.

In the next chapter, we'll explore another critical component of growth: the art of decision-making in uncertain environments. Just as multidisciplinary teams require alignment to succeed, effective decisions require balance—between intuition and analysis, speed and deliberation, risk and reward. Together, these skills will prepare you to lead not just for today's challenges but for the unknown opportunities and obstacles ahead.

An Invitation to Act

The symphony of collaboration is waiting to be conducted. Your teams are ready, their instruments in hand, their ideas rich with potential. The question is: how will you lead them?

The choice is yours. Step onto the podium, raise your baton, and guide your team toward something remarkable. The world needs leaders who can transform diversity into unity, complexity into clarity, and potential into achievement. Be that leader. The stage is set, the music is written—it's time to play.

Chapter 8

The Inner Game of Leadership

"Great leadership starts with self-leadership. The journey to becoming an effective leader begins with understanding, mastering, and growing yourself."

Leadership often feels like standing at the helm of a ship, navigating unpredictable waters. But the greatest storms aren't always external—they often rage within. The doubts that creep in before a high-stakes decision. The endless wrestling with imposter syndrome. The weight of balancing competing priorities while projecting calm and confidence. The most successful leaders don't just navigate external challenges; they master the inner game that shapes every aspect of how they lead.

I once spoke with a founder of a high-growth company, someone whose name is now synonymous with innovation and success. They confided that their toughest battle wasn't entering a new market or scaling operations—it was their relentless inner dialogue. "Every decision," they said, "felt like I was carrying the weight of the world. But it wasn't the world—it was the pressure I put on myself, the constant fear of letting people down."

This raw admission resonates deeply because it reflects a truth we don't talk about enough. Leadership isn't just a job; it's a deeply personal journey that requires confronting your own doubts, emotions, and limitations. And yet, it's this inner work—the willingness to face and navigate those internal storms—that separates those who sustain unstoppable growth from those who burn out along the way.

In *Unstoppable Growth*, we've explored frameworks and strategies for scaling businesses, building systems, and creating impact. But none of it is sustainable without a solid foundation of self-awareness, emotional intelligence, and resilience. This chapter takes a deliberate pause to focus on the most vital asset a leader has: themselves.

The inner game of leadership is about more than surviving moments of self-doubt or stress. It's about recognizing the direct link between your mindset and your ability to lead others. Self-awareness sharpens decision-making. Emotional intelligence fosters trust and alignment in teams. Resilience helps you show up, even when everything feels like it's falling apart.

This isn't about fixing what's "broken" within. It's about acknowledging that growth, both personal and professional, is an ongoing process. Leaders who embrace vulnerability and engage with their inner challenges don't just become stronger—they become more connected to their purpose, more aligned with their values, and more capable of leading through complexity.

In this chapter, we'll explore tools and practices that strengthen the inner game. We'll dive into the research that links emotional intelligence to better leadership outcomes, and we'll hear from leaders who have harnessed self-awareness to overcome their toughest challenges.

Because the truth is, *Unstoppable Growth* doesn't start with market share or quarterly metrics—it starts with the leader. It starts with you. When you master the inner game, you build the foundation for a leadership journey that not only drives results but leaves a legacy. And in a world that increasingly values authenticity and connection, this work isn't optional—it's essential.

Exploring Inner Challenges: Facing the Shadows of Leadership

Leadership is often romanticized as a position of clarity and control, but anyone who has stood at the helm of a growing organization knows that the real picture is far more complex. Beneath the surface of confident decision-making lies a tangled web of internal struggles—self-doubt, decision fatigue, and the emotional strain of carrying the weight of responsibility. These challenges are as universal as they are unspoken, and their impact can ripple through every aspect of leadership.

The Weight of Self-Doubt

Imagine a leader on the verge of launching a new initiative. On the outside, they exude confidence, rallying their team with bold visions and clear directives. But inside, they're wrestling with a question that keeps them awake at night: *What if I'm wrong?* This inner dialogue, familiar to even the most accomplished leaders, reflects the persistent shadow of self-doubt.

Self-doubt isn't necessarily a flaw—it can be a sign of self-awareness and humility. But left unchecked, it can erode confidence, stall decision-making, and seep into the morale of a team. Research published in the *Harvard Business Review* highlights that while self-doubt is common among high-performing leaders, it becomes problematic when it paralyzes action or undermines trust.

Consider Brian Chesky, co-founder of Airbnb, who faced relentless criticism in the early days of his company. The concept of renting a stranger's home seemed absurd to many, and Chesky often questioned whether his vision was misguided. Yet, rather than letting doubt consume him, he leaned into it, seeking input from mentors and his team. By addressing his doubts openly, he not only strengthened his conviction but also built a culture of transparency and resilience within Airbnb.

The Grind of Decision Fatigue

Another silent struggle for leaders is decision fatigue—the mental exhaustion that comes from making countless high-stakes choices. As organizations scale, leaders often find themselves at the center of every critical decision, from strategic pivots to operational details. Over time, the cumulative weight of these choices can lead to burnout, impaired judgment, and a growing sense of overwhelm.

In his book *Thinking, Fast and Slow*, Daniel Kahneman explores how decision fatigue affects even the most rational minds, leading to shortcuts, errors, and indecision. Leaders are particularly vulnerable because their decisions don't just affect themselves—they ripple out to their teams, stakeholders, and the future of their organization.

Take Jeff Bezos during Amazon's rapid expansion. Recognizing the toll of constant decision-making, Bezos famously adopted a principle of "high-quality decisions made before noon," ensuring his most critical choices were made when his energy and focus were at their peak. This approach not only preserved his clarity but also empowered his team to handle decisions independently, lightening his cognitive load.

The Emotional Strain of Leadership

Perhaps the most pervasive challenge leaders face is the emotional strain of carrying the weight of responsibility. Leadership is deeply personal—it requires showing up fully, navigating interpersonal dynamics, and managing one's own emotions while being attuned to the emotions of others. Over time, this constant balancing act can lead to stress, frustration, and even emotional burnout.

Melanie Perkins of Canva recalls the early days of her journey, when the pressures of fundraising, managing a growing team, and meeting user demands often felt overwhelming. She realized that to lead effectively, she needed to manage her own emotional well-being first. By prioritizing reflection, seeking feedback, and developing mindfulness practices, she found a way to sustain her energy and presence, even during the most challenging periods.

Research underscores the importance of emotional regulation in leadership. Studies published in the *Journal of Organizational Behavior* show that leaders who actively manage their emotions not only reduce their own stress but also create a more stable and motivated environment for their teams. Emotional mastery isn't about suppressing feelings—it's about acknowledging them, understanding their roots, and responding with intention.

Why Addressing Inner Challenges Matters

The internal struggles of leadership are not signs of weakness; they're part of the journey. What distinguishes effective leaders is not the absence of these challenges but their ability to confront and address them. Self-doubt can be transformed into thoughtful humility. Decision fatigue can be mitigated with structure and delegation. Emotional strain can be alleviated through reflection and self-care.

When leaders embrace their inner challenges, they not only grow personally but also set an example for their teams. They demonstrate that leadership isn't about having all the answers—it's about the courage to confront uncertainty, adapt, and persevere. By addressing these struggles head-on, leaders build the resilience and clarity needed to guide their organizations through growth and change.

An Invitation to Reflect

As we continue this chapter, take a moment to consider:

- How do self-doubt, decision fatigue, or emotional strain show up in your leadership?
- What practices could you adopt to address these challenges with greater awareness and intention?
- How might your inner growth ripple outward, creating a more grounded and inspired organization?

The next section will delve into research-backed insights and practical strategies to turn these challenges into opportunities for growth, ensuring that the inner game of leadership becomes a source of strength rather than strain.

The Impact of Self-Awareness, Emotional Intelligence, and Resilience in Leadership

The qualities that define a leader's inner strength—self-awareness, emotional intelligence, and resilience—are not abstract ideals; they are measurable, research-backed traits that directly influence organizational success. Studies consistently show that leaders who cultivate these qualities outperform their peers, not just in driving results but in building cultures of trust, collaboration, and adaptability.

Self-Awareness: The Leadership Multiplier

Self-awareness is often referred to as the cornerstone of effective leadership, and for good reason. Research published in the *Harvard Business Review* highlights that leaders with high self-awareness are better decision-makers, more effective communicators, and more adept at aligning their teams with organizational goals. By understanding their own strengths, limitations, and biases, self-aware leaders minimize blind spots and make more thoughtful, balanced choices.

Example: Reed Hastings, co-founder and CEO of Netflix, exemplifies the power of self-awareness in leadership. Hastings recognized early on that his micromanagement tendencies were stifling innovation and team autonomy. By reflecting on this behavior and seeking feedback, he made a deliberate effort to step back, empowering his team to take ownership of decisions. This shift not only freed Hastings to focus on strategic growth but also fostered a culture of accountability and trust within Netflix, a key factor in the company's ability to innovate and adapt.

Self-awareness isn't just about understanding oneself—it's about how that understanding shapes relationships, decisions, and outcomes.

Leaders who invest in self-awareness create ripples of clarity and alignment that extend throughout their organizations.

Emotional Intelligence: Building Trust and Connection

Emotional intelligence (EQ), the ability to recognize, understand, and manage emotions in oneself and others, has been shown to be a stronger predictor of leadership success than IQ or technical skills. A study by Daniel Goleman, a pioneer in the field of EQ, found that nearly 90% of the difference between high-performing leaders and their peers could be attributed to emotional intelligence. Leaders with high EQ are better equipped to build trust, navigate conflict, and inspire their teams.

Example: Melanie Perkins, co-founder of Canva, leaned heavily on emotional intelligence as she built her company. Perkins recognized that fostering a sense of belonging and psychological safety was critical to Canva's success. By creating an environment where employees felt valued and heard, she not only drove engagement but also unlocked her team's creativity and problem-solving abilities. Her ability to connect emotionally with her team became a defining feature of Canva's culture, fuelling its rapid growth.

The business case for emotional intelligence is clear: leaders who prioritize EQ foster stronger relationships, drive better team performance, and create cultures that adapt and thrive.

Resilience: Thriving Amidst Adversity

Resilience is the ability to bounce back from setbacks, adapt to change, and sustain performance under pressure. For leaders of scale-up organizations, where the pace is relentless and challenges abound, resilience is not optional—it's a necessity. Research from McKinsey emphasizes that resilient leaders are more likely to inspire confidence, maintain focus, and drive sustained growth during periods of disruption.

Example: Brian Chesky, CEO of Airbnb, demonstrated extraordinary resilience during the COVID-19 pandemic, when the company's core business—travel—came to a near standstill. Instead of succumbing to despair, Chesky quickly mobilized his team to pivot Airbnb's offerings toward longer-term stays and virtual experiences. His resilience and adaptability not only saved the company but also positioned it to emerge stronger in a post-pandemic world.

Resilient leaders don't avoid adversity; they confront it with composure and creativity, transforming challenges into opportunities for reinvention.

The Interplay of Inner Strengths

Self-awareness, emotional intelligence, and resilience don't exist in isolation—they reinforce one another. A leader who is self-aware can recognize their emotional triggers and regulate their responses, enhancing their emotional intelligence. Similarly, resilience is bolstered by both self-awareness and EQ, as leaders who understand themselves and connect deeply with others are better equipped to navigate setbacks and inspire their teams.

Research from the *Journal of Leadership & Organizational Studies* underscores this interplay, showing that leaders who integrate these qualities are more likely to create high-performing, adaptable organizations. These inner strengths not only enhance individual effectiveness but also shape the collective capacity of teams and businesses to thrive in uncertainty.

A Path Forward

As we explore the inner game of leadership, it's clear that self-awareness, emotional intelligence, and resilience are not fixed traits—they are skills that can be cultivated with intention and practice. The next section will introduce practical frameworks for developing these inner strengths, offering leaders tools to transform self-reflection into action, emotional connection into trust, and personal resilience into organizational success.

The journey inward isn't just about personal growth; it's about unlocking the full potential of leadership to create lasting impact. Let's dive into the strategies that make this possible.

Frameworks for Inner Mastery: Strengthening Leadership from Within

Great leadership begins within. While strategies, decisions, and outward actions define what the world sees, the real work—the foundation of sustained impact—takes place below the surface. The inner game of leadership, with its focus on self-awareness, emotional resilience, and clarity, is where true transformation happens. But how does a leader move from understanding these qualities to embedding them in daily practice?

The **REFLECT** framework offers a path forward. More than a list of principles, it's a guide to cultivating inner mastery through intentional actions. Each step builds on the last, forming a cohesive journey of self-discovery and growth. And while frameworks can feel theoretical, their power lies in how they come alive through real-world application.

The REFLECT Framework: Recognize, Examine, Focus, Learn, Expand, Commit, Transform

The REFLECT framework isn't about quick fixes or surface-level solutions; it's about building habits that sustain growth. Let's explore how it unfolds, weaving in the story of one leader's journey to bring the principles to life.

Recognize: Acknowledging the Inner Landscape

The first step to inner mastery is recognition—pausing to observe what is happening within. This isn't about fixing or judging but about acknowledging emotions, thoughts, and behaviours as they are.

When Melanie Perkins, the co-founder of Canva, faced repeated rejection in her early fundraising pitches, she could have easily dismissed the emotions that came with it. Instead, she took time to recognize the fear and frustration that arose after each "no." By naming these feelings, she avoided suppressing them, creating space to move forward with clarity rather than being weighed down by unacknowledged emotions.

Apply: Start small. At the end of each day, ask yourself: *What emotions did I experience today? What triggered them?* Write these reflections in a journal, not to solve them immediately but to understand the patterns shaping your leadership.

Examine: Understanding the Why

Recognition opens the door to examination—the deeper work of exploring the root causes behind behaviors and emotions. This step asks leaders to look beyond the surface to uncover the beliefs, assumptions, or fears driving their actions.

Perkins reflected on her fundraising challenges and realized her fear wasn't just about rejection—it was about perfectionism. She examined how her desire to have all the answers upfront was holding her back. By understanding this pattern, she began to reframe rejection as a step toward clarity rather than a reflection of failure.

Apply: When you encounter a recurring challenge, ask yourself: *What belief is driving my reaction? How does this belief align—or conflict—with my long-term goals?* This kind of inquiry helps leaders navigate the tension between immediate emotions and deeper values.

Focus: Prioritizing What Truly Matters

With awareness and understanding in place, the next step is focus—aligning actions with long-term priorities and values. This requires filtering out distractions and committing to what will have the most enduring impact.

For Perkins, focus meant staying true to Canva's core mission: simplicity and accessibility. Despite external pressures to build a feature-heavy platform to appeal to niche users, she resisted the distraction, ensuring that every decision served the broader vision. This clarity not only shaped Canva's product but also set the tone for its culture and strategy.

Apply: Define your leadership priorities at the start of each week. Ask: *How does this task or decision align with my values and long-term vision?* By filtering actions through this lens, you can make choices that sustain growth rather than scatter attention.

Learn: Growing Through Feedback

Inner mastery thrives on learning, and learning often begins with feedback. This step invites leaders to seek perspectives beyond their own, using the insights of others to refine their self-awareness and adaptability.

Perkins regularly sought input from her team, investors, and mentors. Rather than avoiding criticism, she leaned into it, treating feedback as a tool for improvement rather than a threat to her confidence. This openness to learning became a hallmark of her leadership, enabling her to adapt Canva's approach while staying rooted in its mission.

Apply: Regularly ask your team: *What's one thing I could do to better support you?* View their responses as gifts, using them to sharpen your leadership without defensiveness or resistance.

Expand: Embracing New Perspectives

Inner growth also requires expansion—stepping beyond familiar patterns to embrace fresh ideas, experiences, and perspectives. This openness fuels innovation and resilience, allowing leaders to adapt to an ever-changing landscape.

For Perkins, expansion wasn't just about the product; it was about leadership itself. She drew inspiration from diverse sources, from the stories of other entrepreneurs to the creative energy of Canva's user base. This willingness to look outward deepened her connection to the broader ecosystem her company served.

Apply: Seek opportunities to broaden your thinking. Attend an event outside your industry, read a book on a topic unrelated to your work, or engage in a conversation with someone who challenges your perspective.

Commit: Turning Reflection into Action

All the insight in the world means little without commitment. This step is where inner mastery takes root, as leaders translate reflection into consistent, intentional action.

Perkins' commitment to her vision was evident in how she approached every decision. She didn't just talk about making design accessible—she embedded that principle into Canva's culture, product, and customer experience. Her ability to stay the course, even when challenges arose, transformed her reflection into results.

Apply: Set a single actionable intention each week. Whether it's improving communication, strengthening relationships, or refining a process, focus on one habit that aligns with your inner growth goals.

Transform: Building Inner Strength That Endures

The final step of the REFLECT framework is transformation—when self-awareness, resilience, and emotional intelligence become ingrained habits. This is where leaders move from reacting to challenges to shaping their trajectory with purpose and clarity.

For Perkins, this transformation wasn't just about personal growth; it was about the ripple effects her leadership had on Canva's culture and impact. By cultivating her inner game, she created a foundation of trust, creativity, and resilience that scaled with the company.

Apply: Periodically reflect on your growth journey. Ask: *How have I evolved as a leader? How has this growth influenced my team and organization?* Celebrate these milestones, and use them as fuel for continued transformation.

The Power of Inner Mastery

The REFLECT framework shows that the inner game of leadership is not an abstract idea—it's a tangible, actionable process. Through recognition, examination, focus, learning, expansion, commitment, and transformation, leaders can cultivate the qualities that sustain growth and inspire others.

Melanie Perkins' journey brings this framework to life, illustrating how self-awareness and resilience can turn challenges into opportunities for innovation and connection. As you integrate these steps into your leadership practice, remember: growth is a journey, not a destination. The work of inner mastery is ongoing, but its impact can resonate far beyond yourself, shaping the culture and success of those you lead.

Inner Growth in Action

Leadership is not defined by the absence of challenges but by how one navigates through them. The inner game of leadership—rooted in self-awareness, emotional resilience, and clarity—becomes most apparent when leaders face their defining moments. Two stories illustrate how embracing these qualities can not only guide organizations through turbulent times but also lay the foundation for long-term success.

Melanie Perkins: Turning Rejection into Resolve

In the early days of Canva, Melanie Perkins often found herself in a precarious position. She had a clear vision for her online design platform, a tool that could democratize design for millions of people. But every pitch meeting brought a new wave of rejection. Investors doubted her ability to scale the concept, dismissing her as a young, inexperienced founder from Australia without connections in Silicon Valley.

For many, these setbacks could have easily bred bitterness or doubt. Yet Perkins chose a different path—one that was guided by self-awareness and emotional resilience. She took the time to reflect on the feedback she received, examining her approach to understand why her pitches weren't landing. Rather than internalizing rejection as a reflection of her worth, she reframed it as an opportunity to refine her strategy and communication.

Perkins also recognized the importance of emotional regulation in sustaining her focus. The sting of repeated rejections was real, but she didn't let it derail her progress. She leaned into practices like deliberate preparation and leaning on her support network to maintain her confidence. Perkins' resilience wasn't about suppressing her feelings; it was about channelling them into determination.

Her perseverance paid off. Canva eventually secured funding and grew into a billion-dollar company used by millions worldwide. But more than the financial success, what stands out is how Perkins' inner growth shaped her leadership. She created a culture at Canva rooted in trust, collaboration, and inclusivity—qualities that mirrored the emotional resilience and self-awareness she cultivated in herself.

Perkins' journey reminds us that growth often emerges from our most challenging moments. By confronting her fears and staying aligned with her vision, she not only transformed her company but also set a powerful example for those around her.

Brian Chesky: Leading Through Crisis with Emotional Depth

When the COVID-19 pandemic brought global travel to a standstill, Airbnb faced an existential crisis. Bookings plummeted overnight, and the company's future hung in the balance. For Brian Chesky, Airbnb's co-founder and CEO, this was a defining moment of leadership. The decisions he made during this period would not only determine the company's survival but also reflect his own growth as a leader.

Chesky began by acknowledging the emotional toll of the crisis—not just on himself but on his team and stakeholders. Instead of retreating behind closed doors, he made a conscious effort to lead with transparency and vulnerability. In an open letter to employees announcing significant layoffs, Chesky shared his thought process and the gravity of the situation with honesty and compassion. He didn't shy away from the emotional weight of the decisions, nor did he try to sugarcoat the reality.

This approach required immense emotional resilience. Chesky had to manage his own fears about the company's future while staying present for his team. He leaned on his self-awareness to balance the need for decisive action with empathy for those impacted. By openly communicating his values and rationale, he preserved trust within Airbnb's workforce, even amid difficult decisions.

Chesky also turned to reflection as a tool for growth. In the aftermath of the layoffs, he revisited Airbnb's mission of creating a sense of belonging. This clarity helped him pivot the company toward new opportunities, such as long-term stays and virtual experiences, ensuring its relevance in a rapidly changing world.

Under Chesky's leadership, Airbnb not only survived the crisis but emerged stronger, going public in late 2020 with one of the most successful IPOs of the year. His ability to lead with emotional depth and clarity underscored the importance of inner growth in navigating uncertainty.

Reflections on Inner Leadership

The stories of Melanie Perkins and Brian Chesky illustrate the transformative power of inner growth in leadership. Both leaders faced immense challenges, yet their self-awareness, emotional resilience, and alignment with their values allowed them to persevere and inspire others. Perkins showed how reframing rejection could fuel innovation, while Chesky demonstrated the impact of vulnerability and reflection in the face of crisis.

These examples remind us that the journey of leadership is as much about the inner work as it is about external outcomes. The ability to pause, reflect, and act with intention doesn't just shape the leader—it ripples outward, influencing the culture, trust, and adaptability of their organizations.

As we continue exploring the inner game of leadership, consider this: How might your own inner growth shape the trajectory of your leadership? What lessons could you draw from Perkins' resilience or Chesky's vulnerability to navigate your own defining moments? The next section will delve into the practical tools and strategies that can help you strengthen your inner game, ensuring that your growth becomes a source of strength and inspiration for those you lead.

Navigating the Dilemma of Short-Term Wins vs. Long-Term Growth

Every leader faces moments where the path forward isn't clear, where competing priorities pull in opposite directions, and where decisions must be made despite uncertainty. One of the most challenging dilemmas is choosing between short-term wins that deliver immediate results and long-term growth that builds enduring success. This choice tests not only a leader's strategic acumen but also their inner clarity—the ability to stay grounded in values and align decisions with a larger vision.

The Temptation of the Quick Win

In the early stages of a company's growth, the pressure to deliver results is immense. Investors demand performance metrics, teams look for immediate validation, and the market rewards those who act decisively. For leaders, the lure of the quick win—a decision that satisfies stakeholders and shows progress—is hard to resist.

Consider the case of a growing tech startup facing stagnant revenue. The CEO is presented with an opportunity to sign a lucrative but short-term contract with a client whose values don't align with the company's mission. On one hand, the deal offers a much-needed revenue boost. On the other, it risks diluting the company's brand and shifting resources away from the innovation pipeline that underpins its long-term strategy.

If the CEO prioritizes the short-term win, the decision may provide immediate relief and satisfy external pressures. But over time, this choice could erode the company's identity, alienate loyal customers, and hinder the development of products that ensure sustainable growth.

The Discipline of Long-Term Thinking

Contrast this with a leader who chooses to prioritize long-term growth, even at the expense of immediate gains. Melanie Perkins, co-founder of Canva, often faced pressure to expand rapidly by adding complex features to the platform. While these features could have appealed to advanced users and increased revenue in the short term, Perkins remained committed to Canva's core mission: simplicity and accessibility for all.

This clarity of purpose required discipline and resilience. By saying no to distractions and staying focused on the long-term vision, Perkins ensured Canva became a platform that scaled inclusively, appealing to millions of users worldwide. The decision to forgo immediate gains paid dividends in building a product with enduring impact and a loyal customer base.

Her story underscores a key lesson: long-term thinking requires leaders to trust their vision, resist external pressures, and make decisions that align with their deeper values, even when the payoff isn't immediate.

The Role of Inner Clarity

The ability to navigate these dilemmas hinges on inner clarity—a leader's capacity to reflect, evaluate, and act with intention. Leaders who lack this clarity may find themselves swayed by external demands or reactive to immediate challenges, leading to decisions that undermine their larger goals.

Self-aware leaders, on the other hand, approach dilemmas with a grounded perspective. They take the time to examine the trade-offs, consult their values, and weigh the potential impact on their vision. This process doesn't eliminate the difficulty of the choice, but it ensures that decisions are made with purpose rather than pressure.

Contrasting Approaches, Diverging Outcomes

Imagine two leaders at a crossroads. One prioritizes the quick win, securing short-term success but compromising the company's ability to innovate and grow sustainably. Over time, this approach creates a culture of reactionary decision-making, where short-term thinking erodes trust and alignment.

The other leader, grounded in inner clarity, chooses the longer, harder road. By aligning decisions with the company's mission and long-term goals, they build a culture of patience, resilience, and purpose. While the immediate rewards may be less tangible, the organization grows stronger, more cohesive, and better positioned to navigate future challenges.

Questions for Reflection

As you consider the role of inner clarity in your decision-making, ask yourself:

- When faced with a dilemma, how do you balance short-term pressures with long-term goals?

- Are your decisions aligned with your values, or are they influenced by external demands?

- How do you ensure that immediate wins don't come at the expense of enduring success?

Leadership isn't about avoiding difficult choices—it's about navigating them with purpose. The inner game of leadership equips you with the tools to reflect deeply, stay grounded, and make decisions that inspire trust and drive impact. As you continue to strengthen this inner foundation, the dilemmas you face will become opportunities to lead with clarity, resilience, and vision.

Expanding Possibilities: Broadening the Path to Inner Growth

The inner game of leadership is as unique as the leaders who navigate it. While self-awareness, emotional resilience, and clarity are universal qualities, the pathways to cultivating them are as diverse as the challenges leaders face. Beyond traditional methods like reflection and feedback, alternative approaches such as journaling, executive coaching, and mindfulness practices offer powerful tools to deepen inner growth. These strategies not only support personal development but also align seamlessly with the diverse demands of leadership across industries.

Journaling: Writing Your Way to Clarity

Leadership often requires making sense of complexity—untangling emotions, processing experiences, and distilling lessons from chaos. Journaling provides a simple yet profound way to do this. By putting thoughts to paper, leaders can create space to explore their inner world without judgment, revealing patterns and insights that might otherwise remain hidden.

A Story in Practice:

Consider Brian Chesky, CEO of Airbnb, who turned to reflective practices during the pandemic's upheaval. While not explicitly a journaler, Chesky frequently documented his thoughts and decisions in real time, creating a written narrative of his leadership journey. This practice allowed him to revisit pivotal moments, learn from his responses, and refine his approach.

For leaders across industries, journaling can become a daily anchor—a quiet moment to pause and process. Whether it's listing lessons learned, exploring emotional triggers, or setting intentions for the day, journaling fosters clarity and self-awareness that ripple outward into decisions and actions.

Executive Coaching: A Mirror for Growth

While leadership can often feel isolating, executive coaching offers a structured partnership to explore challenges, set goals, and cultivate self-awareness. Coaches act as mirrors, reflecting back a leader's patterns and behaviours while challenging them to grow beyond their comfort zones.

A Practical Example:

Vivian Farrell, CEO of Modular Automation, attributes much of her leadership evolution to executive coaching. During a period of rapid expansion, Farrell faced competing priorities and mounting pressures. Through coaching, she identified limiting beliefs that were holding her back, learned to delegate effectively, and sharpened her decision-making processes. The structured conversations not only improved her performance but also empowered her to lead with greater confidence and authenticity.

For leaders navigating complex environments, coaching provides a safe space to process challenges, gain fresh perspectives, and align actions with long-term values. It's a dynamic approach that blends introspection with accountability, ensuring that inner growth translates into tangible outcomes.

Mindfulness Practices: Cultivating Presence in Chaos

Amid the constant demands of leadership, mindfulness practices offer a counterbalance—an opportunity to cultivate presence, reduce stress, and reconnect with purpose. Whether through meditation, breathwork, or focused attention, mindfulness builds the emotional resilience leaders need to stay grounded in turbulence.

A Lesson from the Field:

Reed Hastings of Netflix has spoken about the importance of mindfulness in maintaining his focus and emotional balance. While his practices may not involve formal meditation, Hastings consistently carves out time for reflection and strategic thinking, ensuring he remains present in his decision-making.

Mindfulness doesn't require lengthy retreats or complex rituals. It can be as simple as taking a few deep breaths before a critical meeting, pausing to observe emotions during a stressful moment, or practicing gratitude at the end of a long day. These small moments of presence create a reservoir of calm that leaders can draw upon when navigating uncertainty.

Integrating Diverse Approaches

These alternative strategies—journaling, coaching, and mindfulness—are not standalone solutions. Instead, they complement one another, offering leaders a suite of tools to support their unique journeys. A leader might begin with journaling to explore emotional patterns, engage a coach to refine their goals, and use mindfulness to sustain clarity during implementation. Together, these practices create a holistic approach to inner growth that adapts to the needs of any industry or leadership style.

The integration of these practices reflects a broader truth: there is no single path to inner mastery. Leaders must experiment, adapt, and discover what resonates most with their values and circumstances. By embracing diverse approaches, they not only deepen their inner game but also model the adaptability and openness that inspire those they lead.

Returning to the Core Message

The strategies explored here—journaling, coaching, mindfulness—tie directly to the central themes of this chapter: self-awareness, emotional intelligence, and resilience. Each practice offers a practical way to strengthen these qualities, ensuring that the inner game of leadership becomes a source of strength rather than strain.

As you reflect on these possibilities, consider how they might integrate into your own leadership journey. What small steps could you take today to deepen your self-awareness or cultivate emotional balance? The next section will bring this journey to a close, weaving together the lessons and insights from the inner game of leadership and inspiring you to take action with clarity and confidence. Let's move forward with intention and purpose.

Strength Beneath the Surface

Leadership, like an iceberg, reveals only part of its story to the world. The visible outcomes—decisions made, teams guided, goals achieved—are supported by a much larger, unseen foundation: the leader's inner world. This chapter has delved into the critical components of that foundation—self-awareness, emotional intelligence, and resilience—qualities that shape how leaders respond to challenges, connect with others, and sustain their vision over time.

Through the journeys of leaders like Melanie Perkins and Brian Chesky, we've seen how confronting inner struggles with intentionality can drive transformation, not only for individuals but for entire organizations. We've explored practical frameworks and strategies, such as the REFLECT approach, that offer a roadmap for cultivating inner mastery. From journaling to executive coaching, we've highlighted how diverse practices can support this growth, showing that there's no single path to inner clarity—only the one you choose to walk.

At its core, the inner game of leadership is about alignment: aligning your decisions with your values, your actions with your purpose, and your emotions with your goals. It's a continuous journey of reflection, learning, and adaptation, one that evolves as you do. As you strengthen this inner foundation, you not only enhance your own capacity but also inspire those around you, creating a ripple effect that transforms teams, organizations, and communities.

The work of leadership is never finished, and neither is the journey inward. As we transition to the next chapter, we'll shift our focus outward, exploring the art of creating cultures that amplify collective growth. But before we move forward, let's take a moment to pause, reflect, and integrate the lessons of this chapter into your own leadership journey.

Strengthening Your Inner Game

Take a moment to step back from the noise of daily demands and ask yourself: What lies beneath the surface of your leadership? How does your inner world shape the decisions you make, the relationships you nurture, and the vision you pursue?

Pause and Consider:

Think about a recent leadership challenge. What emotions did it stir within you, and how did those emotions influence your response? Were you guided by clarity, or did external pressures pull you away from your values? Reflect on what you learned from that experience and how it might inform your approach moving forward.

Revisit the Dilemmas:

When faced with a choice between short-term wins and long-term growth, how do you decide what matters most? What role does self-awareness play in guiding your priorities? Consider how you might integrate practices like journaling or mindfulness to ground yourself during these moments of tension.

Chart a Path for Growth:

What practices resonate most with you—journaling, coaching, mindfulness, or another approach? How might you begin to weave these practices into your daily life, not as an obligation but as a resource for clarity and balance?

Look to the Horizon:

As you reflect on the lessons of this chapter, think about the legacy you want to leave as a leader. How can cultivating your inner game not only support your growth but also inspire and empower those you lead?

Leadership isn't about perfection; it's about presence. It's about showing up, again and again, with the courage to reflect, adapt, and grow. As you move forward, take these reflections with you as a compass for navigating the ever-changing tides of leadership. The journey inward is just the beginning, and its impact will resonate far beyond the boundaries of your own growth.

Chapter 9

Health as a Foundation for Resilient Leadership

"True leadership longevity requires not just mental strength but physical and emotional well-being."

For many leaders in the relentless pursuit of growth, health often becomes an afterthought—a "nice-to-have" that's sidelined by the pressing demands of scaling a business. Yet, as the pressures of decision-making mount and the stakes grow higher, it's clear that leadership resilience is intrinsically tied to well-being. Health, in its broadest sense—physical, mental, and emotional—is not just a personal priority but a strategic necessity. Without it, the energy, focus, and clarity required to lead through challenges begin to erode.

A founder I once worked with—let's call her Maria—was in the thick of scaling her tech company. On paper, everything was going right: a surge in customer acquisition, a landmark funding round, and a growing team eager to follow her vision. But behind the scenes, Maria was running on fumes. Her days blurred into nights, meals became afterthoughts, and exercise was perpetually postponed for "when things slow down." That day never came. Eventually, her relentless pace caught up with her. A health scare forced her to step back, and in the weeks that followed, she realized that the very resilience her company needed from her was tied to something she'd been neglecting all along: her own well-being.

Maria's story isn't unique—it's a reality many leaders face. Yet, it underscores a truth that's often overlooked: Leadership doesn't happen in a vacuum. The strength, clarity, and energy we bring to our roles are directly tied to the care we extend to ourselves.

In *Unstoppable Growth*, we've explored strategies to scale businesses, lead with purpose, and create impact. But none of these can be sustained without a foundation of physical, mental, and emotional health. Resilient leadership starts from within. It's not a nice-to-have; it's the fuel that powers everything else.

The intersection of health and leadership isn't just anecdotal—it's supported by research. Studies show that leaders who prioritize their health make better decisions, navigate stress more effectively, and inspire greater trust and performance in their teams. Yet, in the pursuit of growth, health is often the first thing sacrificed.

This chapter is an invitation to rethink that approach. It's not about perfection or adding another item to an already overflowing to-do list. It's about recognizing that caring for yourself is an act of leadership. It's about understanding that the example you set in prioritizing health creates a ripple effect throughout your organization, fostering a culture of resilience and well-being.

We'll explore actionable frameworks for integrating health into your daily leadership practices, hear from leaders who've transformed their approach to well-being, and unpack the research that connects health to sustained success.

Because the truth is, the journey of *Unstoppable Growth* is a marathon, not a sprint. And like any marathoner will tell you, the key to crossing the finish line isn't just about endurance—it's about preparation, care, and pacing yourself for the long haul. Leadership is no different. The health you invest in today will shape not just your capacity to lead tomorrow, but the legacy you leave behind.

The Health-Leadership Connection

Leadership often demands navigating complex challenges, balancing competing priorities, and making decisions with far-reaching consequences. It's no wonder that the pressures of leadership can take a toll on health. Yet, research consistently shows that a leader's physical, mental, and emotional well-being is not just a personal matter—it's a key driver of their effectiveness and resilience.

Physical Fitness: Fuelling Energy and Focus

Physical health forms the foundation for sustained energy and cognitive performance. Studies published in *Harvard Business Review* reveal that regular exercise improves focus, memory, and decision-making abilities. Leaders who prioritize fitness report sharper problem-solving skills and greater stamina to tackle long days. Physical activity also reduces the production of stress hormones like cortisol, promoting emotional stability during high-pressure situations.

Take the example of Richard Branson, the founder of Virgin Group, who credits his daily exercise routine—ranging from swimming to cycling—with giving him the energy and clarity to run a global empire.

Branson's commitment to fitness is more than personal; it's an integral part of his leadership toolkit. "If you take care of your body, your body will take care of your business," he often says.

In organizations, this principle scales. Teams led by health-conscious leaders are more likely to adopt wellness practices, leading to a culture of vitality and productivity. This ripple effect highlights the symbiotic relationship between a leader's health and their organization's performance.

Mental Health: Clarity Amid Complexity

Leadership requires not only physical energy but also mental clarity, particularly in an era of rapid change and information overload. Research from McKinsey emphasizes the importance of mental health in sustaining creativity and strategic thinking. Leaders who address their mental well-being—through mindfulness, therapy, or structured reflection—are better equipped to navigate ambiguity and inspire confidence in their teams.

Arianna Huffington's story is a case in point. After her collapse from burnout, she made sleep and mental health non-negotiable priorities, even founding Thrive Global to promote workplace well-being. Her advocacy isn't just anecdotal; it's backed by data. Studies show that well-rested leaders are 29% more effective at managing teams and 30% better at setting clear goals, according to a *Harvard Business Review* analysis.

Mental health practices such as mindfulness have also gained traction. A study by the *Journal of Occupational Health Psychology* found that leaders who engaged in regular mindfulness practices experienced reduced stress, enhanced emotional regulation, and improved interpersonal relationships—critical factors in high-pressure environments.

Stress Management: Building Resilience Under Pressure

Leadership is inherently stressful, but how leaders manage that stress can make all the difference. Chronic stress impairs decision-making, weakens emotional control, and diminishes creativity—all essential components of effective leadership. However, research shows that leaders who develop proactive stress management strategies are more likely to thrive under pressure.

McKinsey's findings underscore the importance of resilience-building habits, such as exercise, structured downtime, and intentional connection with others. Leaders who manage stress effectively not only maintain their own performance but also create a sense of stability and confidence within their organizations.

Consider Brian Chesky, CEO of Airbnb, who led his company through the chaos of the COVID-19 pandemic. Chesky openly acknowledged the immense stress of making difficult decisions, from layoffs to strategic pivots. By prioritizing reflection and surrounding himself with trusted advisors, Chesky demonstrated how self-awareness and intentional stress management enable leaders to make clear-headed decisions during crises.

The Health-Impact Loop: A Cycle of Growth

The relationship between health and leadership effectiveness isn't linear; it's cyclical. Physical fitness fuels energy, mental health sharpens focus, and stress management builds resilience. Together, these elements create a positive feedback loop, where personal well-being enhances professional performance, which in turn reinforces health through greater clarity and balance.

Leaders who neglect this loop often find themselves in burnout cycles, where declining health erodes their ability to lead effectively, creating further stress and compounding the issue. On the other hand, leaders who invest in their well-being create a foundation for sustained success, not just for themselves but for their teams and organizations.

Setting the Stage for Action

These insights point to a simple but profound truth: resilient leadership starts with personal health. But knowing the importance of health is not enough—leaders need practical tools and strategies to integrate well-being into their demanding lives.

In the sections that follow, we'll explore frameworks designed to help leaders embed health into their leadership practice. From structured approaches like the BALANCE framework to real-world examples of leaders who have embraced well-being, we'll uncover actionable pathways to strengthen the connection between health and resilient leadership.

As we move forward, reflect on your own journey: How might prioritizing your health enhance your ability to lead effectively? And how can you begin to integrate these practices into your daily life? Let's explore these questions together, step by step.

Building Resilience Through BALANCE

Leadership resilience isn't accidental—it's intentional. It's built on daily practices that strengthen physical, mental, and emotional well-being, enabling leaders to sustain their energy and clarity even in the face of relentless challenges. The **BALANCE** framework—Breathe, Align, Listen, Act, Nourish, Centre, Energize—offers a practical roadmap for embedding health into leadership routines. This framework is both actionable and adaptable, designed to guide leaders in cultivating habits that support their ability to lead with strength and purpose.

Let's explore the BALANCE framework in detail, weaving in the story of Arianna Huffington, a leader who transformed her leadership approach by prioritizing well-being.

1. Breathe: Cultivating Calm Through Intentional Pause

The foundation of health-driven leadership begins with the breath. In moments of stress or overwhelm, intentional breathing helps calm the nervous system, creating space for clarity and thoughtful action. It's not just a practice for mindfulness; it's a tool for emotional regulation and decision-making.

Arianna Huffington describes how she incorporates intentional breathing into her daily routine to anchor herself amid demanding schedules. Before important meetings or decisions, she takes a moment to pause, breathe deeply, and ground herself in the present. This simple habit allows her to respond with composure rather than reacting out of stress.

Action: Start small. Practice three deep breaths before beginning a meeting or responding to a high-stakes email. Notice how this brief pause creates space for clearer thinking and intentional action.

2. Align: Grounding Actions in Values and Purpose

Leadership resilience grows when actions are aligned with values and purpose. Misalignment—between what leaders do and what they believe—leads to emotional exhaustion. Aligning daily tasks with personal and organizational purpose brings clarity and focus, reducing decision fatigue and fostering fulfilment.

Example: During Airbnb's pandemic pivot, Brian Chesky continually revisited Airbnb's core mission of creating a sense of belonging. By aligning every decision with this purpose, from workforce reductions to product innovations, he ensured the organization remained true to its values. This alignment gave Chesky the resilience to lead through uncertainty with integrity.

Application: At the start of each day, identify one task or decision that directly supports your values and mission. Aligning even one action with purpose creates momentum for a more intentional day.

3. Listen: Tuning Inward and Outward

Listening is a dual practice: tuning into your inner needs while also remaining attuned to the needs of others. Leaders who prioritize listening develop self-awareness and empathy, creating stronger connections with their teams while staying attuned to their own limits.

Example: Huffington often emphasizes the importance of self-listening—paying attention to the signals of exhaustion or stress in her body. At the same time, she fosters open communication within her teams, encouraging honest conversations about well-being. This balance ensures she leads with both self-care and relational awareness.

Application: Set aside time each day to check in with yourself: *How am I feeling physically, emotionally, and mentally?* Pair this practice with active listening during team interactions, ensuring your leadership remains responsive and empathetic.

4. Act: Taking Intentional Steps Toward Well-Being

Knowledge alone doesn't drive change—action does. Resilient leaders prioritize small, consistent steps toward health, knowing that incremental actions compound into transformative habits.

Example: Huffington's post-burnout journey began with small changes: setting a consistent bedtime, turning off her phone before sleep, and carving out time for reflection. These small but deliberate actions rebuilt her energy and focus over time, ultimately transforming her leadership style.

Application: Choose one health-related habit to implement this week, such as walking for 10 minutes daily or drinking more water. Commit to small actions, and trust their cumulative impact.

5. Nourish: Fuelling the Body and Mind

Resilience depends on nourishment—physically through balanced nutrition and mentally through enriching experiences. Leaders who prioritize nourishment enhance their energy, focus, and emotional stability.

Example: Huffington reframed food as fuel, incorporating nutritious meals that sustain her energy throughout the day. She also nourishes her mind through intentional downtime, such as reading or engaging in creative activities, which helps her recharge.

Application: Examine your current habits: Are you fuelling your body and mind in ways that sustain you? Start by replacing one processed snack with a whole-food alternative or dedicating 15 minutes a day to reading something that inspires you.

6. Centre: Creating Stability Amid Chaos

Centring involves establishing rituals that anchor leaders during turbulent times. Whether it's a morning routine or a reflective practice, centring rituals provide a sense of control and stability.

Example: Huffington starts her day with a centring ritual that includes mindfulness and gratitude. By beginning her day with intention, she sets the tone for resilience and focus, no matter what challenges arise.

Application: Experiment with a centring ritual that resonates with you. It could be as simple as writing down three things you're grateful for each morning or practicing 5 minutes of meditation.

7. Energize: Replenishing Through Movement and Rest

Leadership resilience requires both energy and recovery. Leaders who integrate movement into their day and prioritize rest are better equipped to sustain their performance over time.

Example: Huffington emphasizes the non-negotiability of sleep, noting how rest fuels her ability to lead effectively. Paired with daily movement, this commitment to energy management ensures she shows up fully present for her responsibilities.

Application: Incorporate movement into your routine, whether through a midday walk or a short yoga session. Equally important, set a consistent sleep schedule that prioritizes restorative rest.

Integrating BALANCE into Leadership

The BALANCE framework is not a one-size-fits-all solution; it's a guide that adapts to each leader's needs and circumstances. By embedding these practices into daily routines, leaders can build the resilience, energy, and clarity needed to lead sustainably.

The journey to health-driven leadership doesn't require perfection. It starts with small, intentional steps—breathing deeply before a meeting, aligning actions with values, or committing to better rest. As leaders cultivate these habits, they not only strengthen their inner foundation but also inspire their teams to prioritize well-being, creating a culture of resilience that supports growth and impact.

As we move forward, consider this: Which element of BALANCE resonates most with you? What small shift could you make today to begin embedding health into your leadership? In the next section, we'll explore real-world applications, highlighting leaders who have integrated these principles into their lives and the transformative impact it's had on their organizations.

Health as Leadership's Invisible Power

Behind every successful leader lies a foundation of resilience built on physical, mental, and emotional health. Far from being a secondary consideration, health plays a pivotal role in a leader's ability to inspire, innovate, and sustain their impact. Two leaders—Arianna Huffington and Richard Branson—exemplify how prioritizing well-being can transform not just their own capacity to lead but also the cultures they create within their organizations.

Arianna Huffington: Redefining Success Through Well-Being

Arianna Huffington's story is a wake-up call for leaders who equate success with sacrifice. As co-founder of *The Huffington Post*, Huffington was a model of relentless ambition, often working late into the night to drive her media empire forward. But in 2007, her body sent an undeniable signal: after collapsing from exhaustion in her office, she woke up in a pool of blood with a fractured cheekbone. This moment of crisis forced her to confront a hard truth—her leadership was unsustainable.

Determined to change, Huffington began by addressing her sleep patterns. She made rest a non-negotiable part of her routine, understanding that adequate sleep was essential not just for physical recovery but for emotional balance and mental clarity. Her transformation didn't stop there. Recognizing the broader implications of her personal journey, she founded Thrive Global, an organization focused on combating burnout and promoting well-being in the workplace. Thrive's initiatives, from sleep improvement programs to mindfulness workshops, have helped countless leaders and employees redefine what it means to thrive at work.

Huffington's journey highlights a critical insight: resilience isn't about pushing harder—it's about creating space to recover, reflect, and recharge. By prioritizing her health, she not only sustained her leadership but also amplified her influence, inspiring others to follow suit.

Richard Branson: Energizing Leadership Through Action

For Richard Branson, founder of Virgin Group, health isn't just a personal commitment—it's a strategic advantage. With a portfolio of over 400 companies, Branson's schedule is as demanding as it is dynamic. Yet, he attributes much of his energy and creativity to his unwavering commitment to physical fitness.

Branson begins each day with movement, whether it's kitesurfing, swimming, or cycling. For him, exercise is more than a routine—it's a ritual that sharpens his focus and sustains his stamina. "Staying fit keeps my mind sharp and my energy high," he says. This daily practice not only fuels his ability to lead but also sets an example for his teams, embedding a culture of vitality across his organizations.

Branson's commitment extends beyond his own well-being. At Virgin, he champions employee wellness programs, recognizing that healthy teams are more collaborative, creative, and productive. From flexible work schedules to on-site fitness opportunities, Branson ensures that health is woven into the fabric of Virgin's culture.

His approach underscores a vital principle: leaders who prioritize their health model the behaviors they wish to see in their teams. By doing so, they create environments where well-being and performance go hand in hand.

Lessons in Leadership Resilience

The stories of Huffington and Branson offer profound lessons for leaders at all levels. First, they remind us that resilience isn't a passive trait; it's a skill cultivated through intentional choices. Second, they demonstrate that health isn't a luxury—it's a strategic foundation for sustained impact. Finally, they show that prioritizing well-being isn't selfish; it's an act of service to the teams and organizations leaders support.

Both leaders faced significant challenges: Huffington had to rebuild her approach after a personal health crisis, while Branson balanced the demands of a vast empire with his commitment to fitness. Yet, their strategies converged on a common theme: the importance of health as a driver of leadership effectiveness.

As you reflect on these examples, consider your own leadership journey. Are you prioritizing your health, or is it taking a backseat to your responsibilities? How might a shift in focus—from sacrifice to sustainability—change not only your well-being but also your ability to lead with clarity and resilience?

Health isn't a distraction from leadership; it's a foundation for it. As we move forward in this chapter, we'll explore practical strategies and frameworks that can help you embed well-being into your daily life, ensuring that your health becomes a catalyst for both personal growth and organizational success. Remember: thriving leaders build thriving teams, and it all starts with taking care of yourself.

Innovating Health for Leadership Resilience

As leadership evolves to meet the complexities of modern organizations, so too must the strategies that support well-being. While the foundation of health-driven leadership lies in practices like physical fitness, mental clarity, and emotional balance, alternative and complementary approaches offer fresh opportunities to enhance resilience. These strategies—mindfulness practices, team wellness initiatives, and technology-driven health solutions—expand the possibilities for integrating health into leadership in ways that are adaptable, inclusive, and impactful.

Mindfulness Practices: Cultivating Presence Amid Pressure

Mindfulness, the practice of intentional focus on the present moment, has become a powerful tool for leaders seeking clarity and emotional regulation. Far from being a trend, mindfulness is supported by robust research linking it to reduced stress, improved decision-making, and greater emotional resilience. By creating moments of stillness amid the chaos, leaders can reconnect with their purpose and lead with greater intentionality.

Consider the story of a CEO navigating a turbulent product launch. With deadlines looming and tensions high, she carves out 10 minutes each morning for mindful breathing. This brief ritual doesn't solve the challenges ahead but transforms how she approaches them—grounded, clear, and composed. Her ability to regulate her emotions and remain present trickles down to her team, fostering a culture of calm and collaboration even under pressure.

Mindfulness practices don't require significant time or resources. They can be as simple as taking a few breaths before a meeting, journaling reflections at the end of the day, or practicing gratitude. These small yet transformative habits create a reservoir of resilience leaders can draw upon in moments of strain.

Team Wellness Initiatives: Scaling Health Across Organizations

Health isn't just an individual pursuit—it's a collective value. Leaders who prioritize team wellness initiatives recognize that resilient organizations are built on the well-being of their people. These initiatives can take many forms, from providing gym memberships to hosting wellness workshops or implementing mental health days.

A leading tech company once faced high turnover due to burnout. In response, its leadership team launched a wellness initiative centred on employee health. This included flexible schedules, on-site yoga classes, and an open-door policy for mental health support. The results were transformative: not only did employee engagement soar, but productivity improved, and the culture shifted toward one of mutual care and respect.

For scale-up organizations, fostering team wellness isn't just about perks—it's about creating an environment where individuals feel supported and empowered to bring their best selves to work. Leaders who model this commitment to health inspire their teams to prioritize their own well-being, amplifying resilience across the organization.

Leveraging Technology: The Future of Health-Driven Leadership

Technology offers innovative ways to integrate health into leadership. From wearable devices that monitor physical activity and sleep to apps that facilitate meditation and stress management, tech-driven solutions provide leaders with actionable insights into their well-being.

Imagine a founder of a scale-up who begins each day by reviewing metrics from her smartwatch. The data reveals her sleep quality, stress levels, and readiness for the day ahead. Armed with this information, she adjusts her schedule, incorporating a midday walk to boost energy or prioritizing an earlier bedtime after a demanding day. Over time, these data-informed adjustments enhance her resilience and decision-making capacity.

Technology doesn't replace the human aspects of health-driven leadership but enhances them by offering personalized insights. Leaders can use these tools not only for self-care but also to support their teams, promoting a culture of awareness and balance.

Integrating Diverse Strategies for Greater Impact

These alternative strategies—mindfulness practices, team wellness initiatives, and technology-driven solutions—are not standalone fixes. Instead, they complement foundational health habits, creating a holistic approach to leadership resilience. A leader might begin their day with a mindfulness exercise, monitor their progress through wearable technology, and foster team-wide health through inclusive wellness programs. Together, these practices create a robust framework for sustaining energy, clarity, and balance in the face of leadership challenges.

Tying It All Together

The heart of health-driven leadership lies in its adaptability. Just as no two leaders are alike, no single approach will work for everyone. The key is to experiment, reflect, and integrate the strategies that resonate most deeply with your values and circumstances. Whether through mindfulness, collective wellness, or leveraging technology, these expanded possibilities remind us that health is both a personal commitment and a shared responsibility.

As you reflect on these ideas, consider how they might fit into your own leadership journey. What practices could you adopt to deepen your resilience? How might you inspire your team to prioritize their health as well? Leadership isn't just about guiding others—it's about creating environments where everyone, including you, can thrive. Let these strategies serve as a bridge between intention and action, helping you lead from a place of balance and strength.

Health as Leadership's Bedrock

Leadership is often portrayed as an external endeavour—guiding teams, making decisions, and navigating complex markets. Yet, as we've explored in this chapter, the true foundation of resilient leadership lies within. The metaphor of a sprinter running a marathon at a relentless pace reminds us that health isn't just a personal necessity—it's the core strength that sustains leadership over the long haul.

We've examined how prioritizing physical fitness fuels energy and focus, how nurturing mental health sharpens clarity and creativity, and how managing stress builds resilience under pressure. Through the stories of Arianna Huffington and Richard Branson, we've seen how intentional health practices not only enhance individual performance but also ripple outward, inspiring teams and shaping organizational cultures.

We've also explored practical tools like the BALANCE framework and expanded possibilities such as mindfulness, team wellness initiatives, and leveraging technology. Each strategy offers a path to embedding health into leadership, not as a secondary concern but as a driving force for impact and growth.

As we close this chapter, reflect on the recurring themes: the need for intentionality, the power of small, consistent habits, and the profound connection between personal well-being and professional success. Health isn't a luxury for leaders; it's the very foundation upon which sustainable leadership is built.

Reflect and Refocus: Building Your Leadership Resilience Through Health

Pause for a moment and consider: How is your health shaping the way you lead today? What patterns, habits, or practices are either supporting your resilience or detracting from it?

Reflect on a time when your health—whether physical, mental, or emotional—affected your leadership. How did it impact your ability to make decisions, connect with your team, or sustain your energy? What did you learn from that experience, and how might it inform your approach moving forward?

Think about the strategies discussed in this chapter. Which ones resonate most with you? Is it the grounding simplicity of mindful breathing, the ripple effects of team wellness programs, or the data-driven insights of wearable technology? Consider one practice you can experiment with this week, starting small but staying intentional.

Health isn't just about you—it's about the people you lead and the culture you create. Ask yourself: How can my commitment to health inspire others? What actions can I take to foster well-being within my team or organization, creating an environment where everyone can thrive?

Leadership, like health, is a journey of continuous growth. There will be setbacks and challenges, but each intentional step strengthens your foundation. As you integrate the lessons of this chapter, remember that prioritizing your health isn't an act of indulgence—it's an investment in your ability to lead with clarity, resilience, and purpose.

As we turn the page to the next chapter, we'll explore another dimension of sustainable leadership: creating cultures that thrive. But before we move on, take this moment to commit to one simple, health-driven action. Let it be the seed of a stronger, more resilient you, ready to lead not just for today, but for the marathon ahead.

Chapter 10

Empowering People for Unstoppable Performance

"The real measure of leadership isn't what you achieve alone; it's what you enable others to accomplish."

Leadership isn't about doing it all yourself—it's about unlocking the potential of those around you. For many leaders, the realization comes in a moment of overwhelm, when the sheer magnitude of responsibility becomes impossible to shoulder alone. Yet, what separates great leaders from good ones isn't their ability to take on more—it's their ability to empower others to rise with them.

I once met a CEO named Daniel, who was navigating the rapid growth of his company. Despite his remarkable vision and boundless energy, Daniel found himself at a breaking point. His days were consumed with decisions large and small, and while his team was talented, they often deferred to him out of habit. He felt stuck in a cycle where progress depended on his personal input at every turn.

A mentor offered him a simple but profound piece of advice: "Stop being the bottleneck and start being the bridge." For Daniel, this meant shifting from solving every problem to equipping his team to solve problems on their own. It wasn't easy—letting go rarely is. But as Daniel began to empower his people with clearer roles, trust, and autonomy, something extraordinary happened. His team not only stepped up—they exceeded his expectations. The company thrived, and Daniel discovered a new level of freedom and impact as a leader.

Empowerment isn't a luxury for leaders of scale-up organizations; it's a necessity. In the pages of *Unstoppable Growth*, we've explored how systems, strategy, and resilience fuel organizational momentum. But without empowered people, these elements falter. Teams that are trusted, equipped, and inspired don't just execute tasks—they innovate, adapt, and drive the organization forward.

The science backs this up. Research from Gallup shows that empowered employees are more engaged, productive, and loyal. Trust and autonomy aren't just feel-good principles; they're competitive advantages. Empowered teams make faster decisions, solve complex problems, and foster a culture of ownership that scales with growth.

Yet, empowerment doesn't happen by accident. It requires intentionality from leaders. It's about creating a culture where people feel valued, trusted, and capable. It's about providing clarity on expectations, encouraging collaboration, and celebrating contributions. And, above all, it's about relinquishing control—a challenge for many leaders who equate influence with oversight.

This chapter is about more than delegation. It's about creating an environment where people thrive because they feel empowered to make decisions, take risks, and grow. You'll learn practical frameworks for fostering empowerment, hear stories of leaders who've transformed their organizations by embracing this principle, and discover how empowerment fuels not just individual performance but collective momentum.

Empowering people isn't just a strategy for scaling your organization; it's a mindset shift that redefines leadership itself. Because when you trust your team to rise, they don't just lift the organization—they lift you, too. In the journey of *Unstoppable Growth*, this is where the magic happens.

The Power of Empowerment

Empowerment is not just a feel-good concept; it's a strategic lever for driving exceptional performance, engagement, and innovation. Research consistently underscores its transformative impact on organizations, revealing that when leaders create an environment where individuals feel trusted, autonomous, and recognized, the results ripple across teams and businesses alike.

Trust: The Foundation of High-Performance Teams

Trust is the cornerstone of empowerment. According to a *Harvard Business Review* study, high-trust workplaces outperform low-trust ones by nearly 50% in productivity and employee satisfaction. Trust allows individuals to take risks, share ideas openly, and tackle challenges without fear of failure. Leaders who cultivate trust unlock a sense of psychological safety, where employees feel confident to stretch their capabilities.

Consider the case of Netflix, where CEO Reed Hastings emphasizes trust as a core value. Netflix's famous culture of freedom and responsibility empowers employees to make decisions autonomously, whether it's designing a new user interface or creating original content. This trust-driven approach has fuelled some of Netflix's most groundbreaking successes, from its seamless streaming platform to global hits like *Stranger Things*.

Autonomy: The Catalyst for Innovation

Empowerment thrives on autonomy—the freedom to own one's work and make decisions independently. Gallup's research shows that employees who feel they have autonomy are 22% more likely to be engaged and 15% more likely to report high levels of well-being. Autonomy fosters intrinsic motivation, enabling teams to approach problems creatively and innovate effectively.

At Canva, co-founder Melanie Perkins embraced autonomy as a guiding principle for scaling her company. By trusting her team to explore bold ideas, Canva was able to develop intuitive, user-friendly design tools that democratized creativity for millions worldwide. Perkins' decision to delegate decision-making authority didn't just accelerate product development; it empowered her team to solve complex problems with ingenuity.

Recognition: Fuelling Engagement and Loyalty

Recognition, often overlooked in leadership strategies, plays a pivotal role in sustaining empowerment. Employees who feel valued and appreciated are more engaged, productive, and loyal. A study by O.C. Tanner revealed that recognition increases employees' sense of purpose by 63%, creating a ripple effect of positivity and commitment throughout an organization.

In practice, recognition doesn't need to be elaborate. Simple, meaningful gestures—a handwritten note, a public acknowledgment during a meeting—can create a profound impact. For example, Satya Nadella, CEO of Microsoft, consistently highlights team achievements in company-wide communications, reinforcing a culture where contributions are celebrated. This practice has helped Nadella transform Microsoft's culture into one of collaboration and innovation, driving its resurgence as a tech leader.

The Synergy of Empowerment Principles

Trust, autonomy, and recognition are not standalone ideas; they are deeply interconnected. Trust provides the foundation for autonomy, creating an environment where employees feel safe to take initiative. Autonomy, in turn, fosters innovation and engagement, while recognition reinforces these behaviours, ensuring they are sustained over time. Together, these principles form a powerful cycle that drives high performance and resilience.

A Gallup meta-analysis highlights this synergy, revealing that organizations with empowered teams see a 21% increase in profitability and a 41% reduction in absenteeism. When leaders empower their people, the ripple effects extend beyond individual outcomes, strengthening team cohesion, innovation, and organizational culture.

From Insights to Action

These findings illuminate a simple yet profound truth: Empowered teams are unstoppable. They think creatively, take ownership of their work, and bring their full potential to the table. But empowerment doesn't happen by chance; it requires deliberate leadership practices.

In the next section, we'll explore practical frameworks that leaders can use to foster empowerment within their teams. From building trust to encouraging autonomy and celebrating success, these strategies offer actionable pathways to create cultures of empowerment that fuel growth and performance.

As we move forward, reflect on this: How can you build trust, foster autonomy, and recognize contributions within your organization? Empowerment starts with intention, and the next step is transforming that intention into impact. Let's explore how.

The TRUST Approach

Empowerment is not simply a byproduct of effective leadership—it's a deliberate and intentional process. The **TRUST** framework—Transparency, Respect, Understanding, Support, and Time—provides a practical guide for fostering empowerment within teams. By embracing these principles, leaders can build environments where individuals feel valued, capable, and motivated to achieve their full potential.

Let's delve into each element of the TRUST framework, weaving in the story of Melanie Perkins, co-founder and CEO of Canva, whose leadership exemplifies these principles.

Transparency: Building a Foundation of Openness

Transparency is the cornerstone of empowerment. When leaders communicate openly about goals, challenges, and decisions, they foster trust and alignment within their teams. Transparency creates clarity, reducing uncertainty and enabling employees to act with confidence.

At Canva, Melanie Perkins prioritized transparency from the company's early days. Perkins ensured that her team understood Canva's mission—to make design accessible to everyone—and regularly shared updates about the company's progress. By openly discussing both successes and setbacks, she created a culture where employees felt connected to Canva's vision and equipped to contribute meaningfully.

Leaders can practice transparency by holding regular team check-ins, openly sharing challenges, and being honest about the reasoning behind key decisions. This openness empowers teams to act with clarity and purpose.

Respect: Valuing Every Individual's Contribution

Respect is the recognition of each team member's unique strengths, perspectives, and potential. Empowering leaders foster respect by encouraging diverse ideas, honoring different working styles, and valuing contributions at all levels.

Perkins demonstrated respect for her team by creating an inclusive environment where ideas flowed freely. She valued input from designers, engineers, and marketers alike, knowing that Canva's success depended on the collaboration of diverse perspectives. This culture of mutual respect empowered employees to take ownership of their work, knowing their voices mattered.

Leaders can cultivate respect by actively listening to their teams, encouraging diverse viewpoints, and recognizing individual contributions during meetings or public forums.

Understanding: Cultivating Empathy and Connection

Understanding goes beyond professional roles; it's about acknowledging the human side of leadership. Leaders who take time to understand their team members' strengths, challenges, and aspirations build deeper trust and foster authentic connections.

At Canva, Perkins invested time in understanding her team's needs, both professionally and personally. By creating a workplace that prioritized flexibility and well-being, she showed empathy for the demands her employees faced outside of work. This understanding reinforced a culture where people felt supported and empowered to thrive.

Leaders can build understanding by having one-on-one conversations with team members, asking open-ended questions about their goals and challenges, and tailoring support to individual needs.

Support: Providing Tools and Encouragement

Empowerment isn't about leaving people to figure it out alone; it's about equipping them with the resources and encouragement they need to succeed. Leaders who actively support their teams create conditions where people can take risks and grow.

Perkins ensured her team had the tools and resources needed to innovate at scale. Whether it was investing in new technology or providing professional development opportunities, she actively removed barriers to success, allowing her team to focus on what they did best.

Leaders can offer support by identifying and addressing obstacles, providing constructive feedback, and celebrating progress to boost morale and motivation.

Time: Allowing Space for Growth

Empowerment requires patience. Leaders must give their teams the time and space to develop their skills, test new ideas, and learn from mistakes. By allowing room for growth, leaders cultivate resilience and long-term success.

Perkins understood that great ideas take time to develop. She encouraged her team to experiment, iterate, and refine their work without fear of failure. This patient approach led to groundbreaking features that set Canva apart in the competitive design platform market.

Leaders can embrace this principle by setting realistic timelines, encouraging iterative progress, and viewing setbacks as opportunities for learning and growth.

Bringing TRUST to Life

The TRUST framework offers leaders a roadmap for fostering empowerment within their teams. By practicing transparency, respecting diverse contributions, understanding individual needs, providing active support, and allowing time for growth, leaders can create an environment where people feel valued, capable, and motivated to excel.

As Melanie Perkins' leadership journey demonstrates, these principles are not abstract ideals—they are actionable strategies that unlock potential and drive results. Her commitment to empowering her team didn't just fuel Canva's growth; it built a culture of innovation, resilience, and collaboration that continues to thrive.

Reflect on your own leadership practices: How might you incorporate the TRUST framework into your daily interactions? Which element resonates most with your current challenges, and how can you begin to apply it today? Empowerment starts with intention, and with TRUST, you have a clear path forward.

Leaders Who Embody Empowerment

Empowering leadership is more than delegating tasks or granting autonomy—it's a deliberate act of trust and vision that transforms teams into forces of innovation and resilience. The stories of Melanie Perkins at Canva and Brian Chesky at Airbnb illustrate how fostering empowerment can overcome challenges, unlock potential, and drive extraordinary results.

Melanie Perkins: Designing Empowerment into Culture

When Melanie Perkins co-founded Canva, she was clear about one thing: creating a global design platform that democratized creativity was not a one-person endeavor. As the company scaled rapidly, she recognized the challenges of maintaining innovation and engagement across a growing team. Perkins understood that her role as a leader wasn't to dictate every decision but to empower her team to take ownership of their work.

Her strategy for empowerment revolved around fostering trust and autonomy. Perkins emphasized open communication, ensuring that everyone—from product designers to engineers—had a clear understanding of Canva's mission and how their contributions fit into the bigger picture. By trusting her team to experiment and take risks, she created an environment where people felt confident to push boundaries.

One example of this trust was Canva's development of its real-time collaboration feature. Rather than micromanaging the project, Perkins encouraged her team to approach it with creativity and independence, providing support but allowing space for exploration. The result was a groundbreaking feature that set Canva apart from its competitors, strengthening its market leadership.

The outcomes of Perkins' approach speak volumes. Canva grew into a billion-dollar enterprise with over 60 million users in 190 countries. More importantly, it cultivated a culture where employees felt empowered to innovate, collaborate, and grow. As Perkins often reflects, "Empowering others isn't about giving up control—it's about unlocking possibilities."

Brian Chesky: Redefining Hospitality Through Empowerment

Brian Chesky, co-founder and CEO of Airbnb, faced a critical juncture when the COVID-19 pandemic brought the travel industry to a standstill. As bookings plummeted, Chesky needed to rally his team around a new vision while navigating unprecedented uncertainty. His response? Empowering his employees to innovate their way through the crisis.

Chesky's leadership style is rooted in deep trust and a belief in the creative potential of his team. During the pandemic, he encouraged Airbnb employees to reimagine their offerings, resulting in initiatives like online experiences and long-term rentals tailored to a world of remote work. Instead of imposing top-down directives, Chesky created an environment where his team could experiment, fail, and ultimately succeed.

One of Chesky's key principles is recognizing and amplifying the strengths of his employees. By celebrating successes and learning from setbacks, he reinforced a culture where people felt safe to take risks. His ability to empower his team not only enabled Airbnb to recover but also transformed the company into a more resilient and diversified business.

Under Chesky's leadership, Airbnb's post-pandemic rebound has been remarkable, with the company adapting to new travel trends and achieving one of the most successful public offerings in recent history. Chesky's commitment to empowerment ensured that his team didn't just survive a crisis—they thrived beyond it.

Reflections on Empowerment: A Shared Philosophy

The journeys of Melanie Perkins and Brian Chesky highlight a shared truth: empowering leadership isn't about relinquishing responsibility; it's about creating the conditions for others to succeed. Both leaders faced challenges that required adaptability and resilience, and in each case, their trust in their teams became the catalyst for transformative outcomes.

From Canva's culture of creativity to Airbnb's innovative pivot, these stories reinforce the central themes of this chapter: trust, autonomy, and recognition as the building blocks of empowerment. Their experiences show that when leaders empower their people, they don't just solve immediate problems—they unlock potential that drives long-term growth.

Reflecting on these examples, consider how you might apply their lessons to your own leadership. Are you creating an environment where your team feels trusted and valued? How might you balance guidance with autonomy to foster innovation and resilience?

Empowerment begins with small, intentional acts: granting autonomy in decision-making, recognizing contributions, or simply listening with empathy. As these leaders demonstrate, the impact of empowerment isn't just organizational—it's deeply personal, inspiring individuals to rise to their potential and achieve extraordinary results.

Empowering leadership is about building bridges between vision and action, possibility and performance. As we move forward in this chapter, explore how you can integrate these principles into your leadership approach, transforming challenges into opportunities and unlocking the full potential of your team. The next step in your journey is taking these lessons and turning them into actionable change—both for yourself and for those you lead.

Alternative Strategies for Empowering Teams

Empowerment doesn't come in a one-size-fits-all package. The modern workplace is as dynamic and diverse as the people within it, requiring leaders to adopt creative, tailored approaches to unleash their teams' potential. Beyond traditional methods of trust and autonomy, alternative strategies such as peer-to-peer mentorship programs, cross-functional collaboration, and technology-driven autonomy provide fresh pathways to foster empowerment. By weaving these into their leadership fabric, organizations can unlock new levels of innovation, engagement, and resilience.

Peer-to-Peer Mentorship: Shared Growth Through Collaboration

Traditional mentorship often follows a top-down structure, but peer-to-peer mentorship offers a powerful alternative. By creating a culture where employees at similar levels share knowledge and experiences, leaders enable collaborative growth and mutual support.

A Good example here is Ren Zhengfei, founder of Huawei, who implemented a peer mentorship model to break down silos and foster innovation. Faced with rapid global expansion, Ren realized that top-down directives wouldn't suffice. Instead, he encouraged cross-departmental peer learning, where engineers and marketing professionals regularly collaborated to solve customer challenges. This exchange of expertise not only accelerated problem-solving but also empowered employees to see their contributions in a broader context.

Peer mentorship reinforces the idea that everyone has something to teach and learn, creating a more egalitarian, empowered workforce. Leaders who facilitate these connections help their teams develop critical skills while strengthening relationships across the organization.

Cross-Functional Collaboration: Empowering Through Diversity

Empowerment thrives in environments where diversity of thought flourishes. Cross-functional collaboration brings together individuals from different areas of expertise to tackle complex challenges, fostering innovation and breaking down silos.

When Nandan Nilekani co-founded Infosys and later spearheaded India's Aadhaar project, he leaned heavily on cross-functional collaboration to achieve ambitious goals. In both cases, Nilekani brought together technologists, policymakers, and business strategists to create solutions that were not only innovative but also deeply practical. By empowering diverse teams to contribute equally, he cultivated a culture where ownership and accountability were shared across disciplines.

This approach highlights the power of diversity in driving performance. Leaders who embrace cross-functional collaboration equip their teams to tackle challenges from multiple angles, resulting in well-rounded, impactful solutions.

Technology-Driven Autonomy: Empowerment in the Digital Age

Technology offers unprecedented opportunities to enhance autonomy and empower teams. Tools such as AI-driven project management systems, real-time collaboration platforms, and data visualization dashboards provide employees with the resources to make informed decisions and act independently.

As the founder of ByteDance, Zhang Yiming understood that empowering employees in a tech-driven environment required more than just verbal encouragement. He introduced data-rich platforms that allowed his teams to track content performance and make real-time adjustments without waiting for executive input. This technology-driven autonomy not only sped up decision-making but also inspired a sense of ownership among employees.

By leveraging technology, leaders like Zhang demonstrate that empowerment in the digital age means equipping teams with the right tools and trusting them to deliver results. This approach fosters both agility and accountability, essential qualities for modern organizations.

These alternative strategies—peer-to-peer mentorship, cross-functional collaboration, and technology-driven autonomy—aren't merely tools for empowerment; they are enablers of organizational transformation. Each approach reinforces the core principles of trust, autonomy, and recognition in unique ways, creating pathways for growth that align with the needs of today's workforce.

For leaders, the challenge is to identify which strategies resonate most with their team's dynamics and organizational goals. Empowerment is not about implementing a single formula but about creating a culture where individuals feel inspired to contribute their best, supported by structures that enable success.

As you consider these strategies, ask yourself:

- How can I create opportunities for peer mentorship within my team?
- What steps can I take to foster cross-functional collaboration and break down silos?
- Are there technology tools I could introduce to enhance autonomy and decision-making?

Empowerment is an evolving journey, and these strategies offer new possibilities for enriching that path. By integrating diverse approaches, leaders can cultivate teams that are not just productive but unstoppable, ready to tackle the challenges and opportunities of the future. Let these possibilities inspire you to think expansively and act boldly, empowering your people—and yourself—for sustained performance and growth.

Unlocking the Power of Empowerment

Empowerment is not a leadership tactic—it is a philosophy, a way of creating environments where potential flourishes and extraordinary outcomes emerge. From the trust that nurtures confidence, to the autonomy that inspires innovation, and the recognition that fuels motivation, empowerment transforms individuals into a unified force capable of unstoppable performance.

In this chapter, we've explored how leaders like Melanie Perkins, Brian Chesky, Ren Zhengfei, and Nandan Nilekani have demonstrated the transformative power of empowering their teams. Their successes remind us that empowerment isn't about relinquishing control but about creating a foundation of trust, fostering collaboration, and equipping individuals with the tools and freedom they need to excel.

Through frameworks like TRUST and strategies that expand possibilities—from peer mentorship to leveraging technology—we've uncovered practical pathways to integrate empowerment into your leadership journey. The thread connecting each idea is clear: empowerment begins with the leader's intention and manifests in the culture they cultivate.

Turning Lessons Into Action

As you reflect on this chapter, take a moment to assess your own approach to empowerment. How do you create the conditions for your team to thrive? Are you balancing trust with accountability, freedom with alignment? Consider the following prompts to deepen your reflection and move toward actionable change:

Looking Inward

Think about a recent leadership decision. Did it empower your team to take ownership, or did it hold onto control? Reflect on the emotions and motivations that shaped your choice. What would you do differently if empowerment was your guiding principle?

Exploring Your Culture

How does your current organizational culture support or hinder empowerment? Are there systems or norms that inadvertently limit autonomy or recognition? What small shifts could you make to foster a more empowering environment?

Planning for the Future

What is one action you can take this week to empower someone on your team? It might be delegating a decision, recognizing an achievement, or initiating a conversation about their aspirations. How can this action ripple outward to influence the broader culture?

Empowerment as a Leadership Imperative

Empowerment is not just about enabling others—it's about unlocking your own potential as a leader. It requires courage to let go, trust to believe in others, and a commitment to fostering environments where people can bring their best selves to work. In doing so, you create a culture of resilience, innovation, and shared success—a culture that amplifies the capabilities of every individual and drives the organization forward.

As you close this chapter, consider this thought: Empowerment is not a single act but an ongoing commitment. It is the bridge between vision and execution, between potential and achievement. Let the lessons of this chapter guide you as you continue your leadership journey, building teams that are not just productive but truly unstoppable.

In the next chapter, we'll explore the art of building cultures that thrive—environments where empowerment, purpose, and collaboration come together to create lasting impact. But for now, take this moment to embrace empowerment as your foundation, and let it shape the way you lead from this day forward.

Chapter 11

Cultivating a Culture of Innovation and Impact

"Innovation is not just about new ideas; it's about creating value and making a difference."

Culture isn't just what happens when people come together; it's the invisible force that shapes how they think, work, and dream. It's in the way decisions are made, how risks are taken, and how failure is met—with curiosity or blame. For leaders of scale-up organizations, culture isn't just an abstract idea; it's the engine of innovation and impact.

I'll never forget a conversation I had with a founder, a dynamic leader who had grown her company from a tiny startup to a thriving business. She shared a moment that stopped her in her tracks. Her team had just launched a new product after months of hard work, and while it met expectations, it didn't set the market on fire as she had hoped. Instead of celebrating the effort, the team retreated into silence, reluctant to discuss what went wrong.

"I realized I had built a culture that feared failure," she admitted, "because I had modeled perfectionism, not learning." That moment sparked a shift—not just in her leadership but in the organization itself. She began fostering a culture that embraced curiosity, encouraged experimentation, and valued growth over flawlessness. The results were transformative: employees started taking risks, voicing bold ideas, and innovating in ways that propelled the company forward.

In the journey of *Unstoppable Growth*, we've explored the systems, strategies, and resilience that drive scale-up success. But culture—how it's built, nurtured, and aligned with purpose—might be the most powerful lever of all. A culture that thrives on innovation and impact is the ultimate competitive advantage. It's what allows organizations to adapt to change, inspire their people, and create meaningful value for the world.

Research confirms what many of us feel intuitively: culture matters. Studies from McKinsey show that companies with strong, adaptive cultures are six times more likely to innovate and grow. Psychological safety—a culture where people feel free to voice ideas and take risks—has been linked to higher team performance, as Google famously demonstrated in their Project Aristotle study.

But culture doesn't build itself. It takes intentionality, vulnerability, and a deep commitment to values. Leaders must be willing to ask hard questions: Are we creating space for diverse voices? Are we rewarding curiosity and learning, or only celebrating success? Are we connecting our work to a larger purpose that inspires people to bring their best?

This chapter is about shaping the culture your organization needs to thrive—not just in the market but in the hearts and minds of the people who drive it forward. You'll learn frameworks for building cultures that fuel innovation and create lasting impact. You'll hear stories of leaders who've transformed their organizations by rethinking how culture works.

Because here's the truth: Culture isn't what you say it is. It's what you nurture, reward, and protect. And when you get it right, it becomes the spark that ignites possibility, creating a ripple effect of innovation and impact that extends far beyond the walls of your organization. This is how leaders leave a legacy—not by holding power, but by shaping a culture that empowers others to dream bigger, risk braver, and do work that truly matters.

The Cultural Foundations of Innovation and Impact

Culture is the unseen force that propels organizations forward—or holds them back. It shapes behaviours, fosters collaboration, and provides the foundation for innovation and impact. Research from leading sources underscores that organizations with strong, intentional cultures consistently outperform their peers, particularly in environments that demand agility and creativity.

The Role of Psychological Safety: A Safe Harbor for Innovation

One of the most compelling findings on culture comes from Harvard Business School professor Amy Edmondson, whose research highlights the critical role of psychological safety in innovation. Psychological safety is the shared belief that individuals can take risks, voice ideas, and admit mistakes without fear of ridicule or punishment. In organizations where this safety exists, employees are more likely to experiment, collaborate, and solve complex problems.

For example, Google's Project Aristotle—a landmark study on team dynamics—found that psychological safety was the single most important factor in high-performing teams. Teams with this attribute didn't shy away from difficult conversations or unconventional ideas. Instead, they embraced them, resulting in more creative solutions and stronger outcomes.

The takeaway for leaders is clear: fostering an environment where people feel safe to contribute freely is a non-negotiable foundation for innovation. Without psychological safety, even the brightest ideas may wither before they can take root.

Inclusivity as a Driver of Creativity

A diverse workforce brings a richness of perspectives, experiences, and ideas that fuel creativity and innovation. Research from McKinsey underscores that organizations with greater diversity at leadership levels are 33% more likely to outperform their peers in profitability. This isn't merely a correlation; it's a reflection of how diverse teams approach problem-solving from multiple angles, challenging assumptions and broadening the scope of potential solutions.

One powerful example of inclusivity driving innovation is the story of Ren Zhengfei at Huawei. Zhengfei fostered a culture where engineers, marketers, and frontline employees were encouraged to collaborate and share insights, regardless of hierarchy or background. This inclusivity allowed Huawei to stay ahead of competitors by rapidly iterating products tailored to diverse global markets. Zhengfei's approach illustrates how inclusivity fuels innovation by combining varied perspectives into cohesive, transformative ideas.

Shared Purpose: Aligning for Impact

While innovation is often seen as a product of creativity and strategy, it thrives most when anchored in shared purpose. Organizations with a clear sense of purpose create alignment, inspire engagement, and amplify the impact of their efforts. A shared purpose serves as a north star, ensuring that innovation isn't just about novel ideas but about ideas that matter.

A study by Deloitte reveals that organizations driven by purpose see higher employee engagement, customer loyalty, and long-term growth. Leaders who articulate and embody a clear mission enable their teams to connect their work to a larger vision, fostering motivation and resilience.

Ratan Tata's leadership at Tata Group exemplifies this principle. Tata didn't just build businesses; he cultivated a sense of purpose that extended to improving lives and addressing societal challenges. From pioneering affordable vehicles to launching initiatives in healthcare and education, the Tata Group's innovations consistently aligned with a vision of creating a better world. This alignment galvanized employees and stakeholders alike, transforming purpose into a powerful engine for impact.

Culture: A Strategic Imperative

The interplay of psychological safety, inclusivity, and shared purpose creates the conditions for thriving organizational cultures. These factors aren't incidental; they are intentional choices made by leaders who understand that culture is both a strategic asset and a competitive advantage.

Research consistently demonstrates the tangible benefits of strong cultures. Organizations with thriving cultures report 72% greater employee engagement, 29% higher customer satisfaction, and 19% increased profitability compared to those with weaker cultures (*Gallup*). These findings underscore a simple truth: culture isn't just about how organizations operate—it's about how they succeed.

From Insights to Action

As leaders, the challenge isn't recognizing the importance of culture; it's embedding these principles into the fabric of your organization. The next section will introduce a practical framework to help leaders cultivate cultures that drive innovation and impact. By focusing on psychological safety, inclusivity, and shared purpose, you can create an environment where creativity thrives, collaboration flourishes, and success becomes unstoppable.

Take a moment to reflect: Does your culture encourage bold ideas, celebrate diverse perspectives, and align efforts toward a greater purpose? The answers to these questions aren't just a reflection of your organization—they are a reflection of your leadership. Let's explore how to shape a culture that empowers innovation and amplifies impact.

The IMPACT Model

Creating a culture that fosters innovation and drives meaningful impact requires intentional leadership and actionable strategies. The **IMPACT** framework—Inspire, Model, Promote, Adapt, Connect, and Trust—offers a practical guide for leaders to cultivate environments where creativity, collaboration, and purpose thrive. Each element is designed to align with the principles of psychological safety, inclusivity, and shared purpose, providing a cohesive roadmap for shaping organizational culture.

Inspire: Setting a Vision That Sparks Action

Innovation begins with inspiration. Leaders who articulate a compelling vision create alignment and energize teams to pursue ambitious goals. Inspiration isn't just about words—it's about showing people what's possible and giving them a reason to believe in the journey ahead.

Ratan Tata inspired his team with a bold vision when he launched the Tata Nano, a car designed to be affordable for millions of Indian families. This vision wasn't just about market disruption; it was about addressing a social need. Tata's ability to connect the product's purpose to a larger mission galvanized employees across functions to innovate, resulting in a product that became a global symbol of ingenuity.

Ask yourself: Does your vision ignite excitement and purpose in your team? To inspire effectively, communicate not just what you want to achieve but why it matters.

Model: Leading by Example

Culture is shaped by actions more than words. Leaders who embody the values they wish to instill in their teams set a powerful precedent, demonstrating that innovation and impact aren't just goals—they are ways of working.

Ren Zhengfei of Huawei modeled inclusivity and collaboration by actively participating in cross-functional meetings and valuing input from employees at all levels. His willingness to listen and adapt created a ripple effect, encouraging others to embrace collaboration as a cultural norm.

Reflect on how your actions align with your stated values. Are you modelling the behaviours—such as openness, curiosity, and respect—that you want to see in your team?

Promote: Encouraging Bold Ideas and Risk-Taking

Innovation thrives in environments where people feel encouraged to take risks and propose bold ideas. Leaders who actively promote creativity—by celebrating experimentation and viewing failures as learning opportunities—create cultures that drive continuous improvement.

Zhang Yiming, the founder of ByteDance, created a culture of experimentation by encouraging teams to prototype and test ideas rapidly. This iterative approach led to the development of TikTok, a product that redefined social media by prioritizing user engagement and creativity.

Foster a culture of curiosity by creating platforms for employees to share ideas, no matter how unconventional. Reward experimentation, even when it doesn't yield immediate results.

Adapt: Embracing Change with Agility

Adaptability is the heartbeat of innovation. Leaders who encourage teams to embrace change and iterate quickly create resilience in the face of uncertainty and disruption.

When Airbnb faced a sudden drop in bookings during the COVID-19 pandemic, CEO Brian Chesky empowered his team to pivot rapidly. By embracing adaptability, Airbnb introduced new offerings like online experiences and long-term stays, positioning the company for a strong rebound.

Action

Encourage adaptability by creating mechanisms for teams to analyze challenges, propose adjustments, and execute changes with confidence. Show that change isn't a threat—it's an opportunity.

Connect: Building Relationships and Purpose

Strong cultures are built on connections—between individuals, teams, and the organization's mission. Leaders who create opportunities for collaboration and alignment foster a sense of belonging and shared purpose.

Daniel Ek, the founder of Spotify, cultivated connection within his organization by emphasizing cross-functional collaboration. By aligning product developers, marketers, and data analysts around a common goal—to revolutionize music streaming—Ek ensured that every team's efforts contributed to the broader vision.

Action

Facilitate regular opportunities for cross-functional engagement, from brainstorming sessions to team-building activities. Highlight how each person's role contributes to the organization's larger goals.

Trust: Building a Foundation of Confidence and Autonomy

Trust is the cornerstone of an innovative and impactful culture. Leaders who empower their teams to make decisions and take ownership create environments where creativity flourishes and accountability deepens.

A great example of this is Li Ka-shing, one of Hong Kong's most successful entrepreneurs, exemplified trust by giving his teams the autonomy to make critical decisions while providing guidance when needed. His trust in their capabilities fostered a culture of ownership, enabling the rapid expansion of his diverse business empire.

Delegate decision-making authority where appropriate, and show confidence in your team's abilities. Provide support, but avoid micromanaging.

IMPACT in Action: A Roadmap for Leaders

The **IMPACT** framework isn't just a set of principles—it's a call to action for leaders committed to cultivating innovative and impactful cultures. Each element builds on the others, creating a cohesive approach to shaping environments where individuals and teams thrive.

As you reflect on your leadership, consider this: Are you inspiring with a clear vision, modelling the values you want to see, and promoting bold ideas? Are you embracing adaptability, fostering connections, and building trust? The IMPACT framework offers a guide, but it's up to you to bring it to life.

Empowering cultures aren't built overnight—they are nurtured through daily choices and consistent actions. By committing to this journey, you create not just a successful organization but one that makes a lasting difference in the lives of its people and the world it serves.

Leaders Who Embody Innovation and Impact

Building a culture of innovation and impact requires intentionality, resilience, and a deep understanding of what drives people to collaborate and excel. Leaders like Ratan Tata and Daniel Ek have demonstrated how fostering such cultures can overcome challenges, inspire teams, and create enduring value. Their journeys illuminate the principles of this chapter and provide practical lessons for leaders striving to shape their organizations with purpose and creativity.

Ratan Tata: Driving Innovation with Purpose

When Ratan Tata took the helm of the Tata Group, he inherited an organization steeped in tradition but constrained by outdated practices. Tata understood that to remain relevant and impactful in a rapidly changing world, the company needed to embrace innovation without losing sight of its core values.

One of his boldest initiatives was the creation of the Tata Nano, an affordable car designed to make vehicle ownership accessible to millions of Indian families. This ambitious project was more than an engineering feat; it was a cultural milestone. Tata empowered his teams to think beyond conventional constraints, fostering cross-disciplinary collaboration between engineers, designers, and marketers. His leadership created an environment where bold ideas were not just welcomed but expected.

The challenges were immense—technical hurdles, supply chain complexities, and market skepticism. Yet, Tata's unwavering commitment to purpose-driven innovation inspired his teams to persevere. The Nano became a symbol of ingenuity and impact, demonstrating how shared purpose and inclusivity can drive both innovation and societal progress.

Daniel Ek: Redefining Music with a Culture of Collaboration

Daniel Ek, the founder of Spotify, faced a different challenge: disrupting an entrenched industry while fostering a culture that prioritized creativity and user-centricity. From the outset, Ek emphasized collaboration as a cornerstone of Spotify's culture. He understood that innovation in a digital age required seamless integration of diverse expertise—from software engineers to music industry veterans.

Ek's strategy revolved around aligning teams around a shared vision: making music accessible to everyone, everywhere. By fostering open communication and creating cross-functional teams, Ek enabled Spotify to respond quickly to market trends and user feedback. His commitment to transparency ensured that every employee understood how their contributions supported the company's mission.

Spotify's success wasn't just about the technology; it was about the culture that powered it. Ek's leadership turned Spotify into a global leader, with innovations like curated playlists and algorithm-driven recommendations revolutionizing how people discover music.

Reflections on Leadership and Culture

The journeys of Ratan Tata and Daniel Ek illustrate the transformative power of culture in driving innovation and impact. Tata's story highlights the role of purpose in uniting teams and overcoming challenges, while Ek's approach underscores the importance of collaboration and adaptability in fast-moving industries.

Both leaders recognized that culture isn't an afterthought—it's the foundation upon which organizations build their success. They fostered environments where people felt inspired to contribute their best, empowered to take risks, and connected to a shared vision.

Lessons for Leaders

As you reflect on these examples, consider the following:

- Are you creating a culture where purpose guides innovation? Purpose-driven cultures inspire teams to tackle challenges with creativity and determination, as seen in Tata's leadership.

- How are you fostering collaboration across your organization? Collaboration not only accelerates problem-solving but also deepens engagement, as Ek's Spotify demonstrates.

- What intentional actions are you taking to shape your culture? Culture doesn't evolve by accident. It requires daily choices, consistent behaviours, and clear communication.

The stories of Tata and Ek show that building a culture of innovation and impact isn't just about strategy—it's about leadership that empowers, inspires, and unites. By embracing these lessons, you can transform your organization into a place where bold ideas thrive and meaningful change is possible. Let their journeys be your guide as you cultivate your own path to innovation and impact.

The Balance Between Creative Freedom and Structure

Leadership often feels like walking a tightrope, particularly when it comes to fostering innovation and impact. On one side lies creative freedom, the spark that fuels bold ideas and breakthrough solutions. On the other is structure, the framework that ensures these ideas can be executed and scaled. The challenge is not choosing one over the other but finding the balance that allows both to thrive.

The Dilemma in Action

Imagine two leaders at the helm of growing organizations. One, Priya, believes that creativity flourishes in an unstructured environment. Her approach is hands-off—no rigid processes, minimal oversight, and complete autonomy for her teams. The other, Alex, values control and precision. He introduces strict guidelines, detailed workflows, and frequent check-ins to ensure consistency and efficiency.

Initially, Priya's team bursts with energy. Ideas flow freely, and innovation seems limitless. But over time, cracks begin to appear. Without clear processes, projects stall. Deadlines are missed, and frustration grows as teams struggle to translate ideas into actionable outcomes. The creative spark remains, but the lack of structure dilutes its impact.

Meanwhile, Alex's team operates like a well-oiled machine. Goals are met with precision, and efficiency becomes the hallmark of their work. Yet, over time, a different problem arises. The rigid structure stifles creativity, and employees hesitate to share unconventional ideas, fearing they won't fit within the established framework. Innovation wanes, and the team becomes reactive rather than proactive.

Both leaders face consequences, albeit for different reasons. Priya's lack of structure undermines her team's ability to deliver results, while Alex's overemphasis on control suffocates the very creativity he seeks to harness. The lesson? Neither extreme is sustainable.

A Balanced Approach

Striking the right balance between creative freedom and structure requires intentionality and adaptability. Leaders must create an environment where innovation can flourish within boundaries that guide rather than constrain.

Consider the example of Ingvar Kamprad, founder of IKEA. Kamprad empowered his teams to think outside the box, encouraging unconventional solutions and bold designs. At the same time, he introduced systems and processes—such as IKEA's flat-pack furniture model—that allowed these innovations to scale efficiently. By combining freedom with structure, Kamprad built a culture that not only inspired creativity but also delivered consistent, high-quality results.

Practical Insights for Leaders

1. Define Clear Goals but Allow Flexibility in Execution
   Set the destination, but let your teams determine the path. Providing clarity on outcomes while giving autonomy in how they're achieved fosters both accountability and creativity.

2. Create Safe Spaces for Experimentation
   Encourage teams to test new ideas without fear of failure. Establishing a culture where mistakes are seen as learning opportunities unlocks innovative thinking.

3. Introduce Adaptive Structures
   Instead of rigid frameworks, opt for adaptable systems that can evolve as projects and teams grow. This approach ensures processes support, rather than stifle, creativity.

Reflective Questions for Action

As a leader, where do you fall on the spectrum between creative freedom and structure? Do your teams feel empowered to innovate, or are they bogged down by processes? Conversely, are they so unstructured that they struggle to deliver results?

- How do you encourage creative thinking while ensuring accountability?

- Are there areas where more structure could improve efficiency without dampening innovation?

- What steps can you take to create an environment where both freedom and structure coexist?

The Balancing Act of Leadership

Balancing creative freedom and structure is an ongoing journey, not a fixed destination. It requires self-awareness, a willingness to adapt, and an understanding of what your organization needs at different stages of growth. The most effective leaders are those who can navigate this tension, fostering cultures where innovation and execution are not at odds but in harmony.

As you reflect on this dilemma, remember that balance doesn't mean compromise—it means integration. By thoughtfully combining creative freedom with purposeful structure, you can create a culture where bold ideas come to life and lasting impact is achieved. Let this balance be the foundation of your leadership, guiding your teams toward innovation, resilience, and success.

Unlocking New Pathways for Innovation and Impact

Creating a culture that thrives on innovation and impact is not confined to traditional strategies. While principles like psychological safety and shared purpose form the foundation, leaders who embrace alternative approaches can amplify these efforts, unlocking untapped potential within their teams and organizations. By leveraging diverse perspectives, experimenting with learning practices, and establishing innovation hubs, leaders can push the boundaries of what their cultures can achieve.

The Power of Inclusion

Innovation flourishes in environments where diverse voices are heard. Teams with varied backgrounds, experiences, and viewpoints approach problems from multiple angles, uncovering solutions that might otherwise remain hidden. But diversity alone is not enough; inclusion is the key that unlocks its potential.

Imagine an organization tackling a product launch in an unfamiliar market. Without input from local employees or diverse perspectives, cultural missteps can derail even the best-laid plans. Leaders like Ratan Tata have shown the value of inclusion in driving innovation. Tata's commitment to fostering a culture where all voices mattered enabled his organization to navigate diverse global markets successfully.

Leaders can formalize opportunities for diverse input through advisory boards, employee resource groups, or even cross-functional brainstorming sessions. When people feel valued and heard, they contribute their best ideas, enriching the culture with creativity and innovation.

Experimental Learning: Creating a Culture of Curiosity

Organizations often focus on outcomes, but what if the process of learning itself became a priority? Experimental learning—where teams are encouraged to test, iterate, and adapt—creates a culture of curiosity and continuous improvement. By shifting the focus from perfection to progress, leaders empower their teams to embrace exploration and take calculated risks.

The Case of Koos Bekker at Naspers

Koos Bekker, the South African media tycoon, championed an experimental approach that propelled Naspers into global success. By allocating resources to emerging technologies and nurturing a mindset of "fail fast, learn faster," Bekker created an environment where teams were unafraid to test new ideas. This culture of experimentation led to breakthrough investments, including early stakes in tech giants like Tencent.

How Leaders Can Apply This: Introduce rapid prototyping or pilot programs that allow teams to experiment with new ideas without the pressure of immediate success. Celebrate learnings from failures as much as successes, framing both as integral to growth.

Innovation Hubs: Spaces That Inspire Creation

Physical and virtual innovation hubs provide dedicated spaces for creativity to flourish. These hubs act as catalysts for cross-pollination of ideas, bringing together diverse teams to tackle challenges and develop solutions. More than just spaces, they symbolize an organizational commitment to innovation.

A Lesson from Zhang Yiming of ByteDance

Zhang Yiming's creation of collaborative innovation hubs within ByteDance exemplifies how these spaces drive progress. Teams from engineering, design, and content creation were brought together in dynamic workspaces, fostering a culture of shared problem-solving. The result? Products like TikTok that revolutionized user engagement worldwide.

Building Your Own Hub

Innovation hubs don't require vast resources; they require intention. Leaders can designate physical spaces for brainstorming or create virtual hubs using collaborative tools like Slack or Microsoft Teams. What matters most is fostering an environment where ideas can collide and evolve.

A Culture of Possibilities

These strategies—leveraging diverse perspectives, embracing experimental learning, and establishing innovation hubs—offer leaders new ways to enhance their organizational culture. Each approach ties back to the chapter's central message: intentional leadership shapes the contours of culture, enabling innovation and impact to thrive.

As you consider these possibilities, reflect on what your organization needs to grow and evolve. Are you creating opportunities for diverse voices to be heard? Are you encouraging curiosity and experimentation? Have you dedicated spaces—physical or virtual—where ideas can take flight?

Innovation isn't a one-time event; it's a continuous process fueled by a culture that celebrates exploration, embraces risk, and values inclusivity. By integrating these strategies, you can cultivate a culture that not only adapts to change but drives it, making your organization a beacon of creativity and purpose. Let these possibilities inspire you to think expansively and act boldly, shaping a culture where innovation and impact become inseparable.

Shaping a Culture of Innovation and Impact

Culture is not a backdrop to organizational success—it is the foundation upon which innovation and impact are built. Like the river shaping the landscape in our opening metaphor, culture guides the flow of creativity, collaboration, and purpose, determining whether an organization can rise to meet the demands of growth and transformation.

In this chapter, we explored the critical elements that make cultures thrive. We examined the research-backed principles of psychological safety, inclusivity, and shared purpose, understanding how these factors drive innovation and create meaningful impact. Through the IMPACT framework, we uncovered actionable steps to inspire and model the values that shape culture. The journeys of leaders like Ratan

Tata and Daniel Ek illuminated the power of intentional leadership in fostering environments where teams feel empowered to think boldly and act decisively.

Reflecting on Culture as a Strategic Lever

Culture doesn't evolve by chance—it is cultivated through deliberate action, consistent values, and an unwavering commitment to creating spaces where people feel connected to a greater purpose. As a leader, your role is to be both the architect and steward of your organization's culture, continuously shaping and refining it to support innovation and impact.

Consider these reflective takeaways:

- Are you inspiring your teams with a vision that connects their work to a greater purpose?
- Have you created an environment where diverse perspectives are welcomed and celebrated?
- Do your actions align with the cultural values you aim to instill in your organization?

Reflect and Refocus: Questions for Leadership Growth

Take a moment to reflect on your leadership and its influence on your organization's culture:

- What does your culture say about your leadership?

  Think about the behaviours, values, and norms that define your organization. Do they align with the culture you envision?

- How do you create space for innovation?

Are there processes or practices that enable teams to experiment, take risks, and collaborate? If not, what changes can you make?

- What legacy are you building?

  Culture is the lasting imprint of leadership. What do you want your team to remember and carry forward long after you've moved on?

Closing with Intentional Leadership

As this chapter draws to a close, let it serve as a call to action: prioritize culture as a strategic lever for growth. The most innovative and impactful organizations are not accidental successes—they are shaped by leaders who understand that culture is both a journey and a destination.

When you lead with intention, you create a culture that inspires, empowers, and endures. The work of shaping culture is never finished, but the rewards—resilient teams, groundbreaking innovations, and meaningful impact—are worth every step.

In the next chapter, we'll explore how leaders can build lasting legacies by embedding purpose into the DNA of their organizations. But for now, reflect on the culture you are cultivating today and imagine the possibilities it holds for tomorrow. Let your leadership be the river that shapes the landscape, creating paths for innovation and impact that flow far beyond what you can see.

Chapter 12

Strategic Funding for Unstoppable Growth

"Funding isn't just about capital; it's about aligning resources with the vision that drives your company forward."

Money is never just about money. It's about possibility, courage, and the story we tell ourselves about what's next. For leaders navigating the scale-up journey, funding isn't just a transaction—it's a reflection of their vision, values, and willingness to play big. Yet, so often, the funding process feels like a battle between two fears: the fear of asking for help and the fear of losing control.

I once spoke with a CEO who shared how terrified she felt walking into her first pitch meeting. Her business was growing faster than she could keep up with, and she knew she needed investment to scale. But behind the confidence of her pitch deck, she was wrestling with questions that many leaders face: *Will they believe in my vision? Am I ready to hand over part of what I've built? What if I fail?*

As she sat across from a room of seasoned investors, she decided to take a risk. Instead of masking her vulnerability, she leaned into it. She didn't just talk about her company's numbers; she spoke about her purpose, the lives her product was changing, and her commitment to scaling with integrity. That honesty sparked something unexpected. Not only did she secure funding, but she also built partnerships with investors who shared her values and became champions for her mission.

This chapter is about reshaping how we think about funding. It's not just about raising capital; it's about building strategic relationships that fuel unstoppable growth. It's about understanding that every dollar is a vote of confidence in your vision, and every investor is a potential partner in impact.

In *Unstoppable Growth*, we've explored how leaders cultivate resilience, purpose, and momentum. Funding is another critical piece of the puzzle—a bridge between the resources you have and the future you're building. But it's also a test of your clarity, conviction, and courage.

Research shows that the most successful organizations align their funding strategies with their broader goals and values. A study from Bain & Company found that businesses with a clear strategic narrative attract higher-quality investment. Meanwhile, McKinsey highlights that strong investor relationships often extend beyond capital, providing access to networks, expertise, and opportunities that accelerate growth.

But this isn't just about numbers or strategies—it's about the kind of leader you choose to be in the process. Do you approach funding as a transaction or a partnership? Do you prioritize speed over alignment, or are you willing to take the time to find investors who believe in your mission as much as you do?

In this chapter, we'll explore the strategies and frameworks that help leaders secure funding with confidence and purpose. We'll hear stories of business leaders who navigated the funding journey with courage and clarity, and we'll uncover the lessons they learned along the way.

Because funding isn't just fuel for growth; it's a mirror reflecting what you stand for and where you're going. And when you approach it with intention, it becomes more than a means to an end—it becomes a catalyst for building something truly unstoppable.

The Pillars of Strategic Funding

Securing funding for a scale-up organization is as much an art as it is a science. While financial capital is essential for growth, the approach to raising and managing it determines whether that capital becomes an enabler of success or a potential obstacle. Research from McKinsey, Bain & Company, and CB Insights highlights several key factors that underpin effective funding strategies: timing, alignment with strategic goals, and the cultivation of strong investor relationships.

Timing: The Critical Factor in Funding Decisions

Timing is often the difference between a transformative funding round and a missed opportunity. McKinsey's analysis of growth-stage businesses underscores that organizations with a well-timed funding strategy—one that anticipates market shifts and operational needs—achieve significantly higher valuations than those that wait too long or move prematurely.

Consider Nandan Nilekani, the co-founder of Infosys, who exemplified the importance of timing during the company's scale-up phase. Rather than rushing to secure external capital, Nilekani prioritized building a strong operational foundation. When Infosys eventually sought funding, it was at a stage where the company could negotiate from a position of strength, securing resources that aligned with its growth trajectory. This strategic patience enabled Infosys to scale efficiently without compromising its vision.

Leaders must assess their organization's readiness and the market environment before pursuing funding. Premature funding can dilute equity unnecessarily, while delays can hinder the ability to capitalize on growth opportunities.

Alignment with Strategic Goals

Funding isn't just about raising capital—it's about aligning financial resources with an organization's mission, values, and long-term objectives. Bain & Company's research reveals that businesses with funding strategies tightly linked to their strategic goals are 34% more likely to achieve sustainable growth. Misaligned funding, on the other hand, often leads to operational inefficiencies, conflicts with investors, and challenges in maintaining organizational focus.

An illustrative case is that of Li Ka-shing, the Hong Kong business magnate whose strategic funding decisions were always guided by his broader vision. In his expansion into global markets, Ka-shing sought out investors who not only provided capital but also brought industry expertise and market access. By aligning funding with strategic goals, he ensured that financial partnerships served as accelerators rather than distractions, driving both innovation and international growth.

Leaders must approach funding with a clear understanding of how each dollar supports their mission. This clarity not only ensures that resources are deployed effectively but also signals to investors a strong alignment between leadership vision and operational execution.

The Power of Investor Relationships

At the heart of effective funding lies the ability to cultivate and sustain meaningful relationships with investors. CB Insights notes that 42% of scale-ups cite investor relations as a critical factor in their growth journey. Investors who act as strategic partners, offering mentorship, connections, and expertise, are often the most valuable allies.

Masayoshi Son's Vision Fund demonstrates this principle in action. Through carefully curated partnerships with investors aligned with his bold vision for the future, Son created a network of stakeholders who were invested not just in financial returns but in the shared mission of driving technological innovation. These relationships allowed SoftBank to secure unprecedented funding levels while maintaining alignment with its strategic priorities.

Building investor relationships goes beyond financial transactions—it requires trust, transparency, and a shared sense of purpose. Leaders who invest in these relationships create a foundation for long-term collaboration and mutual success.

From Insights to Action

Timing, alignment, and relationships form the trifecta of effective funding strategies. They are not separate considerations but interconnected elements that together define the success of a funding journey. Leaders who excel in navigating these factors create opportunities for their organizations to grow not just faster but smarter.

As we move into the next section, we will explore a practical framework designed to guide leaders through the complexities of funding. This framework will offer actionable steps to ensure that funding decisions align with organizational goals, foster strategic partnerships, and propel scale-ups toward unstoppable growth.

Take a moment to reflect: How does your current funding approach align with your organization's vision and values? Are you fostering relationships with investors who share your mission? And most importantly, are you pursuing funding at the right time and for the right reasons? The answers to these questions will define your path forward. Let's explore how to navigate it with clarity and purpose.

Frameworks for Funding Success: The GROWTH Model

Strategic funding is not just about securing capital; it's about aligning resources with a vision for sustainable and transformative growth. The GROWTH framework—Goals, Relationships, Options, Weighing Risks, Timing, Harmonization—provides a roadmap for leaders to navigate the complexities of funding. This model integrates the insights explored earlier, offering actionable steps to ensure that funding decisions propel organizations toward their long-term objectives.

1. Goals: Defining the Destination

Every funding journey begins with clarity of purpose. Goals act as the North Star, guiding leaders as they determine how much capital is needed, what it will be used for, and how it supports the organization's broader mission. Without clear goals, funding risks becoming reactive rather than strategic.

Li Ka-shing exemplified goal-oriented funding during Hutchison Whampoa's expansion into global telecommunications. His funding efforts weren't just about raising money—they were meticulously aligned with his vision of becoming a leader in the industry. By defining clear objectives, Ka-shing attracted investors who shared his vision and could provide not just capital but strategic value.

Leaders should start by asking:

- What specific goals will this funding achieve?
- How do these goals align with the organization's mission and long-term vision?

2. Relationships: Cultivating Strategic Partnerships

Funding is not just about financial transactions—it's about building relationships with investors who align with your values and goals. The right investors bring more than money; they offer expertise, networks, and guidance that amplify growth.

Masayoshi Son's Vision Fund demonstrated the power of cultivating investor relationships. Son didn't simply seek capital—he formed partnerships with stakeholders who shared his belief in transformative technology. These relationships provided SoftBank with the strategic resources needed to scale its portfolio companies globally.

Nurture investor relationships by prioritizing transparency and shared purpose. Consider investors as long-term collaborators who contribute to your organization's success beyond financial support.

3. Options: Exploring Funding Pathways

Funding doesn't come in a one-size-fits-all package. Leaders must explore their options—equity financing, debt funding, grants, or strategic partnerships—to determine the best fit for their organization's needs and stage of growth.

Ratan Tata's Tata Group utilized a mix of funding options, including internal reserves, public offerings, and strategic alliances, to finance its global expansion. By diversifying funding sources, Tata ensured stability while pursuing ambitious growth initiatives.

Evaluate all available funding pathways:

- Does the option align with your risk tolerance and growth stage?
- What are the trade-offs in terms of control, repayment obligations, and strategic alignment?

4. Weighing Risks: Balancing Opportunity with Caution

Every funding decision carries risks, from dilution of control to financial overextension. Leaders must weigh these risks against the opportunities that funding provides, ensuring that short-term gains don't compromise long-term sustainability.

Daniel Ek at Spotify faced a critical decision when considering public investment. By carefully weighing the risks of public scrutiny against the opportunity to accelerate global expansion, Ek timed Spotify's IPO to maximize both impact and organizational stability.

Assess the potential risks of each funding option:

- What impact will this funding have on organizational control?
- Are the risks proportionate to the anticipated benefits?

5. Timing: Knowing When to Act

As discussed earlier, timing can make or break a funding strategy. Leaders who raise capital too early risk unnecessary dilution, while those who wait too long may miss critical opportunities.

Arianna Huffington prioritized timing when launching Thrive Global, ensuring the company's foundation was solid before seeking funding. This strategic patience allowed her to attract investors who aligned with her mission of well-being and productivity.

Leaders should evaluate both market conditions and internal readiness:

- Is your organization operationally prepared to scale with new funding?
- Are external conditions favourable for raising capital?

6. Harmonization: Aligning Funding with Organizational Vision

The final step in the GROWTH framework is harmonization—ensuring that funding decisions align with the organization's mission, values, and strategic direction. Misaligned funding can create friction, while harmonious funding accelerates progress.

Naspers' Koos Bekker exemplified harmonization by aligning funding with strategic investments in emerging technologies. His focus on mission-driven capital ensured that every funding decision propelled Naspers closer to its goal of becoming a global technology leader.

Before finalizing funding decisions, leaders should ask:

- Does this funding align with our strategic priorities?
- Will it help us achieve our mission without compromising our values?

Bringing GROWTH to Life

The **GROWTH** framework isn't just a checklist—it's a mindset. It encourages leaders to approach funding as a strategic enabler rather than a transactional necessity. By defining clear goals, cultivating relationships, exploring options, weighing risks, acting with timing, and ensuring harmonization, leaders can secure funding that drives not only growth but also impact.

Take a moment to reflect:

- Are your funding goals aligned with your organization's mission?
- Do your investor relationships reflect shared purpose and long-term collaboration?
- Are you balancing risk, timing, and opportunity in your funding decisions?

Funding is more than a financial milestone; it's a strategic lever for unstoppable growth. With the **GROWTH** framework as your guide, you can navigate the complexities of funding with clarity and confidence, ensuring that every dollar invested propels your organization toward a brighter future.

Funding as a Catalyst for Transformative Growth

Securing and deploying funding effectively is an art that many leaders strive to master. It requires not just financial acumen but a deep understanding of strategic vision, timing, and relationship-building. Two leaders who have exemplified these principles are Masayoshi Son of SoftBank and Jack Dorsey, co-founder of Square and Twitter. Their journeys reveal how strategic funding can fuel unprecedented growth while navigating complex challenges.

Masayoshi Son: Betting Big on Vision

Masayoshi Son's approach to funding has become legendary, marked by his boldness and willingness to take calculated risks. Early in his career, Son demonstrated an uncanny ability to align funding with a larger vision. A defining moment came in the late 1990s when he invested $20 million in Alibaba, a then-fledgling e-commerce startup. Despite scepticism from others, Son's decision wasn't based purely on financial projections—it was rooted in his belief in Alibaba's potential to transform global commerce.

Son's success didn't come without challenges. As he scaled SoftBank, he faced criticism for his high-stakes investments and willingness to bet on unproven technologies. His Vision Fund, launched in 2017, raised over $100 billion and focused on disruptive innovation. By partnering with investors who shared his bold aspirations, Son positioned SoftBank as a catalyst for technological breakthroughs across industries.

Takeaway: Son's story illustrates the importance of aligning funding with visionary goals and cultivating relationships with investors who share a commitment to long-term impact. His approach emphasizes that funding is not just about capital—it's about creating partnerships that amplify innovation.

Jack Dorsey: Scaling Through Strategic Partnerships

Jack Dorsey's journey with Square offers another compelling example of leveraging funding for growth. Launched in 2009, Square began as a solution for small businesses to accept credit card payments. Dorsey recognized the need for funding early on to scale Square's reach and impact, but his strategy wasn't just about raising capital—it was about finding partners who believed in Square's mission to empower small businesses.

Dorsey's challenge was balancing rapid growth with maintaining Square's core values. As the company scaled, Dorsey secured funding from investors who brought not just financial resources but also strategic insights. By carefully timing funding rounds, Square expanded its product offerings, from point-of-sale systems to financial services like Cash App. The result? A company that not only disrupted the payments industry but also became a lifeline for small businesses during economic uncertainty.

Takeaway: Dorsey's journey underscores the importance of aligning funding with purpose. His ability to secure capital that supported both innovation and mission-driven growth highlights the value of strategic partnerships in achieving sustainable success.

Reflections on Funding for Growth

Both Son and Dorsey demonstrate that funding is far more than a transaction—it's a strategic lever that shapes the trajectory of an organization. Their stories reveal several key lessons for leaders:

1. Alignment Is Non-Negotiable: Both leaders secured funding that aligned with their organization's mission and vision, ensuring that capital served as a catalyst rather than a constraint.

2. Timing Is Everything: Whether through Son's bold investments or Dorsey's careful pacing, timing played a crucial role in maximizing the impact of funding decisions.

3. **Relationships Are the Foundation:** Strategic partnerships with aligned investors not only provided financial resources but also brought expertise and networks that accelerated growth.

As you reflect on these examples, consider how your approach to funding aligns with your leadership vision. Are you cultivating relationships with investors who share your purpose? Are your funding strategies designed to support both immediate goals and long-term aspirations?

Funding, when approached strategically, can unlock transformative growth. By learning from the journeys of leaders like Masayoshi Son and Jack Dorsey, you can navigate the complexities of funding with confidence, ensuring that every decision strengthens the foundation of your organization's success. Let these stories inspire you to think boldly and act with intention, turning funding into a cornerstone of unstoppable growth.

The Dilemma of Growth vs. Sustainability

In the dynamic journey of scaling a business, leaders often face a pivotal question: Should we prioritize rapid growth to capture market share, or focus on sustainable scaling to ensure long-term stability? This funding dilemma is not just a financial decision—it's a test of leadership clarity, strategy, and foresight. The consequences of each approach ripple across the organization, influencing everything from team morale to market positioning.

The Tale of Two Leaders: Contrasting Paths

Imagine two founders, each leading a promising scale-up in the renewable energy sector. Both companies are poised to expand, but their funding strategies reveal starkly different approaches to navigating growth.

Leader A: The Sprint Toward Market Dominance

Leader A secures a substantial round of venture capital funding, with the clear mandate to prioritize rapid growth. The strategy is aggressive: scaling operations, launching products quickly, and capturing market share ahead of competitors. For a time, the results are exhilarating—revenue spikes, the company dominates headlines, and investors are thrilled with the trajectory.

But cracks begin to show. The accelerated pace strains the organization's infrastructure. Processes are rushed, product quality suffers, and employee burnout becomes rampant. By focusing solely on speed, Leader A sacrifices sustainability, leaving the company vulnerable to market shifts and operational challenges.

Leader B: The Steady Climb

Leader B takes a different path, raising smaller, strategic funding rounds aligned with measured milestones. This approach emphasizes building robust processes, fostering a resilient company culture, and ensuring each step of growth is manageable. The scaling is slower, but the foundation is solid. When market challenges arise, Leader B's organization adapts effectively, supported by its strong infrastructure and motivated team.

While Leader B's company may initially lag behind its competitors, its stability and adaptability position it for sustained success. The slower, intentional pace proves to be a competitive advantage in the long run.

The Leadership Lens: Weighing Trade-offs

Both leaders made funding decisions based on their vision for growth, but their choices illustrate the trade-offs inherent in this dilemma. Rapid growth offers the allure of immediate results, but it can lead to instability if the organization is unprepared to handle the pressure. Sustainable scaling, while requiring patience, provides a stronger foundation for long-term success—but it risks losing out to faster-moving competitors.

As a leader, the challenge lies in finding the right balance. The decision isn't necessarily about choosing one path over the other—it's about aligning the pace of growth with your organization's capacity and vision.

Reflecting on Your Own Funding Decisions

To navigate this dilemma, leaders must cultivate a deep understanding of their organization's strengths, vulnerabilities, and aspirations. Reflect on these questions:

- What does your organization need most right now?

    Is your immediate priority market capture, or do you need to strengthen your foundation before accelerating growth?

- What is your risk tolerance as a leader?

    Are you comfortable with the volatility that often accompanies rapid scaling, or do you prefer a steadier, more measured approach?

- How will your funding decisions impact your team?

    Consider the human element: Will your strategy energize your employees, or risk overextending them?

- Does your funding approach align with your long-term vision?

    Ensure that your short-term goals support, rather than undermine, the organization's future trajectory.

Embracing the Journey

The tension between rapid growth and sustainable scaling is a natural part of the leadership journey. There is no one-size-fits-all answer—only the path that aligns best with your organization's mission, values, and capabilities. By embracing this dilemma as an opportunity for reflection and intentional decision-making, you can ensure that your funding choices drive not just growth, but lasting impact.

In the words of one experienced entrepreneur, "Scaling is like climbing a mountain. You need the right pace, the right gear, and the right team to reach the summit." As you navigate your funding journey, remember that the choices you make today will shape the landscape of your organization's future. Let your decisions reflect the leader you aspire to be, balancing ambition with resilience, and growth with purpose.

Exploring Alternative Funding Strategies

Funding a scale-up organization requires more than traditional capital-raising methods; it demands creativity, adaptability, and alignment with an organization's core values. While equity funding and venture capital often dominate discussions, alternative strategies such as strategic partnerships, non-dilutive funding options, and crowdfunding offer unique opportunities to fuel growth without compromising mission or control. These approaches not only diversify funding sources but also allow organizations to align financial strategies with their long-term vision.

Strategic Partnerships: Beyond Financial Investment

A strategic partnership is more than a financial transaction; it's a relationship built on shared goals and complementary strengths. Unlike conventional funding, where investors provide capital in exchange for equity, strategic partners bring resources such as expertise, distribution networks, or technology that can amplify an organization's growth trajectory.

Consider the story of Ratan Tata, who used strategic partnerships to expand Tata Group's global footprint. By collaborating with international corporations, Tata was able to access new markets, share risks, and gain valuable insights—all without relying solely on traditional funding mechanisms. These partnerships not only provided financial benefits but also reinforced Tata's commitment to sustainability and innovation, ensuring alignment with the group's long-term goals.

For scale-up leaders, forming strategic partnerships requires identifying organizations whose values and objectives align with their own. It's about asking: What capabilities do we need, and who can help us achieve them while preserving our mission?

Non-Dilutive Funding: Preserving Control and Focus

Non-dilutive funding options, such as grants, loans, and revenue-based financing, offer an alternative path to growth without the need to give up equity or control. These options are particularly valuable for organizations seeking to maintain autonomy while scaling.

Take, for example, a health-tech startup that secured government grants to fund research and development for a groundbreaking medical device. By leveraging non-dilutive funding, the company was able to advance its innovation pipeline without the pressure of external shareholder demands. This approach allowed the founders to remain focused on their mission of delivering impactful solutions, rather than diluting their vision to meet investor expectations.

Leaders considering non-dilutive funding should evaluate their organization's eligibility for grants or loans, as well as the potential trade-offs in terms of flexibility and repayment timelines.

Crowdfunding: Building Community and Capital

Crowdfunding has emerged as a powerful tool for organizations looking to raise capital while building a community of supporters. By leveraging platforms such as Kickstarter or Indiegogo, businesses can generate funding from a broad base of individuals who believe in their mission.

Zhang Yiming, the founder of ByteDance (the parent company of TikTok), tapped into a version of this strategy by fostering early user investment—both financial and emotional—through grassroots marketing efforts. While not traditional crowdfunding, his ability to galvanize communities created a base of advocates who contributed to the company's meteoric rise.

For scale-ups, crowdfunding offers more than financial benefits; it creates an engaged audience that feels personally connected to the organization's success. It's an opportunity to turn early adopters into brand ambassadors, fueling both funding and loyalty.

Connecting Possibilities to Purpose

These alternative strategies—strategic partnerships, non-dilutive funding, and crowdfunding—offer leaders a chance to think beyond conventional paths. They highlight the importance of creativity and intentionality in funding decisions, ensuring that financial growth supports rather than detracts from organizational values.

Reflect on the possibilities:

- Are there partners whose resources could amplify your impact while preserving your autonomy?
- Can non-dilutive funding provide the stability you need to scale without compromising control?
- How might crowdfunding or community-driven efforts align with your mission while creating a loyal base of advocates?

By exploring these paths, leaders can craft funding strategies that not only meet immediate financial needs but also position their organizations for sustainable, values-driven growth. Funding, after all, is not just about capital—it's about creating opportunities to align resources with purpose and transform vision into reality.

Funding as a Strategic Lever for Growth

Funding, as we've explored throughout this chapter, is far more than a financial necessity—it's a powerful lever that can propel an organization toward sustainable and transformative growth. Like the sapling in our opening metaphor, the lifeblood of funding must be carefully chosen and strategically deployed to ensure that growth is not only rapid but resilient.

From aligning funding strategies with organizational goals to building meaningful relationships with investors and exploring creative alternatives, this chapter has emphasized that funding is a journey of intentional choices. Leaders who approach it with clarity, courage, and a long-term perspective lay the groundwork for sustained impact and success.

Reflective Takeaways

As we conclude, consider the core lessons that emerged:

- Timing and Alignment: Funding decisions should align with your organization's mission and readiness, ensuring that resources fuel growth without compromising values.

- Relationships Matter: Investors and partners should not only bring financial resources but also align with your vision, creating synergies that amplify success.

- Creative Thinking: Alternative funding strategies such as strategic partnerships, non-dilutive funding, and crowdfunding offer new avenues for achieving growth while maintaining control and purpose.

Ultimately, funding is not an end in itself but a means to achieve something greater: the realization of your organization's potential. By taking a strategic approach, you can ensure that every funding decision supports your larger vision and strengthens your foundation for the future.

As you reflect on your organization's funding journey, ask yourself these critical questions:

- Does your funding strategy align with your mission and long-term goals?

- Are you building relationships with investors who share your values and vision?

- Have you explored alternative funding options that might better suit your needs and stage of growth?

These questions are not meant to simplify the complexity of funding decisions but to inspire a mindset of intentionality. The choices you make today will ripple across your organization's future—affecting not just its financial health but its culture, values, and impact.

Setting the Stage for What's Next

As we move forward in this leadership journey, remember that funding is just one piece of the larger puzzle. It connects to broader themes of strategy, empowerment, and innovation—each playing a critical role in the growth and resilience of your organization.

The next chapter will build on these insights, exploring how to harness the collective potential of your team to turn vision into action. Together, these strategies will create a roadmap for not just growth, but unstoppable, purpose-driven leadership.

As you consider your funding approach, reflect on this: How can your financial decisions serve not just your organization's goals but also its higher purpose? The answer will guide you toward funding choices that don't just sustain growth but amplify it in meaningful and transformative ways.

Chapter 13

Financial Planning and Intelligent Resource Allocation

> *"Effective financial planning is about more than just balancing budgets; it's about directing resources in a way that propels growth and mitigates risk."*

If I asked you to describe your relationship with money in one word, what would it be? For many leaders, the answer isn't pretty. Words like *stressful*, *complex*, or even *distrustful* often come up. And when we're honest, these words don't just describe how we handle personal finances—they seep into how we approach financial decisions in our businesses, too.

I once sat with a founder who described financial planning as her least favorite part of leadership. "I got into this to build something meaningful," she said, "not to obsess over spreadsheets and cash flow." And yet, as her organization scaled, she realized that purpose without planning wasn't enough. Growth demands structure, and structure demands clarity—not just about where you're going but about how you're allocating the resources to get there.

Here's the truth: financial planning isn't about controlling every detail or micromanaging every dollar. It's about creating the freedom to lead boldly. It's about aligning your resources with your vision so that every choice reflects what matters most to your organization.

Think about it this way: money is a tool, not a solution. It won't tell you where to go or what to build, but it will amplify whatever direction you choose. And if you don't take the time to plan, to align your financial decisions with your purpose, that amplification can lead to chaos just as easily as it can lead to growth.

In *Unstoppable Growth*, we've talked about resilience, adaptability, and the power of vision. But here's where the rubber meets the road. A compelling vision without a financial foundation is like a car with no fuel—it's not going anywhere. And in the fast-paced world of scaling businesses, failing to plan isn't just risky; it's often the difference between thriving and surviving.

Research backs this up. Studies from Harvard Business Review and McKinsey consistently show that organizations with robust financial planning processes outperform their peers. These companies don't just survive downturns—they emerge stronger because they've built the flexibility to adapt while staying grounded in their strategic priorities.

But financial planning isn't just a numbers game—it's a leadership practice. It requires courage to face hard truths, creativity to navigate limited resources, and discipline to stay aligned with your goals. Most importantly, it requires trust: trust in yourself, in your team, and in the systems you've built to guide your decisions.

In this chapter, we're going to dive into the art and science of financial planning. We'll explore frameworks that make resource allocation less overwhelming and more intentional. We'll learn from leaders who've turned financial clarity into a competitive advantage. And we'll reflect on how to shift your mindset from seeing financial planning as a chore to embracing it as a cornerstone of impactful leadership.

Because when you take control of your financial strategy, you're not just managing resources—you're creating the conditions for sustainable, purpose-driven growth. And isn't that what unstoppable leadership is all about?

The Strategic Role of Financial Planning

In the world of scale-up organizations, financial planning is often the silent engine driving sustainable growth. Yet, many leaders underestimate its power, treating it as a task for back-office functions rather than a cornerstone of strategic decision-making. Research consistently reveals that organizations with robust financial planning and resource allocation practices outperform their peers in resilience, innovation, and long-term success.

A study by **Harvard Business Review** underscores the importance of aligning budgets with strategic priorities. Companies that actively allocate resources toward growth-focused initiatives, rather than spreading budgets evenly across departments, are more likely to achieve their objectives. This concept, often referred to as "dynamic resource allocation," allows leaders to pivot quickly in response to market changes while ensuring that high-impact areas receive the attention they deserve.

Take the case of **McKinsey's research** on adaptive financial planning. The study revealed that organizations embracing agile financial strategies—characterized by regular budget reviews and reallocation of resources based on real-time data—achieved a 30% higher return on investment in growth initiatives. This adaptability not only optimized resource usage but also created a culture of proactive decision-making, empowering leaders to stay ahead in competitive markets.

Bain & Company takes this insight further, emphasizing the role of data-driven decision-making in resource allocation. Companies leveraging predictive analytics and financial modelling tools reported improved efficiency and reduced waste. By identifying which projects and initiatives yielded the highest returns, these organizations ensured that every dollar was purposefully spent, reinforcing their strategic goals.

Aligning Budgets with Strategic Priorities

At the heart of effective financial planning lies the principle of alignment. Budgets are not just numbers on a spreadsheet; they are a reflection of an organization's values and priorities. Research shows that organizations that tie their financial planning processes directly to their strategic goals achieve greater clarity and focus.

Consider the example of a global manufacturing firm transitioning toward sustainability. Rather than evenly distributing its financial resources, the company allocated a significant portion of its budget to R&D for renewable energy solutions, positioning itself as an industry leader in green innovation. This strategic alignment not only advanced the company's mission but also opened doors to new markets and partnerships.

The Role of Data-Driven Decision-Making

In a world saturated with information, the ability to make sense of data is a critical advantage. Financial leaders who embrace data-driven decision-making create clarity amidst complexity. Predictive analytics, scenario planning, and financial dashboards allow leaders to anticipate trends, assess risks, and allocate resources with precision.

For instance, a tech startup looking to scale its operations used predictive models to forecast customer demand across different markets. By aligning its financial strategy with these insights, the company was able to avoid overinvestment in low-demand regions while maximizing returns in high-growth areas. This approach not only optimized its budget but also fostered confidence among investors and stakeholders.

Ensuring Adaptability in Financial Strategies

Adaptability is no longer a luxury—it is a necessity. As markets evolve and uncertainties arise, organizations must remain agile in their financial planning. McKinsey's research highlights that organizations with flexible budgetary processes are better equipped to navigate disruptions, from economic downturns to technological advancements.

One compelling example is a healthcare company that pivoted during a global crisis. By reallocating resources from planned marketing campaigns to bolster supply chain resilience, the company ensured operational continuity and strengthened its reputation in the market. This ability to adapt quickly while staying true to its strategic vision exemplifies the power of flexible financial planning.

A Transition to Action

The insights above illustrate that financial planning is far more than a numbers game—it's a strategic lever that can determine the success or failure of an organization's growth journey. Aligning budgets with strategic priorities, leveraging data, and fostering adaptability are critical components of effective financial leadership.

As we transition to the next section, we will explore a practical framework that empowers leaders to implement these principles in their organizations. This framework will provide a roadmap for navigating the complexities of financial planning and resource allocation, turning insights into actionable strategies for sustainable success. Let's delve into the tools and approaches that can make intelligent resource allocation a reality.

The ALIGN Approach

Effective financial planning for scale-up organizations requires more than instinct or intuition; it demands a structured approach that aligns resources with strategic priorities while allowing room for adaptability and growth. The **ALIGN framework**—Assess, Link, Iterate, Guide, Navigate—offers leaders a practical roadmap for making informed financial decisions that drive sustainable success.

1. Assess: Understanding the Current Landscape

The first step in intelligent financial planning is a thorough assessment of your organization's current financial health and market positioning. This means diving deep into key financial metrics, evaluating cash flow, and identifying existing resource inefficiencies. But assessment isn't limited to internal data—it also involves understanding external trends, competitive landscapes, and market opportunities.

For example, consider a scale-up in the renewable energy sector. As the company sought to expand, leadership conducted a comprehensive assessment to identify underperforming markets and areas ripe for investment. This analysis revealed that reallocating resources toward solar panel production would yield higher returns than continuing to focus on wind energy in certain regions. Armed with these insights, the company was able to align its financial strategy with market opportunities, ensuring that every dollar was purposefully deployed.

2. Link: Aligning Resources with Strategic Goals

Once the financial landscape is clear, the next step is to link resources directly to your organization's strategic objectives. This alignment ensures that budgets reflect not just immediate needs but long-term priorities, such as innovation, talent development, or market expansion.

For instance, when Ratan Tata led Tata Group's expansion into global markets, financial resources were meticulously allocated to reflect the organization's broader vision of sustainable and inclusive growth. Investments were made in industries like renewable energy and electric vehicles—areas aligned with Tata's commitment to innovation and environmental stewardship. By linking financial decisions to strategic goals, Tata Group not only scaled successfully but also reinforced its core values.

3. Iterate: Embracing a Dynamic Approach

Financial planning is not a one-and-done exercise; it's a dynamic process that requires ongoing refinement. Leaders must regularly revisit their plans, incorporating new data and adjusting strategies as circumstances evolve. This iterative approach allows organizations to remain agile, responding effectively to challenges and opportunities.

Take the example of a global tech company navigating a rapidly changing digital landscape. By implementing quarterly financial reviews, the leadership team was able to identify emerging trends and pivot resources accordingly. When demand for artificial intelligence solutions surged, the company quickly reallocated funding from other projects, ensuring they capitalized on the opportunity without losing momentum elsewhere. Iteration allowed them to stay competitive while maintaining focus on their overarching goals.

4. Guide: Engaging Teams in Financial Decision-Making

Financial planning isn't just the responsibility of senior leaders or finance departments—it's a collaborative process that benefits from the input of cross-functional teams. Engaging employees in financial discussions fosters transparency, encourages innovation, and builds trust across the organization.

Consider a healthcare scale-up preparing to launch a new product line. Leadership invited managers from operations, marketing, and R&D to participate in budget discussions, ensuring that diverse perspectives shaped the financial plan. This collaborative approach uncovered hidden inefficiencies and led to creative solutions for maximizing resources. By guiding teams to take ownership of financial decisions, the organization created a culture of accountability and alignment.

5. Navigate: Steering Through Uncertainty

The final step in the ALIGN framework is navigating uncertainty with confidence and resilience. This involves leveraging predictive analytics, scenario planning, and contingency strategies to prepare for the unexpected. Leaders must balance risk and opportunity, ensuring that their organizations are ready to weather challenges while seizing growth opportunities.

During a global supply chain crisis, a manufacturing scale-up used predictive analytics to forecast disruptions and adapt its financial strategy accordingly. By reallocating funds to strengthen supplier relationships and diversify sourcing options, the company minimized downtime and maintained customer trust. This proactive navigation not only safeguarded operations but also positioned the organization for long-term success.

Bringing ALIGN to Life

The ALIGN framework provides leaders with a structured yet flexible approach to financial planning. By assessing their current landscape, linking resources to strategic goals, iterating their plans, guiding their teams, and navigating uncertainty, scale-up organizations can optimize their financial strategies to fuel sustainable growth.

Reflect on your own leadership practices:

- Are you regularly assessing both internal and external financial landscapes?
- How effectively are your budgets linked to your organization's mission and goals?
- Are you fostering a culture of collaboration in financial decision-making?

Financial planning isn't just about managing resources—it's about shaping the future of your organization. By applying the ALIGN framework, leaders can turn financial strategies into powerful tools for resilience, innovation, and unstoppable growth.

Intelligent Financial Leadership in Action

Effective financial planning and resource allocation are not abstract concepts; they are strategies that have been tested and refined by some of the most successful leaders in the business world. By examining their journeys, we can uncover valuable insights that transcend industries and offer practical lessons for scale-up leaders.

Ingvar Kamprad: The Power of Frugality and Purpose

Ingvar Kamprad, the founder of IKEA, built his empire on principles of frugality and long-term vision. From its early days as a small mail-order business in Sweden, IKEA's financial strategy was rooted in Kamprad's belief that every resource should be allocated with purpose. Kamprad famously avoided wasteful expenditures, channelling funds into areas that would directly enhance the customer experience, such as streamlined supply chains and innovative product design.

One of Kamprad's defining moments in financial leadership came during IKEA's rapid international expansion. The company faced significant challenges, including high operating costs in new markets and fierce competition. Rather than chasing short-term gains, Kamprad doubled down on cost efficiency and reinvested savings into creating a global distribution network. This allowed IKEA to scale without sacrificing affordability, which was central to its brand promise.

Kamprad's approach to resource allocation also extended to his employees. He ensured that funds were available for training and professional development, recognizing that an engaged and empowered workforce was key to sustaining growth. His ability to align financial planning with IKEA's mission of "creating a better everyday life for the many people" cemented the company's reputation as an industry leader.

For today's scale-up leaders, Kamprad's story offers a powerful lesson: financial discipline doesn't mean stifling ambition. By allocating resources with clarity and purpose, leaders can fuel growth while staying true to their core values.

Bernard Arnault: Strategic Investments for Lasting Impact

Bernard Arnault, the chairman and CEO of LVMH, has mastered the art of leveraging financial resources to drive innovation and growth. Under his leadership, LVMH has become a global powerhouse in luxury goods, encompassing brands such as Louis Vuitton, Dior, and Moët Hennessy. Arnault's success lies in his ability to make bold, strategic investments while maintaining a meticulous focus on long-term value creation.

One pivotal moment in Arnault's journey was his acquisition of Christian Dior in the 1980s. At the time, the brand was struggling financially, but Arnault saw untapped potential. By carefully reallocating resources to revitalize Dior's product lines and marketing strategies, he transformed the brand into a cornerstone of LVMH's portfolio. This strategic risk not only paid off but also set the stage for LVMH's aggressive yet calculated expansion into other luxury sectors.

Arnault's financial leadership extends beyond acquisitions. He consistently prioritizes innovation, allocating significant funds to R&D for sustainable practices and digital transformation. For example, LVMH's investment in blockchain technology to authenticate products reflects Arnault's commitment to staying ahead of industry trends while addressing consumer demands for transparency.

What sets Arnault apart is his ability to balance bold financial moves with a disciplined approach to risk management. By aligning his investments with LVMH's vision of timeless luxury and innovation, he has ensured the group's enduring relevance in a highly competitive market.

Reflections on Financial Leadership

Both Kamprad and Arnault demonstrate that intelligent financial leadership is not a one-size-fits-all strategy—it's about understanding the unique needs and values of an organization and allocating resources accordingly.

Kamprad's emphasis on frugality and operational efficiency offers a model for leaders navigating resource constraints, while Arnault's bold investments highlight the power of strategic risk-taking. Together, they illustrate that successful financial planning is both an art and a science, blending data-driven decisions with an intuitive understanding of what will drive long-term success.

As you consider your own approach to financial planning, reflect on these questions:

- Are your financial strategies aligned with your organization's mission and goals?
- How do you balance bold investments with prudent risk management?
- What lessons can you draw from leaders like Kamprad and Arnault to optimize resource allocation in your organization?

By learning from these real-world examples, scale-up leaders can develop financial strategies that are not only intelligent but transformative, paving the way for sustainable growth and impact.

Balancing Innovation and Cost Efficiency

Financial planning often feels like walking a tightrope, with one side pulling toward bold investments in innovation and the other demanding the restraint of cost efficiency. For scale-up leaders, this dilemma is both familiar and complex: How do you fuel the creativity and growth needed to scale without compromising financial stability?

The Story of Two Approaches

Consider the journey of two companies in the renewable energy sector, each poised for growth but with distinct approaches to financial planning. The first company, SolarNext, prioritized innovation at all costs. Determined to outpace competitors, its leadership allocated the majority of its budget to R&D, aiming to create groundbreaking solar panel technology. However, in its zeal for innovation, SolarNext overlooked the operational efficiencies needed to sustain its aggressive strategy. Cash flow constraints began to emerge, and by the time the technology was ready to launch, the company lacked the resources to scale production effectively. What started as a bold vision ended as an underwhelming execution.

In contrast, GreenLight Power, another scale-up in the same industry, took a more balanced approach. While committing a significant portion of its budget to R&D, the leadership team ensured that operational costs were tightly managed and that funds were set aside for contingency planning. This careful balance allowed GreenLight to innovate without jeopardizing its financial health. When its new technology was ready, the company had both the resources and the operational efficiency to scale production, securing a leading position in the market.

The contrasting outcomes of these two companies underscore a fundamental truth: innovation and cost efficiency are not mutually exclusive. The challenge lies in striking a balance that aligns with the organization's unique goals and circumstances.

The Trade-Offs in Focus

Balancing these priorities requires leaders to navigate a series of trade-offs. Investing heavily in innovation can position a company as a market leader but may expose it to financial risks if not paired with operational discipline. On the other hand, focusing solely on cost efficiency can stifle creativity and limit the organization's ability to seize growth opportunities.

This tension often manifests during budget planning. Imagine a scale-up tech company deciding whether to allocate funds toward developing a new AI-driven product or enhancing its existing operational infrastructure. The product has the potential to revolutionize the industry, but it also comes with significant risks and long development timelines. Meanwhile, the operational investment promises immediate gains in efficiency and customer satisfaction but lacks the same transformative appeal.

These decisions require leaders to weigh immediate needs against long-term aspirations, factoring in variables such as market conditions, organizational capacity, and the availability of funding.

Questions for Reflection

For scale-up leaders, resolving this dilemma begins with self-awareness and strategic clarity. Ask yourself:

- Are your financial decisions rooted in the organization's long-term vision, or are they driven by short-term pressures?
- How do you evaluate the risks and rewards of investing in innovation versus maintaining cost efficiency?
- What safeguards can you put in place to ensure that bold investments do not compromise financial stability?

Bridging the Gap

The most successful leaders recognize that financial planning is not about choosing one side of the spectrum but about finding harmony between competing priorities. This balance might involve setting clear criteria for funding decisions, using scenario planning to anticipate outcomes, or fostering cross-functional collaboration to ensure that diverse perspectives shape the financial strategy.

By embracing this nuanced approach, leaders can transform financial dilemmas into opportunities for growth, ensuring that their organizations remain both innovative and resilient. As you reflect on your own leadership journey, consider how you can bridge the gap between vision and discipline, creating a financial strategy that propels your organization toward unstoppable growth.

Alternative Strategies for Financial Agility

Financial planning, much like navigating a complex and shifting landscape, often demands a mix of traditional tools and innovative strategies. For scale-up organizations aiming to align resources with long-term vision, alternative approaches such as scenario planning, zero-based budgeting, and predictive analytics offer opportunities to enhance agility and precision. These methods not only refine decision-making but also provide a competitive edge in today's dynamic markets.

Scenario Planning: Anticipating the Unknown

Imagine a tech scale-up preparing to expand into international markets. The leadership team is excited about the opportunities, yet they're aware of the risks: currency fluctuations, regulatory challenges, and varying market demand. Traditional financial planning might struggle to account for such variables, but **scenario planning** provides a roadmap to navigate the unknown.

By modelling multiple potential outcomes—best-case, worst-case, and likely scenarios—the company creates a set of adaptable financial plans. Each scenario highlights key triggers, such as a sudden rise in shipping costs or a delay in regulatory approvals, and outlines pre-emptive actions to mitigate risks. This approach enables the leadership team to allocate resources flexibly, ensuring the organization remains resilient regardless of external conditions.

Scenario planning not only strengthens financial agility but also fosters a culture of preparedness. It empowers leaders to make informed decisions, grounded in a clear understanding of potential challenges and opportunities.

Zero-Based Budgeting: Starting Fresh

Traditional budgeting often builds on the previous year's allocations, perpetuating inefficiencies and misaligned priorities. **Zero-based budgeting (ZBB)** flips this approach by requiring leaders to justify every expense from the ground up. It's not about cutting costs indiscriminately—it's about ensuring that every dollar contributes to the organization's goals.

Consider a manufacturing company looking to improve profitability while investing in sustainability initiatives. Through ZBB, the leadership team evaluates each department's spending, identifying areas where resources can be reallocated without compromising operations. For instance, funds previously used for outdated marketing channels are redirected to green energy solutions, aligning financial decisions with both short-term efficiency and long-term purpose.

ZBB challenges organizations to think critically about their priorities and eliminates complacency in resource allocation. It's a powerful tool for aligning financial planning with strategic intent, particularly during periods of rapid growth or change.

Predictive Analytics: The Power of Data-Driven Insights

In the age of big data, predictive analytics has emerged as a game-changer for financial planning. By analyzing historical data and identifying patterns, organizations can forecast future trends, assess risks, and optimize resource allocation with unprecedented accuracy.

Take the example of a retail scale-up leveraging predictive analytics to anticipate seasonal demand. By analyzing customer purchasing behavior, the company identifies peak sales periods and adjusts its inventory and staffing accordingly. This data-driven approach not only minimizes waste but also ensures that resources are concentrated where they'll have the greatest impact.

Predictive analytics doesn't just enhance financial efficiency—it also unlocks new opportunities for innovation and growth. By providing leaders with actionable insights, it enables them to make proactive decisions that keep their organizations ahead of the curve.

Bridging Innovation and Discipline

These alternative strategies—scenario planning, zero-based budgeting, and predictive analytics—are more than financial tools; they are pathways to smarter, more adaptable leadership. They reflect the chapter's core themes: aligning resources with strategic goals, fostering agility, and empowering organizations to thrive in uncertainty.

As you consider these possibilities, reflect on how they might fit into your organization's financial planning practices:

- Are you prepared for multiple future scenarios, or do your financial plans hinge on a single assumption?
- How well do your budgets reflect current priorities versus outdated habits?
- Are you leveraging technology to gain insights that inform and refine your decisions?

Incorporating these approaches can transform financial planning into a dynamic and empowering process. By combining the discipline of traditional methods with the creativity of innovative strategies, leaders can build organizations that are not only resilient but poised for unstoppable growth.

Financial planning, much like constructing the foundation of a great structure, is about creating stability while leaving room for innovation and growth. Throughout this chapter, we've explored how thoughtful financial leadership serves as the bedrock for scaling organizations. From aligning resources with strategic goals to embracing frameworks like ALIGN and learning from the experiences of seasoned leaders, the message is clear: financial planning is not a static process but a dynamic, strategic enabler.

A recurring theme in this chapter is intentionality. Just as a builder carefully selects materials to withstand time and elements, leaders must make deliberate financial choices that reflect their organization's mission and long-term vision. The stories of leaders like Ingvar Kamprad and Bernard Arnault remind us that success lies not in following a formula but in adapting strategies to unique circumstances, blending bold innovation with disciplined resource allocation.

Another essential insight is the importance of adaptability. Markets evolve, challenges arise, and opportunities emerge unexpectedly.

Leaders who incorporate tools like scenario planning, zero-based budgeting, and predictive analytics are better equipped to navigate these changes with confidence, ensuring their organizations remain resilient in uncertainty.

Finally, financial planning is as much about people as it is about numbers. Engaging teams in financial decision-making fosters trust, creativity, and alignment. It transforms budgeting from a task into a shared vision, ensuring that every stakeholder understands their role in driving the organization's growth.

Reflective Takeaways

- Intentionality Drives Growth: Financial decisions must reflect and reinforce your organization's mission and values. Alignment is not a luxury; it's a necessity.

- Adaptability Creates Resilience: Embrace tools and strategies that prepare you for uncertainty. A flexible financial plan is your organization's safety net and springboard for opportunity.

- Collaboration Fuels Success: Involve your team in financial planning to unlock innovative solutions and build a culture of shared accountability.

As you reflect on this chapter, consider how your financial planning aligns with your leadership vision. Are you creating a solid foundation for your organization to grow sustainably, or are there gaps that need addressing? Financial planning is not a one-time exercise but an ongoing commitment to intentionality, adaptability, and collaboration. Take the first step by reviewing your current strategies and identifying areas for refinement.

Reflect and Refocus

1. Alignment: How well do your financial strategies reflect your organization's mission and long-term goals? Are there areas where resources could be better allocated to drive impact?

2. Adaptability: Are you prepared for unforeseen challenges and opportunities? What tools or approaches could enhance your financial agility?

3. Collaboration: How engaged is your team in financial decision-making? What steps can you take to foster a culture of shared responsibility in this area?

Financial planning isn't just about spreadsheets and budgets—it's about creating the conditions for your organization to thrive. As you consider these questions, remember that every decision you make today shapes the trajectory of your organization tomorrow. Approach financial planning with intention, and it will become a powerful lever for growth, resilience, and lasting impact.

With this foundation in place, we now turn to the next chapter, exploring how to navigate the complexities of building impactful partnerships and collaborations—another critical component of scale-up success.

Chapter 14

Building Strong Partnerships with Investors and Stakeholders

"Great partnerships are built on trust, transparency, and a shared vision for the future."

If there's one thing I've learned from studying relationships—whether personal or professional—it's this: the quality of our connections determines the quality of our outcomes. Partnerships, at their core, are a form of relationship. And just like any relationship, they thrive on trust, alignment, and communication.

I once heard a CEO describe her approach to partnerships as "transactional." She said, "It's about the numbers, the terms, and the deliverables. Emotions don't belong in business." But then her voice softened as she admitted, "That mindset got us through the early days, but as we've grown, I'm seeing cracks in that approach." Her team was strained, her investors felt disconnected, and her most promising partnerships were unraveling.

The truth is, partnerships built solely on transactions are like houses built on sand—they may stand for a while, but they crumble under pressure. To build something lasting, something resilient, you need a foundation of shared values and mutual respect.

Think about your own partnerships, whether they're with investors, board members, or other key stakeholders. Are they grounded in trust? Do they align with your organization's purpose? Do they feel like a collaboration or a competition?

The leaders who build enduring, impactful partnerships understand that these relationships are about more than funding or influence—they're about shared vision and co-creation. They recognize that the best partnerships amplify the strengths of everyone involved, creating something far greater than the sum of its parts.

In *Unstoppable Growth*, we've explored how purpose, resilience, and alignment fuel organizational success. This chapter is where all of that comes together. Strong partnerships don't just happen; they're built intentionally. They require leaders to balance vulnerability with conviction, curiosity with clarity, and ambition with humility.

And here's the beauty of it: when you invest in your partnerships, they invest in you. When you show up authentically and with integrity, you set the tone for collaboration that transcends the ordinary and drives extraordinary results.

Research from McKinsey and Bain & Company shows that organizations with well-aligned stakeholder relationships grow faster, weather crises more effectively, and sustain their competitive edge longer. But this isn't just about metrics—it's about the energy and commitment you bring to the table. Partnerships thrive when you treat them as relationships, not transactions.

In this chapter, we'll dive deep into what it takes to build partnerships that last. You'll learn from leaders who've transformed their organizations through strategic collaboration. We'll explore practical frameworks for nurturing trust and alignment, and we'll reflect on how your leadership sets the tone for every relationship your organization creates.

Because at the end of the day, partnerships aren't just about shared goals—they're about shared humanity. And when we lead with purpose and connection, we don't just build organizations—we build legacies.

The Foundations of Strong Partnerships

Successful partnerships are not built overnight. They require intentional effort, clear communication, and a foundation of mutual trust. Research consistently shows that strong partnerships—whether with investors, stakeholders, or collaborators—are a critical driver of organizational growth and resilience. According to McKinsey, businesses that foster high-trust relationships with their stakeholders see significantly greater long-term performance, including improved decision-making and increased agility during periods of uncertainty. Yet, trust doesn't emerge in isolation—it is cultivated through transparency, shared purpose, and consistent alignment of expectations.

One study by Bain & Company highlights that organizations with well-defined partnership strategies experience 20–25% faster growth compared to their peers. These companies prioritize communication and work to understand their partners' goals, ensuring that both parties feel invested in the relationship. For example, businesses that co-create strategies with their investors—rather than treating them as passive funders—report stronger alignment and higher levels of satisfaction on both sides. This collaborative approach fosters a sense of shared ownership, turning what could be a transactional relationship into a dynamic partnership.

The role of shared purpose is equally vital. The Stanford Social Innovation Review emphasizes that partnerships grounded in aligned values are more likely to endure challenges and adapt to changing circumstances. When organizations articulate a clear vision that resonates with their investors or stakeholders, they create a unifying force that transcends individual agendas. This shared purpose not only enhances collaboration but also ensures that decisions are guided by principles rather than short-term pressures.

Transparent communication is the final pillar of successful partnerships. Transparency builds confidence, reduces misunderstandings, and creates a platform for constructive dialogue. A report from PwC found that businesses practicing open communication with stakeholders and investors were better positioned to navigate crises and maintain trust, even during challenging times. Clear reporting, regular updates, and honest discussions about risks and opportunities all contribute to the kind of transparency that deepens relationships.

Take, for instance, the example of a rapidly growing technology company that faced mounting pressures from investors to scale aggressively. Rather than conceding to every demand, the leadership team initiated regular town-hall-style meetings with investors, sharing both successes and setbacks. This approach not only earned trust but also opened the door for collaborative problem-solving, enabling the company to scale in a way that aligned with its long-term vision. This blend of transparency and shared purpose turned potential friction into a stronger, more unified partnership.

These insights underscore the relational nature of partnerships. They are not merely agreements on paper but living, evolving connections that require nurturing. As we transition into actionable frameworks, we'll explore how leaders can embed trust, shared purpose, and transparency into their approach, ensuring their partnerships are positioned to thrive in a competitive and dynamic business environment.

TRUST in Action

Building strong partnerships with investors and stakeholders requires more than good intentions—it demands a deliberate approach guided by clear principles. The TRUST framework—Transparency, Reciprocity, Understanding, Shared Goals, and Timeliness—offers a practical roadmap for leaders to cultivate relationships that drive growth and resilience. This framework, rooted in research and tested in real-world scenarios, ensures that partnerships are built on a foundation of trust, aligned purpose, and mutual benefit.

Transparency: Building Confidence Through Open Communication

Transparency is the cornerstone of trust. Partners—whether investors or stakeholders—need to feel they have a clear view of the organization's vision, challenges, and opportunities. Transparency means sharing the good and the bad with honesty and consistency. This isn't about overloading your partners with data but offering them meaningful insights that empower collaboration.

For example, a fast-growing e-commerce company in Southeast Asia faced pressure from its investors to accelerate market expansion. Instead of succumbing to vague assurances, the leadership team invited their investors into the decision-making process, presenting detailed growth scenarios with accompanying risks and opportunities. By providing clarity, the team not only gained their investors' confidence but also fostered a sense of partnership in navigating these challenges together.

Reciprocity: Fostering Mutual Value

Partnerships thrive when both sides feel valued and supported. Reciprocity ensures that the relationship isn't one-sided; it's about creating win-win scenarios where both parties see tangible benefits. For investors, this might mean delivering strong financial returns alongside meaningful involvement in shaping the business. For stakeholders, reciprocity often looks like listening to their concerns and incorporating their input into the organization's strategy.

Consider the example of a renewable energy startup collaborating with local communities to establish solar farms. Instead of imposing decisions, the company involved community leaders in the planning process, ensuring the projects addressed both environmental goals and local needs. This reciprocal approach not only built goodwill but also created advocates who actively supported the project's success.

Understanding: Deepening Connection Through Empathy

Empathy is essential for building enduring partnerships. Understanding your investors' and stakeholders' motivations, concerns, and goals helps foster meaningful connections. It's not just about what your organization needs—it's about aligning those needs with the priorities of your partners.

Take the case of a technology scale-up that secured funding from a venture capital firm known for its hands-on approach. The CEO took the time to understand the firm's broader portfolio and strategic goals, tailoring updates and discussions to align with these priorities. By showing empathy and alignment, the CEO positioned the organization as a valued partner, not just another investment.

Shared Goals: Aligning Visions for Success

The most successful partnerships are anchored in shared goals. Whether it's a financial target, a sustainability initiative, or a long-term growth vision, alignment ensures that both parties are moving in the same direction. Shared goals also provide a guiding light during periods of uncertainty or disagreement, reinforcing the partnership's purpose.

For instance, a luxury fashion brand collaborating with its investors during a market downturn ensured alignment by reasserting its commitment to long-term brand equity over short-term profit. By reaffirming this shared goal, the brand secured its investors' patience and trust, enabling a steady recovery.

Timeliness: Respecting Commitments and Momentum

Timeliness reflects respect for your partners' time and the urgency of shared goals. Whether it's delivering reports, responding to inquiries, or meeting milestones, adhering to timelines builds reliability and strengthens the relationship. Timeliness is also about recognizing when to act decisively and when to pause for thoughtful reflection.

A South African telecommunications scale-up demonstrated timeliness by providing real-time updates to its investors during a critical product launch. This proactive communication not only reassured stakeholders but also ensured alignment and timely adjustments to their strategies, contributing to a successful rollout.

TRUST in Practice: From Framework to Growth

The TRUST framework isn't just a checklist—it's a philosophy that shapes how leaders engage with investors and stakeholders. By embedding transparency, reciprocity, understanding, shared goals, and timeliness into your partnerships, you create a foundation for enduring relationships that amplify your organization's resilience and impact.

As we move forward, we'll explore real-world examples and leadership insights that bring the TRUST framework to life, illustrating how these principles drive meaningful and measurable success in scale-up organizations. Partnerships built on TRUST are more than collaborations—they are catalysts for unstoppable growth.

The Art of Building Transformative Partnerships

Strong partnerships are often forged in the crucible of challenges, where vision, trust, and intentionality are tested. Two leaders who exemplify the art of cultivating impactful relationships with investors and stakeholders are Nandan Nilekani, co-founder of Infosys, and Strive Masiyiwa, founder of Econet. Their journeys provide valuable lessons on navigating the complexities of partnerships while staying true to core values.

Nandan Nilekani: Aligning Vision with Stakeholder Trust

Nandan Nilekani's leadership journey at Infosys offers a masterclass in building partnerships grounded in shared purpose and trust. When Infosys was still an emerging IT services company, Nilekani and his co-founders recognized that to scale globally, they needed more than financial backing—they needed long-term partners who believed in their vision of delivering world-class IT solutions from India.

The challenge was significant. At the time, global investors were skeptical about India's ability to compete in the high-tech industry. Nilekani took a transparent approach, showcasing not only Infosys's capabilities but also the integrity and long-term vision of its leadership team. This transparency was paired with rigorous communication—regularly updating investors on both progress and setbacks. Over time, Nilekani's ability to foster trust helped Infosys secure not only funding but also strategic partnerships with global clients.

Nilekani's approach extended beyond investors to Infosys's employees and clients. He emphasized shared goals, ensuring that every stakeholder felt aligned with the company's mission. This alignment built resilience during periods of economic uncertainty, allowing Infosys to emerge as one of the most respected IT companies in the world. His success underscores the importance of combining trust, clear communication, and shared purpose in building enduring partnerships.

Strive Masiyiwa: Empowering Communities Through Collaboration

Strive Masiyiwa's journey with Econet illustrates how partnerships can extend beyond financial stakeholders to include communities, governments, and other key players. When Masiyiwa sought to launch Econet in Zimbabwe, he faced immense regulatory barriers. Rather than viewing the government solely as an obstacle, he sought to engage policymakers as partners in his vision of connecting underserved communities.

Masiyiwa's strategy was rooted in reciprocity and understanding. He framed Econet's mission not just as a business venture but as a means of driving socioeconomic development, creating jobs, and improving access to communication. By aligning Econet's goals with the government's aspirations for national development, Masiyiwa was able to build a coalition of support that eventually allowed him to break through the barriers.

Econet's partnerships didn't end there. Masiyiwa actively fostered relationships with local communities, reinvesting in education and healthcare initiatives. This holistic approach to partnership-building strengthened Econet's brand and created a network of advocates who were deeply invested in the company's success. Today, Econet is a telecommunications giant, and Masiyiwa is celebrated for his ability to build bridges where others saw walls.

Lessons from Nilekani and Masiyiwa

The experiences of Nilekani and Masiyiwa highlight several critical principles of partnership-building:

1. Trust is foundational: Whether engaging with investors or governments, both leaders demonstrated the power of transparency and ethical leadership in building trust.

2. Shared purpose amplifies impact: Aligning goals with stakeholders' aspirations creates partnerships that are resilient and mutually beneficial.

3. Intentional communication strengthens relationships: Regular updates and open dialogue ensure that all parties feel informed and valued.

4. Beyond transactions, relationships drive success: Both leaders approached partnerships as long-term collaborations, emphasizing reciprocity and mutual respect.

As leaders of scale-up organizations, the lessons from Nilekani and Masiyiwa serve as a reminder that partnerships are not just about securing resources—they are about creating a foundation for sustainable growth and shared success. By prioritizing trust, alignment, and empathy, leaders can transform partnerships into powerful engines of innovation, resilience, and impact.

The question for you, as a leader, is this: How can you approach your own partnerships with the same intentionality and clarity? What steps can you take to align your vision with the values and goals of your investors and stakeholders? Partnerships are not destinations—they are dynamic, evolving relationships that require care, attention, and a commitment to mutual growth.

Balancing Investor Expectations and Organizational Values

Every leader faces moments where the demands of investors seem to collide with the core values of their organization. These moments, though challenging, reveal the heart of leadership—the ability to make decisions that balance immediate needs with long-term vision, and financial imperatives with ethical commitments. The dilemma of balancing investor expectations with organizational values is one that defines partnership-building in scale-up organizations.

Consider a hypothetical scenario inspired by many real-world leadership journeys. A technology startup, let's call it "GreenTech Solutions," has developed an innovative clean energy product that has garnered significant attention. Early-stage investors are eager to see rapid commercialization and higher returns, but the company's leadership team is committed to ensuring the product's affordability for underserved markets. The tension is palpable: Should GreenTech prioritize speed to market to meet investor demands or take the slower, more deliberate route to maintain their commitment to accessibility and social impact?

Two Contrasting Paths

On one hand, the CEO could prioritize investor expectations, fast-tracking production and marketing efforts to deliver impressive short-term financial results. This approach might secure continued funding and build investor confidence, but it risks alienating key stakeholders, including employees and community partners, who believed in the company's mission to drive equitable change. Over time, the divergence from core values could erode trust and damage the brand's authenticity.

On the other hand, the CEO could lean into the company's values, transparently communicating to investors the importance of staying true to their mission. This path would involve fostering a deeper dialogue with investors, presenting a roadmap that balances profitability with purpose. While this might delay returns and require additional effort to align stakeholders, it could strengthen the company's long-term positioning, attracting mission-aligned partners and building a more resilient brand.

Consequences of Leadership Choices

The choice a leader makes in such dilemmas reverberates across the organization. Prioritizing investor expectations at the expense of values may deliver short-term gains but often results in long-term instability, as trust and alignment are compromised. Conversely, standing firm on values can be more challenging in the moment, but it establishes a foundation of integrity and sustainability that builds enduring partnerships.

Reflecting on Your Own Leadership

As you navigate your own partnerships, ask yourself:

- Are your organizational values clearly defined and communicated to investors and stakeholders?
- How do you handle moments where short-term financial pressures conflict with your mission and long-term goals?
- What mechanisms can you put in place to ensure transparency and alignment in these critical relationships?

The balance between expectations and values is not a static one—it is an ongoing negotiation that requires clarity, empathy, and strategic thinking. Leadership, in this context, is about finding harmony in tension, creating solutions that honor the needs of all parties while remaining steadfast in your commitment to purpose.

By embracing the complexities of these dilemmas, you not only build stronger partnerships but also strengthen your own leadership resilience. The ability to navigate these moments with integrity and vision is what transforms transactional relationships into transformative collaborations.

Reimagining Partnerships for a Dynamic Future

Partnerships, like organizations, must evolve to meet the demands of an increasingly interconnected and dynamic world. While trust, transparency, and shared purpose remain the cornerstones of successful relationships, leaders can unlock new potential by embracing innovative strategies. From leveraging digital tools for enhanced communication to fostering cross-sector collaborations, these approaches can transform partnerships into engines of innovation and growth.

Leveraging Digital Tools for Connection and Alignment

In today's digital age, technology has redefined how partnerships are formed and maintained. Tools like data visualization platforms, collaborative dashboards, and real-time communication apps enable leaders to enhance transparency and foster engagement with investors and stakeholders. For example, a renewable energy startup might use digital dashboards to provide investors with real-time updates on project milestones, energy outputs, and financial performance. This level of transparency not only strengthens trust but also empowers investors to feel actively involved in the company's progress.

Similarly, tools like Slack, Asana, or Microsoft Teams can facilitate seamless communication between diverse stakeholder groups. By creating a virtual space where ideas can be shared and challenges addressed collaboratively, leaders can break down silos and foster a sense of collective ownership. In a world where face-to-face interactions are often limited, these digital innovations provide a pathway for building strong, resilient partnerships.

Exploring Stakeholder Co-Creation Models

Partnerships thrive when stakeholders feel that their voices are not just heard but actively shape outcomes. Co-creation models—where investors, community members, or other partners are invited to collaborate on strategy or product development—are becoming increasingly popular. These models go beyond consultation, empowering stakeholders to contribute meaningfully to the organization's vision.

Consider the case of a healthcare scale-up developing an affordable diagnostic tool for underserved regions. By inviting local healthcare providers and community leaders to co-create the product's design and distribution strategy, the organization ensures that the solution is not only effective but also culturally and contextually relevant. This approach builds deeper trust and engagement while creating a product that meets real-world needs.

Fostering Cross-Sector Collaborations

The most impactful partnerships often transcend traditional boundaries. Cross-sector collaborations, where businesses partner with governments, nonprofits, or academia, allow organizations to tackle complex challenges that no single entity could solve alone. For instance, a technology company focused on digital literacy might collaborate with educational institutions and government agencies to design and implement large-scale training programs. Each partner brings unique strengths to the table, creating a synergy that amplifies impact.

Leaders who embrace cross-sector collaborations must be adept at aligning diverse priorities and navigating potential conflicts. However, the rewards—greater reach, increased credibility, and innovative solutions—are well worth the effort.

Tying It All Together

These alternative strategies—leveraging digital tools, embracing co-creation, and fostering cross-sector collaborations—reflect the evolving nature of partnerships in a complex world. They challenge traditional notions of transactional relationships, inviting leaders to think creatively and expansively about how they engage with investors and stakeholders.

As you consider these possibilities, reflect on how you can integrate them into your own leadership journey. Are there opportunities to use technology to strengthen transparency and alignment? Could a co-creation model deepen your stakeholders' connection to your mission? How might cross-sector collaborations expand your organization's reach and impact?

By exploring these avenues, you move beyond the conventional, unlocking the full potential of partnerships to drive innovation, resilience, and growth. The future of your organization depends not just on who you partner with, but how you partner—and the possibilities are limitless.

Strengthening the Ties That Drive Growth

Throughout this chapter, we've explored the vital role of partnerships in propelling organizations toward sustainable growth and lasting impact. Partnerships, whether with investors or stakeholders, are more than just functional arrangements—they are relational investments that shape the trajectory of a business. By cultivating trust, aligning with shared goals, and fostering open communication, leaders can transform these relationships into dynamic forces that amplify resilience, innovation, and success.

The metaphor introduced earlier—a network of interconnected bridges—reminds us that partnerships are not static structures. They are living, evolving connections that require care and maintenance. Each bridge you build, whether with a major investor or a key community stakeholder, strengthens the path toward your organization's goals. Neglect the bridges, and the journey becomes fraught with obstacles. Nurture them, and they can carry the weight of your boldest aspirations.

Key Insights to Take Forward

- Trust as the Foundation: Transparency, authenticity, and consistent communication form the bedrock of any successful partnership.

- Shared Vision and Reciprocity: Aligning goals and creating mutual value elevate partnerships from transactional to transformative.
- Adaptability and Innovation: Embracing new tools and strategies—such as digital platforms, co-creation models, and cross-sector collaborations—ensures partnerships remain relevant and impactful.

Strong partnerships are built on intentional leadership. They demand a commitment to understanding your partners' motivations, aligning those with your organizational vision, and navigating the inevitable complexities with empathy and strategic clarity. They are not without their challenges, but the rewards—trust, collaboration, and shared growth—make the effort worthwhile.

Examining Your Own Partnerships

As we close this chapter, take a moment to reflect on the partnerships you are cultivating in your own leadership journey:

- Are you approaching your relationships with investors and stakeholders as dynamic collaborations rather than transactions?
- How transparent are you in sharing both the successes and challenges of your organization's journey?
- Do your partnerships reflect a shared vision and a commitment to mutual success?
- Are you exploring innovative ways to engage and collaborate with your stakeholders?

Your partnerships are not merely tools for achieving goals—they are the very foundation upon which your organization's resilience and growth are built. By prioritizing these relationships, you lay the groundwork for a future filled with opportunity, impact, and purpose.

As we transition into the next chapter, consider how these lessons might shape your approach to leadership at every level. Partnerships are bridges—but you are the architect. How will you design the connections that define your organization's legacy?

Chapter 15

Sustaining Growth Momentum in Changing Markets

"The only constant in today's business environment is change. Leaders who can adapt while staying focused on their mission are the ones who thrive."

For leaders in scale-up organizations, the challenge of sustaining growth often feels deeply personal. It's not just about the numbers or the strategy—it's about the pressure of keeping the dream alive in a world that's constantly shifting. Growth can be exhilarating, but when the pace of change accelerates, it's easy to feel like you're trying to run uphill in a rainstorm, carrying the weight of expectations, responsibilities, and an uncertain future all at once.

Let me tell you a story. A few years ago, I sat down with the CEO of a fast-growing company. She had built something remarkable from the ground up—a product that was solving real problems and a team that believed in her vision. But as we talked, it was clear that the joy of building had been replaced by the fear of losing momentum. "It feels like we're on a treadmill that keeps speeding up," she said. "If I slow down for even a second, I'm afraid everything will fall apart."

Her words struck a chord because they captured a truth many leaders are reluctant to admit: sustaining growth isn't just about the business; it's about the leader. It's about their ability to adapt, to make hard decisions, and to show up with clarity and courage in the face of uncertainty. It's about balancing the demands of agility and focus, innovation and stability, ambition and patience.

Markets are unpredictable—technology advances, customer preferences shift, and economic conditions evolve. What worked yesterday won't necessarily work tomorrow. Leaders who succeed in sustaining growth understand this. They don't cling to what's familiar; they embrace the discomfort of change. They lean into the tension between moving fast and staying grounded, finding a rhythm that allows their organizations to thrive even when the world feels chaotic.

This chapter is about navigating that tension. It's about understanding how to maintain momentum in changing markets without losing sight of what matters most. Together, we'll explore the research on what drives sustained growth, introduce frameworks to help you navigate uncertainty, and share stories of leaders who've faced the storm and found a way through.

But before we dive into strategies and examples, I want to ask you this: What does momentum mean to you? Is it a relentless push forward, or is it the ability to keep moving with intention, even when the winds of change blow hard? As you reflect on this question, remember that growth isn't just about what you achieve—it's about who you become in the process. Let's explore how you can lead with courage, clarity, and resilience, ensuring that your organization doesn't just survive in changing markets, but thrives.

Key Factors for Sustaining Growth in Changing Markets

The ability to sustain growth amidst shifting market conditions is a hallmark of enduring organizations. Research consistently highlights three critical factors that enable scale-ups to navigate uncertainty and maintain momentum: market adaptability, customer-centric innovation, and agile leadership. These elements work in tandem, creating a resilient foundation that allows organizations to respond effectively to change while staying true to their core mission.

Market Adaptability: Staying Ahead of Change

A study by McKinsey revealed that adaptable companies—those capable of rapidly adjusting their strategies and operations in response to external shifts—are 2.5 times more likely to outperform their peers in terms of revenue growth. Market adaptability involves more than reacting to change; it requires proactive anticipation of trends and the agility to pivot when necessary.

Consider the experience of Zara, the global fashion retailer renowned for its "fast fashion" model. When customer preferences began shifting toward sustainability, Zara didn't resist the change. Instead, it adapted its supply chain to include sustainable materials and introduced repair and recycling programs. This proactive approach allowed Zara to remain relevant while deepening customer loyalty, demonstrating the power of adaptability in sustaining growth.

Customer-Centric Innovation: Aligning with Evolving Needs

Harvard Business Review research emphasizes that organizations prioritizing customer-centric innovation are better positioned to sustain momentum. By aligning product and service offerings with evolving customer needs, companies not only maintain relevance but also create opportunities for differentiation.

Take the example of Spotify. As music consumption transitioned from downloads to streaming, Spotify didn't just offer a platform for listening—it introduced personalized playlists and data-driven recommendations. These innovations kept the platform ahead of competitors and reinforced its position as a market leader, showing that deep customer insights can fuel sustained growth even in highly competitive industries.

Agile Leadership: Guiding Through Uncertainty

Agility at the leadership level is critical for sustaining growth in changing markets. Bain & Company's analysis of top-performing scale-ups found that organizations led by agile leaders—those who foster experimentation, empower their teams, and make informed yet swift decisions—are significantly more resilient during periods of upheaval.

For instance, during the COVID-19 pandemic, many restaurant chains struggled to stay afloat. In contrast, companies like Domino's Pizza thrived by leveraging agile leadership. Domino's quickly pivoted to enhance its delivery capabilities, introduced contactless solutions, and doubled down on digital platforms. The result was not only survival but record-breaking sales, underscoring the importance of leadership adaptability in uncertain times.

Tying It Together

These three factors—market adaptability, customer-centric innovation, and agile leadership—form the foundation for sustaining growth in dynamic environments. They emphasize the importance of being proactive rather than reactive, deeply understanding customer needs, and fostering a leadership style that thrives on flexibility and experimentation.

As we move into the next section, we'll explore actionable frameworks that translate these insights into practical strategies for leaders of scale-up organizations. How can you anticipate market shifts while maintaining focus on your long-term mission? What frameworks can help you align innovation, adaptability, and leadership to ensure sustained growth? Let's delve into the tools that will enable you to thrive in changing markets.

Using The ADAPT Approach

Navigating changing markets requires more than intuition—it demands a structured approach that empowers leaders to assess, adjust, and advance with clarity. The **ADAPT** framework—Analyze, Design, Act, Pivot, Thrive—provides a roadmap for sustaining growth in dynamic environments. Each step focuses on aligning strategy with resilience, enabling organizations to respond effectively to uncertainty while maintaining momentum.

Analyse: Understanding the Landscape

The foundation of adaptability lies in understanding. Leaders must assess internal strengths and weaknesses, external opportunities, and potential threats. This phase involves deep analysis of market trends, customer needs, and competitor actions.

Consider a technology company preparing to launch a new product in an increasingly competitive industry. By analysing customer feedback and industry reports, the company identifies a gap in user-friendly software solutions for small businesses. This insight not only shapes its product design but also ensures that its offering aligns with real market demands.

Design: Creating Flexible Strategies

Once the landscape is clear, leaders must design strategies that are both ambitious and adaptable. Flexibility doesn't mean a lack of focus; it means building plans with contingencies and options for recalibration.

An example is Patagonia, the outdoor apparel company. As sustainability became a dominant customer priority, Patagonia's leadership designed strategies that embedded environmental stewardship into every aspect of its operations. This included developing sustainable product lines and committing to transparent supply chain practices. The company's ability to design flexible strategies allowed it to lead the market rather than react to it.

Act: Executing with Purpose

Strategies are only as effective as their execution. Acting decisively, with clear goals and accountability, ensures that plans translate into tangible results. In this phase, communication and alignment across teams are critical.

Take the example of Nando's, the global restaurant chain, which adapted quickly to shifting consumer preferences during the pandemic. By acting swiftly to enhance digital ordering and delivery capabilities, the company maintained customer engagement and revenue streams, even as traditional dining options declined.

Pivot: Embracing Change

No plan is immune to disruption. The ability to pivot—adjusting course when new data or circumstances arise—is what differentiates resilient organizations from those that falter. Pivoting is not about abandoning strategy but refining it in response to evolving realities.

During its early years, Slack started as a gaming company. When its initial product struggled to gain traction, the leadership recognized an opportunity in its internal communication platform. By pivoting its focus to this tool, Slack transformed into a global leader in workplace collaboration, demonstrating the power of adaptability.

Thrive: Sustaining Growth

The final step in the ADAPT framework is about more than surviving change—it's about thriving because of it. Thriving organizations leverage their adaptability to build lasting competitive advantages, deepen customer loyalty, and fuel innovation.

For instance, LEGO's journey from near bankruptcy in the early 2000s to becoming one of the world's most valuable toy brands illustrates thriving through adaptability. By reevaluating its product lines, engaging customers through digital innovation, and streamlining operations, LEGO not only recovered but set new benchmarks for growth.

A Roadmap for Resilient Growth

The ADAPT framework is not a one-time solution—it's a mindset and a process. By continuously analyzing the environment, designing flexible strategies, acting with purpose, pivoting when needed, and striving to thrive, leaders can navigate uncertainty while building sustainable momentum.

As you reflect on this framework, consider the areas where your organization excels and those where greater adaptability might unlock new opportunities. How well does your current strategy align with the dynamic nature of your market? The answers may hold the key to your organization's next phase of growth.

Sustaining Growth in Changing Markets

Zhang Yiming, the visionary behind ByteDance, offers a masterclass in sustaining growth amidst volatile markets. ByteDance, the parent company of TikTok, has navigated rapid expansion and intense scrutiny while redefining how users engage with digital content globally.

The challenge was immense: scaling a platform in an industry dominated by tech giants like Facebook and YouTube, while adapting to diverse regulatory environments and cultural nuances across markets. Early on, Zhang recognized that sustaining ByteDance's growth required two key strategies: relentless innovation and adaptability to market dynamics.

ByteDance invested heavily in advanced AI systems, allowing the platform to deliver highly personalized content. This not only set TikTok apart from competitors but also created a level of user engagement that became its hallmark. Beyond technology, Zhang led the company with a sharp focus on localization. By tailoring TikTok's content and features to resonate with specific regions, ByteDance ensured its relevance across disparate markets.

However, success didn't come without obstacles. TikTok faced significant regulatory challenges, particularly in the U.S. and India. Instead of retreating, Zhang demonstrated resilience by pivoting strategies, enhancing transparency, and fostering partnerships to address concerns. These decisions not only mitigated immediate risks but solidified ByteDance's position as a global leader in its field.

Zhang's leadership exemplifies the principles of agility, customer-centric innovation, and resilience. His ability to anticipate market trends, invest in scalable technologies, and adapt swiftly to external pressures underscores the importance of combining vision with flexibility to sustain growth.

Ren Zhengfei, the founder of Huawei, has built one of the world's largest telecommunications companies, despite facing immense geopolitical and economic pressures. Huawei's journey serves as a compelling example of how organizations can maintain momentum by doubling down on innovation and leveraging strategic partnerships.

In the face of trade restrictions and supply chain disruptions, Huawei's growth trajectory could have faltered. Instead, Ren focused on fostering internal resilience. The company accelerated its investments in R&D, developing proprietary technologies that reduced reliance on external suppliers. By prioritizing innovation, Huawei launched competitive products like its 5G solutions, solidifying its leadership in telecommunications despite external headwinds.

Ren also understood the value of building strong relationships with key stakeholders. Huawei expanded collaborations with governments, academic institutions, and local industries, positioning itself as an indispensable partner in global technology ecosystems. This emphasis on stakeholder trust enabled Huawei to maintain its market position, even as it faced significant challenges.

The resilience demonstrated by Ren and Huawei reflects the principles discussed in this chapter: adaptability, long-term vision, and the ability to pivot without losing focus on the core mission. Through strategic investments and stakeholder engagement, Ren ensured Huawei not only weathered storms but emerged stronger.

Lessons for Sustained Growth

The stories of Zhang Yiming and Ren Zhengfei offer invaluable lessons for leaders aiming to sustain growth in changing markets. Both exemplify the importance of innovation, adaptability, and relationship-building in navigating complex landscapes. Their journeys show that sustaining momentum requires not only responding to immediate challenges but also anticipating and preparing for the opportunities that lie ahead.

As you reflect on these examples, consider the following: How can you invest in resilience within your organization? What steps can you take to adapt proactively to market shifts? By embracing these principles, you too can lead your organization toward sustainable, unstoppable growth in even the most dynamic environments.

Balancing Agility with Strategic Focus

Leadership in scale-up organizations often feels like navigating a tightrope. On one side lies the need for agility—the ability to pivot, innovate, and respond swiftly to changing markets. On the other is strategic focus—the discipline to stay aligned with long-term goals, avoiding distractions that can dilute efforts. Balancing these forces is no small task, yet it is essential for sustaining growth momentum.

The Dilemma: Agility vs. Strategic Focus

Imagine a mid-sized tech company, Synergia Solutions, at a pivotal moment in its journey. Synergia has carved out a niche in developing software solutions for remote work. As the pandemic-era boom in demand subsides, the company faces a choice: Should it invest heavily in diversifying its product line to capitalize on adjacent market opportunities, or should it refine its existing offerings to build deeper loyalty among its core customer base?

The leadership team is divided. The CEO advocates for agility, seeing diversification as a way to mitigate risks in a cooling market. The COO, however, warns against spreading the team too thin, arguing for a laser-focused strategy to solidify their position in their existing niche.

Contrasting Approaches and Consequences

The CEO's approach initially leads to a flurry of innovation. New product lines are launched, and Synergia captures attention in adjacent markets. However, the rapid diversification stretches resources, creating inconsistencies in product quality and support. As core customers begin to feel neglected, retention rates decline, eroding the company's once-strong foundation.

In contrast, the COO's approach prioritizes deepening relationships with existing customers. By enhancing core offerings and improving service delivery, Synergia reinforces its reputation as a reliable partner. While the company misses out on short-term opportunities in adjacent markets, its loyal customer base drives steady revenue and provides a platform for sustainable growth.

Finding the Balance

This story illustrates the complexities of leadership in changing markets. Neither agility nor focus alone guarantees success—it's the balance between the two that defines resilient organizations. Leaders who can adapt without losing sight of their vision are better positioned to navigate uncertainty while maintaining momentum.

Reflective Questions for Leaders

As you consider your own leadership approach, reflect on these questions:

- When faced with new opportunities, how do you evaluate whether they align with your organization's core mission?
- Are there areas where agility has diluted your focus, and how can you recalibrate?
- How can you empower your team to remain flexible while staying committed to long-term goals?

Balancing agility and strategic focus is not a one-time decision—it's an ongoing practice of intentional leadership. By cultivating the ability to pivot with purpose, you can guide your organization through change, ensuring that momentum is not only sustained but accelerated.

Exploring Alternative Strategies for Sustained Momentum

In a world where markets shift with unprecedented speed, the ability to explore and implement alternative strategies becomes a crucial element of sustained growth. Leaders who embrace innovative approaches not only position their organizations for resilience but also unlock new opportunities for long-term success. This section explores three strategies that can transform the way scale-up organizations maintain momentum: leveraging predictive analytics, fostering partnerships for market innovation, and adopting sustainable growth practices.

Leveraging Predictive Analytics: Seeing Around the Corner

Imagine a retailer preparing for an uncertain holiday season. Consumer preferences are evolving, supply chain disruptions loom, and competition is fierce. By utilizing predictive analytics, the retailer analyzes historical trends, customer behavior data, and market signals to forecast demand with remarkable precision. This insight allows them to optimize inventory, tailor marketing campaigns, and ensure timely delivery, creating a competitive edge.

Predictive analytics empowers organizations to move from reactive to proactive decision-making. By harnessing advanced data models and AI, leaders can anticipate market trends, identify potential risks, and allocate resources more effectively. Companies like Amazon have long used predictive analytics to fine-tune operations, ensuring they remain steps ahead of competitors. For scale-ups, adopting this approach can mean the difference between stagnation and sustained momentum.

Fostering Partnerships for Market Innovation: The Power of Collaboration

Growth often accelerates when organizations collaborate to expand their capabilities and reach. Consider the case of a renewable energy start-up teaming up with a global automotive company to develop cutting-edge electric vehicle batteries. The partnership enables both organizations to leverage complementary expertise, share risks, and accelerate time-to-market for innovative solutions.

Strategic partnerships can unlock growth in ways that might be unattainable through solo efforts. Collaborating with other organizations—whether through joint ventures, co-creation initiatives, or cross-sector alliances—can foster innovation, deepen market penetration, and enhance brand credibility. For scale-up leaders, building partnerships with aligned goals ensures shared success and adaptability in dynamic markets.

Adopting Sustainable Growth Practices: Building for the Future

Sustainability is no longer just a value-driven consideration; it's a strategic imperative. Companies that embed sustainable practices into their growth strategies are better positioned to thrive in markets increasingly shaped by environmental, social, and governance (ESG) considerations.

For example, IKEA has committed to becoming a fully circular business by 2030, designing products with reusability and recyclability in mind. This commitment not only aligns with consumer values but also secures long-term resilience by reducing dependency on finite resources. Scale-up organizations can similarly adopt sustainable growth practices, ensuring that their business models are adaptable and future-proofed in the face of global challenges.

Bringing It Together

These strategies—predictive analytics, partnerships for innovation, and sustainable growth practices—illustrate the expansive possibilities available to leaders navigating changing markets. Each offers a pathway to resilience, adaptability, and sustained success.

As you consider these approaches, reflect on their potential within your organization. What role could predictive analytics play in enhancing your decision-making? Which partnerships might accelerate your growth trajectory? How can sustainability become a cornerstone of your strategy?

Sustaining momentum requires more than perseverance; it demands a willingness to embrace new ideas and reimagine what's possible. By exploring these alternative strategies, leaders can not only navigate change but thrive within it, setting the stage for enduring growth in any market landscape.

Sustaining Momentum in Changing Markets

As we close this chapter on sustaining growth momentum in changing markets, it's clear that adaptability and resilience are not just desirable qualities but essential strategic levers. The organizations that thrive in dynamic environments are those that embrace change as an opportunity rather than a threat, constantly aligning their actions with their vision while staying flexible enough to pivot when needed.

Key Insights for Sustained Momentum

Throughout this chapter, we've explored how organizations can harness adaptability and resilience to maintain their growth trajectory. From leveraging predictive analytics to fostering collaborative partnerships and embedding sustainable practices, the strategies shared illustrate that the path to sustained momentum is multifaceted. Success comes from not only anticipating change but also proactively shaping it through informed decisions and innovative approaches.

The **ADAPT** framework serves as a practical guide, emphasizing the need to analyze changing landscapes, design flexible strategies, act decisively, pivot when required, and ultimately thrive. Real-world examples like Zhang Yiming's ByteDance and Ren Zhengfei's Huawei underscore how these principles come to life in practice, offering lessons for any leader seeking to sustain growth in turbulent times.

Calls to Action

Sustaining momentum is a journey, not a destination. It requires constant reflection and recalibration. As you think about your own organization, consider the following:

- Resilience as a Priority: Are you cultivating a culture of resilience that empowers your team to navigate uncertainty with confidence?

- Strategic Alignment: How well do your current initiatives align with your long-term vision and market dynamics?

- Adaptability in Action: Are you creating systems that enable your organization to pivot without losing focus on your core mission?

By embedding adaptability and resilience into your leadership approach, you can ensure that your organization not only survives but thrives, regardless of external challenges.

Reflect and Refocus

Before moving forward, take a moment to reflect:

- How do you currently respond to market changes? Are your strategies reactive or proactive?

- In what ways can you foster greater resilience within your team and processes?

- What steps can you take to balance agility with long-term focus in your leadership decisions?

These questions are not just for contemplation but for action. Use them to identify areas where your organization can strengthen its foundation for sustained momentum.

Looking Ahead

As we move into the next chapter, we will delve into the essential elements of creating a legacy through leadership. The principles of adaptability and resilience you've explored here will continue to be central, serving as the bridge between navigating the present and shaping a meaningful future. Let this chapter be a call to lead with both vision and agility, ensuring that your organization not only keeps pace with change but drives it forward with purpose.

Chapter 16

Beyond Growth: Evolving Leadership for Lasting Success

"True leadership isn't just about growing a business—it's about evolving in ways that leave a lasting impact on others."

Legacy. It's a word that carries the weight of permanence, of the footprints we leave behind. Yet for many leaders, it feels like a distant horizon—something to consider when the work slows down or the successes accumulate. But here's the truth: we are shaping our legacy every day, whether we're intentional about it or not. The way we show up in a meeting, the decisions we make under pressure, the values we uphold when no one is watching—these moments weave the threads of our leadership legacy.

Let me take you back to a conversation I had with a seasoned entrepreneur whose company had just crossed the billion-dollar valuation mark. He looked successful on every surface level—industry accolades, financial growth, a workforce that admired him. But over coffee, he leaned in and said something that stuck with me: *"I'm proud of what we've built, but sometimes I wonder…am I proud of how we've built it? When my name comes up in the years ahead, will people talk about what we accomplished or how we treated people along the way?"*

That question—*how will we be remembered?*—is at the heart of this chapter. Legacy isn't something we write into our company values statement or reserve for grand gestures. It's the quiet accumulation of our values, actions, and the ripples they create. It's the courage to ask hard questions about the kind of impact we want to leave and to take consistent steps to align our work with those answers.

As leaders of scale-up organizations, the pace is relentless, the decisions are complex, and the stakes are high. It's easy to fall into the trap of measuring success purely by quarterly earnings, market share, or the latest innovation. But building a legacy isn't about sacrificing results—it's about broadening the definition of success to include the kind of impact that endures long after we've left the room.

In this chapter, we'll explore what it takes to lead with a legacy mindset—how to prioritize long-term impact without losing sight of short-term goals. We'll uncover how values-driven leadership builds trust, fosters purpose, and creates organizations that are not just profitable but deeply meaningful. Through stories of leaders who have left remarkable legacies and research that connects leadership to lasting impact, we'll look at how to navigate this journey in a way that feels both ambitious and authentic.

So, as we embark on this final chapter together, let me ask you this: If your leadership were a story, what would you want the last chapter to say? Not just about what you achieved, but about who you were, what you stood for, and how you made others feel. Because legacy isn't a final destination—it's the map we create every day with our actions, our decisions, and our unwavering commitment to something bigger than ourselves. Let's draw that map with intention.

The Role of Leadership in Shaping Legacy

When we think about legacy, it's easy to conjure images of towering achievements or iconic leaders whose impact reshaped industries or society. But the research tells a more human story—one where legacy is less about the size of our achievements and more about the depth of our impact.

Studies from *Harvard Business Review* and *Stanford Social Innovation Review* consistently highlight that values-driven leadership is the cornerstone of lasting legacies. Leaders who align their actions with their values foster trust, deepen connections, and inspire sustained purpose within their organizations. They create a culture where the work isn't just about transactions but transformations—of people, systems, and communities.

In one landmark study, researchers found that organizations led by purpose-driven leaders were 50% more likely to retain top talent and 70% more likely to outperform their peers over a 10-year period. The reason? Employees weren't just working for a pay check—they were connected to something larger, something meaningful. When leaders articulate a clear vision rooted in shared values, they build trust that doesn't just bind teams together—it ripples outward to customers, investors, and entire communities.

A striking example comes from the global non-profit sector. A study by Bain & Company showed that non-profits with leaders who prioritized collaborative, values-driven leadership achieved significantly higher community engagement and long-term impact. These leaders didn't just focus on immediate goals—they nurtured relationships, modelled empathy, and built systems that aligned daily actions with their mission.

But the power of legacy isn't confined to non-profits or social enterprises. Consider Bernard Arnault's LVMH, where a commitment to craftsmanship and innovation has elevated luxury brands into cultural icons. His leadership has shown that legacy is built by threading long-term vision into every aspect of an organization—from the way artisans create products to how partnerships are formed. It's about intention at every level.

At its heart, legacy-building is deeply relational. Studies highlight that trust is the foundation of lasting leadership impact. Trust isn't built in grand gestures or polished statements—it's earned in moments of vulnerability, consistency, and courage. Studies have shown that, when leaders embrace their humanity—acknowledging uncertainty, owning mistakes, and listening deeply—they create spaces where people feel valued and seen. And when people feel seen, they show up more fully, more creatively, and with a deeper commitment to shared goals.

The idea of legacy also intersects with purpose. Research shows that purpose-driven organizations—those where leaders embed values into strategy, operations, and culture—are not only more resilient in changing markets but also more innovative. Purpose becomes a guiding light, allowing leaders to navigate uncertainty with clarity and align their actions with long-term goals.

As we move forward in this chapter, we'll explore how these insights translate into actionable strategies. We'll look at frameworks for embedding values into leadership, creating ripple effects that extend far beyond an individual's tenure. Because legacy isn't just something we leave behind—it's something we actively create, moment by moment.

The question for all of us isn't just, What will people remember about my leadership? It's, What will endure because of it? Let's take a deeper look at how to lead with that kind of intention.

Using The LEGACY Framework

When we talk about legacy, it's tempting to think of it as a distant milestone—a plaque on the wall or a story told long after we're gone. But legacy isn't created in the distance. It's built here and now, through the everyday moments where our values, decisions, and actions align to shape the world around us. To make this process tangible, let's explore the LEGACY framework:

- Listen
- Empower
- Guide
- Act
- Connect
- Yield

Each element of this framework offers a pathway for leaders to move from intention to impact, creating a legacy that's not just remembered but lived.

Listen: Start with Curiosity

Legacy begins with listening—deep, intentional listening. It's about tuning in not just to what's being said but to what's unsaid. It's about understanding the needs, fears, and aspirations of your team, your community, your family and yourself.

Example in Action:

When Ratan Tata took the helm of the Tata Group, he spent his early days meeting employees at all levels and listening to their stories. From factory workers to executives, he sought to understand their challenges and dreams. This practice of listening informed his decisions for years to come, allowing him to lead with empathy and precision.

How You Can Apply It: Begin your next meeting or strategy session with open-ended questions:

- What do we most need to address?
- How are we showing up for each other?
- What's getting in the way of our shared purpose?

Empower: Trust Others to Lead

Legacy isn't built by one person—it's a shared endeavour. Empowerment means trusting others to take ownership of their roles, equipping them with the tools and authority they need to succeed.

Example in Action: At LVMH, Bernard Arnault fosters empowerment by giving creative directors autonomy to innovate within their brands. This balance of trust and accountability has allowed iconic brands like Louis Vuitton and Dior to thrive.

How You Can Apply It: Identify an area where your team could benefit from greater ownership. Offer them not just responsibility but the resources and trust to make meaningful decisions.

Guide: Lead with Vision and Purpose

A legacy leader provides guidance by articulating a clear vision rooted in shared values. This isn't about micromanaging—it's about offering a compass for the journey ahead.

Example in Action: When Satya Nadella became CEO of Microsoft, he guided the organization with a renewed focus on empathy and a "learn-it-all" culture. His leadership redefined Microsoft's purpose, fostering innovation and collaboration at every level.

How You Can Apply It: Take time to articulate your vision to your team. How does it connect to your shared purpose? What story are you writing together?

Act: Align Actions with Intentions

Legacy is shaped not by what we say but by what we do. Acting with intention means ensuring that every decision, every policy, and every initiative aligns with the values we claim to uphold.

Example in Action: Patagonia's decision to donate 100% of its Black Friday sales to environmental causes wasn't just a marketing move—it was a reflection of their core values. This bold action solidified their legacy as a purpose-driven brand.

How You Can Apply It: Reflect on a recent decision you made. Did it align with your values and your organization's mission? If not, what can you do differently next time?

Connect: Build Relationships That Endure

Legacy lives in relationships—how we connect with those we lead, serve, and partner with. Connection fosters trust, and trust is the foundation of lasting impact.

Example in Action:

Strive Masiyiwa, founder of Econet, emphasizes the power of relationships in building a sustainable telecommunications empire across Africa. By nurturing partnerships with communities and governments, he created a network of trust that fuels growth and innovation.

How You Can Apply It: Invest in your relationships. Reach out to a colleague or partner to ask: How can I better support you? How can we strengthen our connection?

Yield: Make Space for Others to Thrive

The final piece of legacy leadership is yielding—creating space for others to grow, lead, and carry the mission forward. This isn't about stepping back entirely; it's about recognizing that true impact is shared.

Example in Action: When Gina Rinehart, one of Australia's most prominent entrepreneurs, transitioned leadership responsibilities within Hancock Prospecting, she ensured the next generation was prepared to uphold the company's values while driving innovation.

How You Can Apply It: Consider your current role. How are you creating opportunities for others to lead? What legacy are you enabling others to build?

Bringing It All Together

The LEGACY framework isn't a checklist—it's a mindset. It's an invitation to lead with purpose, clarity, and compassion, building something that lasts far beyond your tenure. As you reflect on your own leadership, ask yourself:

- How am I listening to those I lead?
- What actions am I taking to empower and guide my team?
- Am I aligning my decisions with the values I hope to pass on?

Legacy isn't built in one grand moment—it's crafted in the choices we make every day. What will yours be?

People Building Legacies That Last

Legacy isn't a monument—it's the ripple effect of our actions, values, and leadership. In the world of business and impact, there are leaders whose lives and work exemplify the art of leaving an enduring mark. Let's explore the journeys of two such leaders: **Strive Masiyiwa**, the visionary founder of Econet, and Arianna Huffington, whose work transcends the traditional boundaries of success to redefine well-being and purpose in leadership.

Strive Masiyiwa: Empowering a Continent Through Connection

Strive Masiyiwa didn't just build a telecommunications empire—he reshaped the way millions of people across Africa access opportunities. Econet, which started as a bold idea to provide mobile connectivity, became a vehicle for social and economic transformation.

Masiyiwa's journey was far from smooth. He faced fierce opposition from government regulators in Zimbabwe during Econet's early years, enduring years of legal battles just to launch the company. Many would have given up, but Masiyiwa's commitment to his vision was unwavering. His leadership was deeply rooted in a sense of purpose: connecting people to each other and to opportunities that could change their lives.

His strategy wasn't just about building towers or rolling out infrastructure; it was about creating partnerships with communities, governments, and global organizations. By combining business acumen with a clear social mission, Masiyiwa extended Econet's impact far beyond connectivity. Initiatives like the Higherlife Foundation, which provides scholarships and support to underprivileged children, demonstrate how his legacy is woven into every layer of his work.

Reflections for Leaders: Masiyiwa's story challenges us to think beyond quarterly results. It invites us to ask: How can we embed purpose into every decision we make? What partnerships can we cultivate to extend our impact?

Arianna Huffington: Redefining Success Through Well-Being

For Arianna Huffington, legacy isn't just about what we achieve; it's about how we achieve it. After building a media empire with The Huffington Post, Huffington experienced a personal wake-up call when she collapsed from exhaustion. That moment became a turning point—not just for her life but for the way she would lead and inspire others.

Huffington founded Thrive Global, a company dedicated to ending the epidemic of workplace burnout. Her mission? To shift the narrative of success from relentless hustle to a model that values well-being, mindfulness, and balance. Through Thrive, Huffington has helped leaders and organizations reimagine productivity, showing that prioritizing health and purpose leads to more sustainable and impactful success.

Her approach is deeply personal and profoundly actionable. By sharing her own vulnerabilities, Huffington has created a space where leaders feel permission to embrace their humanity. She reminds us that legacy isn't just about what we leave behind—it's about how we show up today.

Reflections for Leaders: Huffington's story asks us to reconsider: What does success really look like? Are we prioritizing the well-being of ourselves and our teams? How can redefining productivity help us create a more enduring impact?

Tying It All Together: The Power of Purpose-Driven Leadership

Strive Masiyiwa and Arianna Huffington offer two very different paths to legacy, yet their stories converge on a common theme: leadership rooted in values, resilience, and a deep commitment to making a difference.

Their journeys remind us that legacy is less about perfection and more about persistence. It's about asking ourselves hard questions, taking bold actions, and staying true to a purpose greater than ourselves.

As you reflect on their stories, consider:

- What is the legacy you're building in your organization and community?
- How can you align your actions today with the values you hope to leave behind?
- What steps can you take to extend your impact beyond your immediate circle?

The legacies of leaders like Masiyiwa and Huffington inspire us to lead with intention, courage, and compassion. They show us that the mark we leave isn't just about what we build—it's about how we make others feel, grow, and thrive in the process.

Balancing Short-Term Results with Long-Term Impact

Leadership often feels like walking a tightrope. On one side, the urgency of short-term results demands immediate attention—quarterly profits, looming deadlines, or the need to appease stakeholders. On the other side, the enduring pull of long-term impact beckons—decisions that build a legacy, shape culture, and leave something meaningful for future generations. This tension isn't just theoretical; it's the reality every leader faces.

The Tug-of-War Between Now and Later

Imagine a thriving tech startup, led by a dynamic CEO named Maya. Investors are pushing for rapid growth, urging her to scale aggressively to capture market share. Maya knows that hiring quickly could help her meet those goals, but she also recognizes the risk: rushing the process might sacrifice the strong, values-driven culture she has painstakingly built.

In one meeting, Maya's COO presents a plan to onboard 50 new team members within three months. The projected revenue increase is compelling, but Maya can't shake a nagging feeling. "If we grow too fast, will we lose the trust and collaboration that make us special?" she asks. Her leadership team is split—some prioritize the numbers, while others champion the slower, more deliberate approach.

This is the crossroads many leaders find themselves at: the immediate allure of short-term gains versus the patience required for long-term legacy. Choosing one over the other is never easy, and the stakes can feel impossibly high.

Two Contrasting Paths

Leaders often take one of two approaches to this dilemma, each with its own consequences:

1. **The Short-Term Sprint:**

Some leaders lean heavily into the immediate demands. They prioritize quarterly results, meet investor expectations, and focus on scaling fast. While this approach can deliver impressive short-term wins, it often comes at a cost. Teams may experience burnout, cultural cohesion may erode, and decisions driven by urgency may lack alignment with core values.

In Maya's case, choosing this path might mean onboarding the 50 employees quickly, only to find that the team becomes fractured, with new hires struggling to integrate and long-term employees feeling disillusioned. The financial gains may materialize, but at what expense?

2. **The Legacy Lens:**

Other leaders take the long view, prioritizing foundational decisions that align with their values and the future they hope to build. This often requires patience and resilience, especially in the face of external pressures.

For Maya, this approach might involve scaling slower, investing in robust onboarding systems, and ensuring that each new hire aligns with the company's purpose. The immediate growth might be modest, but the cultural integrity and long-term sustainability could position the company for enduring success.

The Hard Truth

Neither path is inherently right or wrong—it's about making choices that align with your values and the legacy you hope to leave. The challenge is recognizing when short-term wins serve the long-term vision and when they undermine it.

Reflective Questions for Leaders

Maya's dilemma invites us all to reflect on our own leadership priorities:

- Are you prioritizing short-term results at the expense of your long-term vision?

- How do your daily decisions align with the legacy you hope to create?

- What pressures—external or internal—are shaping your choices, and how can you navigate them with clarity and courage?

Legacy-driven leadership isn't about avoiding hard decisions; it's about embracing the tension with integrity. It's about balancing the urgent with the enduring, the immediate with the meaningful. And, as Maya learns, it's about staying rooted in purpose, even when the path forward is uncertain.

When we lead with the long view in mind, we don't just build organizations—we build legacies. And that, ultimately, is what transforms leadership from a role we hold to a mark we leave.

Broadening the Path to Legacy

When we think of legacy, it's tempting to envision a single, monumental contribution—a groundbreaking invention, a transformative policy, or a company that redefines an industry. But the truth is, legacy is often built in layers, with each decision, strategy, and action forming the foundation for something enduring. As leaders, expanding our approach to legacy means embracing diverse strategies that amplify impact, stretch across generations, and align deeply with our values.

Fostering Intergenerational Leadership

Imagine a founder who builds a company not just for today but for tomorrow, embedding the seeds of leadership in the next generation. This isn't about succession planning in the traditional sense; it's about mentorship, empowerment, and creating a culture where leadership is a shared responsibility.

Take the example of Ren Zhengfei, the founder of Huawei. Known for his commitment to intergenerational leadership, Ren established a rotating CEO structure, empowering younger leaders to step into decision-making roles. By sharing power, he ensured that the company could sustain its vision even as leadership evolved.

For your own organization, consider these questions:

- How are you preparing emerging leaders to carry forward your mission?
- What structures could you create to foster cross-generational dialogue and collaboration?

By viewing legacy through an intergenerational lens, we recognize that our greatest contribution may be enabling others to lead with courage and clarity.

Leveraging Technology for Social Impact

In a world increasingly defined by digital transformation, technology is one of the most powerful tools for amplifying impact. Leaders who integrate technological innovation into their legacy-building efforts not only enhance their reach but also create scalable solutions for pressing challenges.

Consider the work of Zhang Yiming, the founder of ByteDance, whose platforms like TikTok have not only disrupted the entertainment industry but also created spaces for social awareness and connection. While not without challenges, the potential to leverage technology for education, equity, and empowerment remains immense.

For leaders exploring this path:

- How can technology extend your impact beyond the walls of your organization?
- Are there digital tools that could amplify your mission in ways previously unimaginable?

When aligned with purpose, technology becomes more than a tool—it becomes a bridge to broader impact, helping leaders leave marks that ripple outward.

Embedding Sustainability into Business Practices

Few strategies align as deeply with legacy as sustainability. It's about more than reducing carbon footprints or improving supply chains; it's about redefining success to include the health of the planet and the communities we serve.

Leaders like Mo Ibrahim, who founded Celtel to bring mobile technology to Africa, demonstrate the power of embedding sustainability into business models. His work has not only driven economic growth but also connected millions, transforming lives across the continent. By prioritizing long-term value over short-term gains, he created a legacy that balances profitability with responsibility.

Ask yourself:

- How can sustainability become a core part of your decision-making?
- What practices can you adopt to ensure your impact benefits future generations?

When sustainability becomes integral to leadership, it elevates legacy beyond personal achievement—it becomes a collective gift to those who follow.

Legacy isn't one-dimensional, nor is it confined to a single approach. By fostering intergenerational leadership, leveraging technology, and embedding sustainability, leaders expand the possibilities for what their legacy can be.

These strategies challenge us to think beyond individual success and consider the systems, values, and ripple effects we set in motion. They remind us that legacy isn't just about what we achieve but how we empower others, adapt to changing times, and ensure our impact lasts far beyond our tenure.

As we close this chapter, reflect on these possibilities:

- What areas of your leadership could benefit from a fresh perspective or expanded approach?
- How can you ensure that your legacy aligns not only with your vision but also with the evolving needs of the world around you?

Legacy-driven leadership is about building bridges—between generations, industries, and ideals. It's about creating a path that others can follow, adapt, and expand upon, ensuring that the work we do today continues to make a difference tomorrow.

The Leadership Legacy: Creating Impact That Endures

Legacies are not accidental. They are built deliberately, moment by moment, decision by decision. As we've explored throughout this chapter, a legacy is the culmination of our values, our actions, and the way we lead—both in public and in private. It's not confined to what we achieve but how we achieve it, and the ripples we create in the lives of others.

One of the most profound truths about legacy is that it's never about perfection. It's about intention. The stories of visionary leaders who shaped industries, communities, and lives remind us that it's the daily choices—the ones that often feel small or inconsequential—that shape the greater story we leave behind. The way we listen, empower, and invest in others becomes the scaffolding of a legacy that endures far beyond any singular accomplishment.

Throughout this chapter, we've discussed the frameworks and strategies that enable leaders to align their values with their actions. We've seen how creating trust, fostering meaningful connections, and focusing on sustainable impact can build a leadership legacy that is both authentic and profound. But as we bring this journey to a close, it's essential to recognize that legacy-driven leadership isn't a destination; it's a practice. And like any practice, it requires self-awareness, vulnerability, and an unrelenting commitment to growth.

Reflective Takeaways and Calls to Action

As you reflect on your own leadership journey, consider the threads of your legacy already in motion. What values are evident in the way you lead? Are your decisions today creating the kind of impact you want to be remembered for tomorrow? Legacy is not something we build in hindsight; it's a narrative we shape with intention in the here and now.

To help you deepen this reflection and take meaningful steps forward, consider these guiding questions:

- **Values in Action:** How do your daily decisions reflect your core values? Where might there be gaps between intention and impact?

- **Ripple Effects:** What kind of emotional and professional impact are you leaving on the people you lead? How do you want them to describe your influence years from now?

- **Sustainable Impact:** Are the strategies and structures you're building today designed to outlast your tenure? What steps can you take to ensure your work creates lasting value?

- **Courage in Leadership:** Where do you need to lean into vulnerability, take a stand, or make a difficult decision to align your actions with your vision for the future?

Drawing the Final Map

As this chapter comes to a close, it's important to remember that leadership is both a privilege and a responsibility. We have the power to shape not only our organizations but also the lives of those within them. That power requires us to ask the hard questions, to embrace the moments of discomfort, and to keep showing up with the courage to lead authentically.

Your legacy isn't written in the grand gestures or singular victories; it's etched in the moments you choose to listen, to act with integrity, and to make decisions that honour something greater than yourself. It's a map you create one step at a time, with each conversation, each decision, and each act of leadership.

As you step into the final chapter of this book, I invite you to carry this truth with you: The story of your leadership legacy isn't something that happens to you; it's something you write with every choice you make. So write boldly, write with intention, and write in a way that makes an indelible mark—not just on the world, but on the hearts and lives of those you lead.

Conclusion

Your Roadmap to Lasting Impact and Unstoppable Growth

Opening Reflection: Revisiting the Journey

"Growth is not a destination; it's a journey that requires resilience, adaptability, and a commitment to continuous evolution."

As we reach the end of this book, it's worth taking a moment to reflect on the journey we've explored together. We've walked through the stages of growth, from building scalable systems and fostering innovation to sustaining momentum in changing markets and building a culture of purpose-driven leadership. This book has been about more than just strategies—it's been a guide to becoming the kind of leader who can navigate the challenges of scale, inspire teams, and create lasting value.

Each chapter has focused on different facets of growth, but the underlying message is universal: building an enduring business requires intentionality, adaptability, and a commitment to values that align with your mission. The strategies and insights shared here are stepping stones for anyone who aspires to lead with purpose, create impact, and, ultimately, leave a legacy that transcends individual success.

The Core Principles for Unstoppable Growth

As you look ahead, let these core principles serve as your guiding compass. Each is a reminder of what it means to lead in a way that promotes both growth and sustainability:

1. **Lead with Purpose**: Purpose is the heart of growth. It's what will keep you grounded in challenging times and inspire those around you to contribute their best.
2. **Adapt with Resilience**: The world is unpredictable, but the ability to adapt with a strong core of resilience allows you to thrive in any environment.
3. **Empower Your People**: Sustainable growth is achieved by unlocking the potential of those around you. Empowerment isn't just a strategy; it's a commitment to building a culture where people can flourish.
4. **Balance Innovation with Consistency**: Innovation fuels growth, but consistency builds trust. Strike a balance between these forces to stay agile while maintaining the core integrity of your brand.
5. **Invest in Continuous Learning**: Growth doesn't stop. Commit to learning—not only as a leader but as an organization. The

more you evolve, the more you can inspire change and growth in those around you.

6. **Focus on Long-Term Impact, Not Just Success**: True growth goes beyond immediate wins; it's about creating something that endures. Let your legacy be defined by the impact you've made on people, industry, and society.

These principles are not mere strategies but a mindset—a way of approaching every decision, challenge, and opportunity. They remind us that growth and leadership are dynamic, requiring us to continually refine, reflect, and re-align with our purpose.

Practical Takeaways and Next Steps

To help you internalize these principles and bring them into your daily practice, here's a set of actionable steps and questions to guide your path forward:

1. **Define Your Non-Negotiables**: Identify three to five core values that will guide your decisions, especially in times of growth. How does each align with your long-term mission?

2. **Empower a Leadership Team**: Reflect on areas where you can delegate more. Who in your organization can you empower to take on a leadership role? Set clear goals and provide resources to help them grow.

3. **Create a Resilience Plan**: Review your contingency plans and assess your organization's adaptability. What systems do you have in place to respond to unexpected changes? Consider implementing regular "Resilience Reviews" to stay prepared.

4. **Launch a Continuous Learning Initiative**: Establish learning opportunities for both yourself and your team. Can you create a

mentorship program or provide access to courses and workshops? Emphasize learning as a core value.

5. **Celebrate Purpose-Driven Wins**: Take time to recognize milestones that align with your mission and impact. How can you reinforce the importance of these achievements within your culture?

These steps are designed to keep you focused on what matters most. They're not just about increasing revenue or market share; they're about nurturing a culture and mindset that sustain your mission, team, and long-term impact.

Vision for the Future: A Call to Continuous Evolution

"The journey doesn't end here—this is just the beginning of what you can achieve."

Growth, by its nature, is ongoing. As you move forward, keep in mind that leadership is an evolving process. You've already demonstrated the drive to scale and grow; now it's about sustaining that momentum and expanding your impact. Embrace the mindset of continuous evolution, not just as a business strategy but as a personal commitment.

The leaders who achieve the most lasting success are those who remain open to change, who learn from each experience, and who constantly refine their approach. This is a journey that will test you, challenge you, and ultimately reward you as you adapt and grow alongside your organization.

Invitation to Engage and Additional Resources

As you continue this journey, remember that you're not alone. This book is only the beginning, and there are resources available to support you as you take these ideas forward. Consider engaging with the following tools and opportunities:

- **Online Growth Diagnostic Tools**: Access personalized insights to evaluate where your organization stands in areas like adaptability, innovation, and resilience.
- **Workshops and Training Modules**: Join live sessions and online courses designed to deepen your understanding of key growth strategies.
- **Community and Networking**: Connect with other leaders who share your values and are on similar growth journeys. These relationships can become a source of inspiration, support, and accountability.

Take advantage of these resources to deepen your knowledge, connect with others, and continuously adapt and grow in alignment with your purpose.

Final Words: Leaving a Legacy of Impact and Inspiration

"The true measure of success isn't just what we achieve; it's the impact we leave behind."

Leadership is about more than meeting metrics and achieving targets. It's about creating something that matters, that resonates with people, and that makes a difference. The principles and strategies in this book are designed to help you do just that—not only to grow your organization but to make a meaningful contribution to the lives of those around you and the communities you serve.

As you move forward, let your focus be on building a legacy of integrity, purpose, and impact. Commit to leading in a way that inspires others to bring their best selves to their work and challenges them to pursue their own path of growth and purpose. Your journey is part of something greater, a ripple effect that extends beyond yourself to inspire, uplift, and drive positive change.

Thank you for taking this journey, for your commitment to growth, and for the impact you will make. Lead with purpose, adapt with resilience, and always remember that the legacy you leave is in the lives you touch and the difference you make.

Bibliography

Foundational Texts on Growth and Scaling

1. **Zook, C., & Allen, J.** (2016). *The Founder's Mentality: How to Overcome the Predictable Crises of Growth.* Harvard Business Review Press.

    o Foundational insights into the predictable crises of growth, supporting themes of resilience and scalability.

2. **Ismail, S., Malone**, M. S., & van Geest, Y. (2020). *Exponential Organizations 2.0: The New Playbook for 10x Growth and Impact.* Diversion Books.

    o Updated insights on building organizations that scale rapidly and sustainably.

3. **Horowitz, B**. (2014). *The Hard Thing About Hard Things: Building a Business When There Are No Easy Answers.* Harper Business.

    o Practical guidance on navigating challenges during growth and leading effectively.

4. **Gerber, M. E.** (2020). *Beyond the E-Myth: The Evolution of an Enterprise.* Harper Business.

    o Focuses on systems essential for sustainable growth, reinforcing strategies for scaling.

5. **Hoffman, R., & Yeh, C.** (2021). *Masters of Scale: Surprising Truths from the World's Most Successful Entrepreneurs.* Currency.

    o Key lessons on scaling businesses, supported by interviews with leading entrepreneurs.

Leadership and Purpose

6. **Sinek, S. (2020**). *The Infinite Game.* Portfolio.

    o Discusses purpose-driven leadership and the benefits of long-term thinking.

7. **Handy, C. (2016).** *The Second Curve: Thoughts on Reinventing Society.* Random House.

    o Explores reinvention and purpose, relevant to sustainable leadership.

8. **Brown, B. (2021).** *Atlas of the Heart: Mapping Meaningful Connection and the Language of Human Experience.* Random House.

    o Examines vulnerability and empathy, core themes in resilient leadership.

9. **Brooks, A. C. (2022).** *From Strength to Strength: Finding Success, Happiness, and Deep Purpose in the Second Half of Life.* Portfolio.

    o A modern take on balancing personal and professional growth for enduring success.

10. **Kouzes, J. M., & Posner, B. Z.** (2017). *The Leadership Challenge: How to Make Extraordinary Things Happen in Organizations.* Jossey-Bass.

- Offers actionable strategies for leading with purpose and building trust.

Innovation, Adaptability, and Resilience

11. **Christensen, C. M., Raynor, M., & McDonald, R.** (2017). *The Innovator's Dilemma: When New Technologies Cause Great Firms to Fail.* Harvard Business Review Press.

- Classic exploration of innovation and adaptability in leadership.

12. **Kahneman, D., Sibony, O., & Sunstein, C. R**. (2021). *Noise: A Flaw in Human Judgment.* Little, Brown Spark.

- Examines judgment, bias, and decision-making in leadership.

13. **Gates, B. (2021).** *How to Avoid a Climate Disaster: The Solutions We Have and the Breakthroughs We Need.* Knopf.

- Focuses on sustainable innovation and its integration into leadership.

14. **Osterwalder, A., & Pigneur, Y.** (2020). *The Invincible Company: How to Constantly Reinvent Your Organization with Inspiration from the World's Best Business Models.* Wiley.

- Examines resilience and adaptability in scaling organizations.

15. **McKeown, G. (2021).** *Effortless: Make It Easier to Do What Matters Most.* Currency.

- Explores simplicity and focus in building resilient systems.

Human Health and Resilient Leadership

16. **Goleman, D. (2020).** *Emotional Intelligence: Why It Can Matter More Than IQ.* Bantam Books.

- Highlights emotional intelligence as a cornerstone of resilient leadership.

17. **Asprey, D. (2021).** *Fast This Way: Burn Fat, Heal Inflammation, and Eat Like the High-Performing Human You Were Meant to Be.* Harper Wave.

- Connects personal health optimization to effective leadership.

18. **Seppälä, E., & Cameron, K. S.** (2021). *The Happiness Track: How to Apply the Science of Happiness to Accelerate Your Success.* HarperOne.

- Discusses well-being and resilience in leadership contexts.

19. **Huffington, A. (2014).** *Thrive: The Third Metric to Redefining Success and Creating a Life of Well-Being, Wisdom, and Wonder.* Harmony.

- Examines the role of health and well-being in sustainable leadership.

20. **Loehr, J., & Schwartz,** T. (2003). *The Power of Full Engagement: Managing Energy, Not Time, Is the Key to High Performance and Personal Renewal.* Free Press.

- Focuses on energy management for resilience and leadership effectiveness.

Funding, Partnerships, and Strategic Planning

21. **Kawasaki, G.** (2020). *Wise Guy: Lessons from a Life.* Portfolio.

- Insights into funding, partnerships, and entrepreneurial growth.

22. **Damodaran, A.** (2021). *Investment Valuation: Tools and Techniques for Determining the Value of Any Asset.* Wiley.

- Comprehensive guide to funding and capital allocation.

23. **Blank, S., & Dorf, B**. (2020). *The Startup Owner's Manual: The Step-By-Step Guide for Building a Great Company.* Wiley.

- Practical advice for funding and scaling businesses.

24. **Cialdini, R. B.** (2021). *Influence, New and Expanded: The Psychology of Persuasion.* Harper Business.

- Updated insights on building investor and stakeholder relationships.

25. **Lerner, J.** (2020). *The Boulevard of Broken Dreams: Why Public Efforts to Boost Entrepreneurship and Venture Capital Have Failed—and What to Do About It.* Princeton University Press.

- Examines strategic funding challenges and solutions.

Additional Influences on Leadership and Legacy

26. **Erhard, W., Jensen, M. C., & Granger, K.** (2020). *Creating Leaders: An Ontological/Phenomenological Model.* Harvard Business School.

- Explores transformative leadership and personal growth.

27. **Pfeffer, J.** (2015). *Leadership BS: Fixing Workplaces and Careers One Truth at a Time.* Harper Business.

- Challenges leadership myths, advocating practical, values-driven leadership.

28. **Brown, T. (2020).** *Change by Design: How Design Thinking Creates New Alternatives for Business and Society.* Harper Business.

- Emphasizes creative problem-solving in leadership.

29. **Senge, P. (2006).** *The Fifth Discipline: The Art & Practice of the Learning Organization.* Currency.

- Examines systems thinking for sustainable growth and leadership.

30. **Olalla, J.** (2021). *The Art of Transformation: How Leadership Can Facilitate Personal and Social Transformation.* Newfield Press.

- Explores transformational leadership and its societal impact.

Case Studies and Leadership Profiles

1. **Nadella, S.** (2017). *Hit Refresh: The Quest to Rediscover Microsoft's Soul and Imagine a Better Future for Everyone.* Harper Business.

    - Chronicles Satya Nadella's leadership in transforming Microsoft's culture, emphasizing empathy and a growth mindset.

2. **Branson, R.** (2011). *Losing My Virginity: How I've Survived, Had Fun, and Made a Fortune Doing Business My Way.* Virgin Books.

    o A personal account of building Virgin into a global brand through bold leadership and calculated risks.

3. **Kapferer, J.-N.** (2019). *The Luxury Strategy: Break the Rules of Marketing to Build Luxury Brands.* Kogan Page.

    o Profiles Bernard Arnault's strategic approach to scaling LVMH into a global luxury conglomerate.

4. **Vance, A.** (2015). *Elon Musk: Tesla, SpaceX, and the Quest for a Fantastic Future.* Ecco.

    o Explores Musk's drive for innovation and resilience across multiple industries.

5. **Iger, R.** (2019). *The Ride of a Lifetime: Lessons Learned from 15 Years as CEO of the Walt Disney Company.* Random House.

    o Details Bob Iger's leadership lessons in transforming Disney into a powerhouse of creativity and acquisition.

6. **Masiyiwa, S.** (2022). *The African Leadership Advantage. Forbes Africa.*

    o Highlights Strive Masiyiwa's visionary leadership in the telecommunications sector and his impact on African entrepreneurship.

7. **Huffington, A.** (2014). *Thrive: The Third Metric to Redefining Success and Creating a Life of Well-Being, Wisdom, and Wonder.* Harmony.

- Shares Arianna Huffington's insights on integrating health and well-being into leadership for sustained impact.

8. **Perkins, M.** (2020). *The Canva Growth Journey. TechCrunch.*

    - Examines Melanie Perkins' leadership in scaling Canva into a global design platform through innovation and inclusivity.

9. **Chesky, B.** (2022). *Leading in Uncertain Times. Harvard Business Review.*

    - Describes Brian Chesky's approach to navigating Airbnb through the pandemic, balancing empathy and strategy.

10. **Tata, R.** (2021). *The Visionary Legacy of Ratan Tata. The Economic Times.*

    - Reflects on Ratan Tata's impact on Indian industry and his commitment to ethical leadership and innovation.

11. **Hastings, R.** (2020). *No Rules Rules: Netflix and the Culture of Reinvention.* Penguin Press.

    - Co-authored by Netflix CEO Reed Hastings, exploring how a culture of freedom and responsibility drove innovation.

12. **Bekker, K.** (2021). *Innovative Strategies for Media Growth. The Times.*

    - Chronicles Koos Bekker's transformation of Naspers into a global digital leader, leveraging strategic investments.

13. **Dorsey, J.** (2022). *Innovation through Simplicity. Tech Journal.*

    o Examines Jack Dorsey's leadership at Twitter and Square, emphasizing simplicity and focus in decision-making.

14. **Ren, Z.** (2021). *Huawei's Resilience in a Volatile World. Financial Times.*

    o Details Ren Zhengfei's strategies for navigating geopolitical challenges and maintaining Huawei's growth trajectory.

15. **Son, M.** (2020). *Vision Fund and Beyond: Investing for the Future. The Wall Street Journal.*

    o Explores Masayoshi Son's bold investment strategies and their impact on global tech startups.

16. **Kamprad, I.** (2018). *The IKEA Way: Building a Sustainable Empire. Fast Company.*

    o Reflects on Ingvar Kamprad's frugal leadership style and commitment to affordability and sustainability.

17. **Arnault, B.** (2021). *Crafting Luxury at Scale. The Luxury Observer.*

    o Examines how Bernard Arnault combined creativity and discipline to grow LVMH's influence worldwide.

18. **Ek, D.** (2021). *Spotify's Rise to Global Dominance. Forbes.*

- Highlights Daniel Ek's leadership in disrupting the music industry through innovation and customer-centricity.

19. **Ortega, A.** (2020). *The Inditex Success Story: Lessons in Agility. Business Insider.*

    - Chronicles Amancio Ortega's journey in building Zara and Inditex into a global leader in fast fashion.

20. **Nilekani, N.** (2022). *Scaling Technology for Social Impact. The Indian Express.*

    - Reflects on Nandan Nilekani's leadership in Infosys and his vision for leveraging technology for societal change.

21. **Hoffman, R.** (2021). *Blitzscaling: The Lightning-Fast Path to Building Massively Valuable Companies.* Currency.

    - Discusses Reid Hoffman's insights on scaling organizations quickly while managing risk.

22. **Rinehart, G.** (2022). *Mining the Future: Leadership in Australia's Resource Sector. Mining Weekly.*

    - Profiles Gina Rinehart's impact on Australia's mining industry and her strategies for scaling resource operations.

23. **Farrell, V.** (2022). *Innovative Automation Strategies. The Manufacturer.*

    - Details Vivian Farrell's leadership in expanding Modular Automation's global presence.

24. **Thakrar, S., & Thakrar, K.** (2021). *Dishoom: Creating a Culinary Legacy. The Times.*

    o   Highlights the Thakrar brothers' leadership in scaling Dishoom while preserving cultural authenticity.

25. **Jianlin, W.** (2021). *Wanda Group: Leadership in Real Estate and Entertainment. China Daily.*

    o   Chronicles Wang Jianlin's strategic growth of Wanda Group into a global brand.

Appendix

Tools, Exercises, and Additional Resources for Unstoppable Growth

1. Growth Diagnostic Checklist

- A practical checklist for assessing your organization's growth stage, including prompts for evaluating market position, financial health, team dynamics, and scalability.
- **Suggested Companion Resource**: For an interactive version of this checklist, visit impactthinking.net/Unstoppable-growth/.

2. Purpose and Vision Alignment Worksheet

- A guided worksheet to help leaders articulate and refine their purpose, mission, and vision, including prompts for aligning personal and organizational values.
- **Suggested Companion Resource**: Access additional purpose-alignment exercises online at impactthinking.net/Unstoppable-growth/.

3. Leadership Self-Assessment Tool

- Reflect on your leadership strengths, blind spots, and development areas, covering core traits like adaptability, resilience, emotional intelligence, and decision-making.

- **Suggested Companion Resource**: Take a digital version of this assessment and receive a personalized report at impactthinking.net/Unstoppable-growth/.

4. Financial Planning and Resource Allocation Templates

- Templates and guidelines for effective budgeting, financial forecasting, and strategic resource allocation tailored for growth-stage businesses.
- **Suggested Companion Resource**: Explore more financial planning tools and tutorials on advanced resource management at impactthinking.net/Unstoppable-growth/.

5. Stakeholder and Investor Communication Guide

- A guide to crafting purpose-aligned messages for stakeholders and investors, with sample email structures and presentation tips.
- **Suggested Companion Resource**: Downloadable guides and templates are available at impactthinking.net/Unstoppable-growth/.

6. Case Studies and Reflective Questions

- A recap of the real-world case studies featured in the book, along with reflective questions to encourage deeper understanding and application.
- **Suggested Companion Resource**: For extended case studies and interviews, visit impactthinking.net/Unstoppable-growth/.

7. Personal Development and Mindset Exercise

- Reflection exercises focused on mindset, resilience, and adaptability, with journaling prompts to guide deeper exploration of your personal leadership journey.

- **Suggested Companion Resource**: Access a digital course on developing a growth-oriented mindset at impactthinking.net/Unstoppable-growth/.

8. Team Empowerment and Culture Building Toolkit

- A toolkit to help leaders foster a culture of collaboration, inclusivity, and innovation, with tips, prompts, and templates.
- **Suggested Companion Resource**: Find additional team-building guides and downloadable handouts at impactthinking.net/Unstoppable-growth/.

9. Innovation and Adaptability Framework

- A framework to help leaders assess their organization's innovation potential and foster a culture of adaptability.
- **Suggested Companion Resource**: Interactive tools to analyze innovation readiness are available at impactthinking.net/Unstoppable-growth/.

10. Next Steps: Engaging with Your Community of Leaders

- Guidance on leveraging your professional network for inspiration, learning, and identifying potential mentors or collaborators.
- **Suggested Companion Resource**: Join a community of like-minded leaders and explore peer support resources at impactthinking.net/Unstoppable-growth/.

Final Note

For those who wish to explore these tools further, additional resources and advanced versions of these exercises are available online at impactthinking.net/Unstoppable-growth/. Visit us to continue your journey toward unstoppable growth.

Glossary

A

- **Adaptive Leadership**
  A leadership approach focused on responding flexibly to challenges, fostering resilience, and encouraging innovation within teams to address rapidly changing environments.
- **Agile**
  A project management and organizational framework designed to prioritize flexibility, responsiveness, and iterative progress, often used in software development but applicable across various sectors.
- **Anchor Purpose**
  A deeply rooted organizational purpose that guides decision-making, strategy, and culture, ensuring alignment with long-term values and goals.

B

- **Bootstrapping**
  The practice of building a business from the ground up with personal savings, operational revenue, and minimal external funding. Often associated with lean, self-sustaining growth.
- **Burnout**
  A state of mental, physical, and emotional exhaustion due to prolonged stress, commonly experienced by leaders and entrepreneurs during intense periods of growth or high-stress environments.
- **Business Model Innovation**
  The process of redefining how an organization creates, delivers, and captures value, often as a response to market changes or competitive pressures.

C

- **Cash Flow Management**
  The process of tracking, analysing, and optimizing the inflow and outflow of cash in a business to maintain liquidity, support operations, and fuel growth initiatives.
- **Core Values**
  Fundamental beliefs that guide an organization's behaviours, decision-making, and strategic direction. Core values often serve as a foundation for organizational culture and brand identity.
- **Culture of Innovation**
  An organizational environment that encourages creativity, experimentation, and continuous improvement, where employees feel empowered to explore new ideas and challenge traditional ways of thinking.
- **Customer Acquisition Cost (CAC)**
  The total cost of acquiring a new customer, including marketing and sales expenses, divided by the number of new customers acquired. A critical metric for understanding profitability and scaling potential.
- **Customer Lifetime Value (CLV)**
  An estimation of the total revenue generated from a customer over their relationship with the business, minus the acquisition and retention costs. This metric helps assess customer profitability and long-term business growth.

D

- **Disruptive Innovation**
  An innovation that significantly alters an existing market or creates a new market, often displacing established products or services. Coined by Clayton Christensen, this term is central to understanding innovation and market shifts.
- **Digital Transformation**

The integration of digital technology into all areas of a business, fundamentally changing how it operates and delivers value to customers.

E

- **Emotional Intelligence (EI)**
  The capacity to recognize, understand, and manage one's own emotions, as well as empathize with others' emotions. A vital skill for effective leadership, resilience, and relationship-building.

- **Entrepreneurial Spirit**
  A mindset characterized by creativity, risk-taking, adaptability, and a drive to pursue new opportunities, often essential for the success of growth-stage businesses and startups.

- **Exit Strategy**
  A plan for an owner or investor to sell their stake in a business, often through acquisitions, mergers, or public offerings, to realize their investment gains.

F

- **Founder's Mentality**
  A business framework emphasizing core attributes like entrepreneurial energy, customer focus, and employee loyalty, often essential for sustaining growth and overcoming internal obstacles as a company scales.

- **Future-Proofing**
  Strategies designed to prepare an organization for long-term challenges and opportunities, ensuring resilience and relevance in a rapidly changing environment.

G

- **Growth Mindset**
  The belief that abilities, intelligence, and potential can be developed through effort, learning, and resilience. A growth mindset is linked to adaptability, innovation, and long-term success.

I
- **Innovation Grant**
  A form of funding provided to employees or departments to pursue new ideas, products, or processes within an organization, fostering a culture of innovation and experimentation.

K
- **Key Performance Indicators (KPIs)**
  Measurable metrics used to assess the effectiveness of an organization's activities and progress toward its strategic objectives. KPIs are crucial for tracking performance and guiding decision-making.

L
- **Lean Startup**
  A methodology focused on developing businesses and products with minimal waste and maximum efficiency by quickly testing assumptions, gathering customer feedback, and iterating based on results.

M
- **Mission Statement**
  A brief description of an organization's core purpose, values, and goals, providing a clear guide for decision-making and direction. Often serves as a foundation for strategic planning.
- **Multidisciplinary Team**
  A team composed of members with diverse skills and expertise who collaborate to achieve a common objective. In a business context, this approach fosters creativity, innovation, and problem-solving.

P
- **Pivot**
  A strategic shift in a business's direction, often involving a change in product, market, or business model, to better align with customer needs or market opportunities.

- **Product-Market Fit**
  The point at which a product meets the needs of a well-defined target market and gains traction. Achieving product-market fit is essential for growth and scaling.

R
- **Resilience**
  The ability to recover from setbacks, adapt to change, and continue forward despite adversity. A critical trait for leaders in fast-paced or high-growth environments.

S
- **Scalability**
  The ability of a business or system to grow and manage increased demand without compromising performance, efficiency, or quality. Scalability is a key focus for growth-stage businesses.
- **Sustainable Growth**
  Growth that is maintained without compromising financial stability, environmental health, or social responsibility. Sustainable growth focuses on balanced progress across multiple dimensions.
- **Systems Thinking**
  A framework for understanding the interconnections within an organization or ecosystem, emphasizing how changes in one area can impact the whole. Useful for building scalable systems and anticipating challenges.

T
- **Transformational Leadership**
  A leadership style that inspires and motivates employees to exceed expectations, often by focusing on vision, values, and the individual growth of team members.

V
- **Value Proposition**
  A clear statement explaining how a product or service solves a customer's problem, meets their needs, or provides specific

benefits. A strong value proposition is key to differentiation and customer acquisition.

- **Vision Statement**

    A forward-looking declaration of an organization's long-term goals and aspirations, often meant to inspire and guide strategic planning and decision-making.

About the Author

Ben Botes is a seasoned entrepreneur, leadership coach, and growth strategist with over 31 years of industry experience. Having successfully led four business exits and supported scale-ups across Sub-Saharan Africa and beyond, Ben combines practical expertise with a deep understanding of purpose-driven leadership. With a career spanning venture capital, executive education, and human development, Ben's work focuses on helping leaders build resilient organizations, scale sustainably, and achieve lasting impact. His holistic approach bridges strategy and personal growth, making him a trusted advisor for leaders navigating the complexities of growth.

Printed in Dunstable, United Kingdom

64468226R00224